PEMBROKESHIRE

THE HISTORIES OF WALES
SERIES EDITOR: CATRIN STEVENS

PEMBROKESHIRE

THE CONCISE HISTORY

ROGER TURVEY

University of Wales Press
Cardiff
2007

British Library Cataloguing-in-Publication Data
A catalogue record for this book is available from the British Library.

ISBN 978-0-7083-1948-2

Printed in Malta by Gutenberg Press, Tarxien

For my mother
Maryl Elizabeth Turvey

Acknowledgements

I wish to thank Dillwyn Miles, president of the Pembrokeshire Historical Society, and Professor Gareth Elwyn Jones for reading and commenting on the book.

Contents

Series Editor's Preface   ix

Preface   xi

Introduction: 'Ynglond be yond Walys' or
'Little England beyond Wales'   1

I
Prehistoric Pembrokeshire: From Stone Age to Iron Age   7

II
Ancient Pembrokeshire: 'Celts' and Romans   14

III
Early Medieval or 'Dark Age' Pembrokeshire: An Age of
Kings, Kingdoms and Saints   22

IV
Late Medieval Pembrokeshire: Conquests, Castles and Kings   36

V
Early Modern Pembrokeshire: Reorganization,
Reformation and Revolution   60

VI
Modern Pembrokeshire: From an 'Age of Enlightenment'
to an 'Age of Reform'   93

VII
Contemporary Pembrokeshire: The Twentieth Century   127

References   144

Select Bibliography   147

Index   149

Series Editor's Preface

The 'Histories of Wales' series is intended to enrich our knowledge and understanding of the colourful diversity of the local and regional cultures and heritage of Wales. When the series is complete, when all the counties, regions and cities have been duly chronicled in all their distinctiveness and complexity, each volume will contribute in its own unique way to the composite and intricate jigsaw which constitutes the history of Wales.

The first two volumes published in the series, the concise histories of Anglesey (David A. Pretty, 2005) and Carmarthenshire (Dylan Rees, 2005) respectively, have paved the way admirably and have been well received by both professional and amateur historian as well as by the general, interested reading public. In some ways, however, writing the concise history of Pembrokeshire presents an even greater challenge for its author, since the 'county', from Norman times onwards, has traditionally been seen as a 'county' of two halves: the more populated and anglicised world of the 'down-belows' in 'Little England beyond Wales' to the south of the virtual line of the *landsker* on the one hand and the more sparsely populated Welsh-speaking culture of north sir Benfro on the other. Perhaps, therefore, the fact that the author, Roger Turvey, is not a native of the county, but of neighbouring Carmarthenshire, has been of advantage to him, for it has enabled him to view Pembrokeshire with a measure of dispassion and to encompass both traditions with equal empathy. This impartiality has not, however, produced an arid, impassive text; rather he seems to have adopted Pembrokeshire as his own and the county, in turn, has absorbed him. Indeed, he has already made his mark upon Pembrokeshire history, with his studies of the Elizabethan Perrott family and especially Sir John Perrott (d.1592) and he is the dedicated editor of the *Journal of the Pembrokeshire Historical Society*. He is also a Fellow of the Royal Historical Society and a Fellow of the Society of Antiquarians.

In this concise history Turvey frequently reflects upon his debt to those eminent 'local' historians of Pembrokeshire, in whose footsteps he walks tall. These are his 'cloud of witnesses', to quote Waldo Williams, Pembrokeshire and one of Wales's finest poetic voices, whose writings have helped him unlock the county's past. The works of Giraldus Cambrensis, George Owen of Henllys, Richard Fenton, and in more recent times Brian Howells and David W. Howell, editors of the monumental County Histories, have served him well but ultimately this is his own interpretation which will make its own invaluable contribution to this erudite tradition. He traces Pembrokeshire's rich history chronologically, from prehistoric times to the present day; from Pentre Ifan as a Neolithic 'cromlech' to its status today as a major tourist attraction and icon in twenty-first century Wales. He has undertaken the journey with resourcefulness and scholarship and as editor I am greatly indebted to him for his perseverance and devotion and for producing such a readable and comprehensive book.

Catrin Stevens
Series Editor, The Histories of Wales

Preface

After ignorance of Holy Writ, nothing could be more grave than
lack of knowledge of antiquity and histories.

(John Twyne (d.1581), *Communia Loca*)

The pursuit of county or local history has its origins in the sixteenth
century being fostered by the likes of Twyne, a schoolmaster, author and
sometime mayor and MP of Canterbury. Deeply influenced by the great
awakening of interest in history and antiquities which marked the age of
Elizabeth, Twyne's enthusiasm for antiquarian study and its sources
was shared by others, principal among them William Lambarde (d.1601)
whose *Perambulation of Kent*, published in 1576, is usually reckoned to
be the earliest 'county history'. Yet it is to John Leland (d.1552), the earliest
of modern British antiquaries, that we must turn if we are to appreciate
the true beginnings of the writing and study of local history. A clerical
scholar and absentee pluralist who attracted royal favour, Leland intended
to write 'as many bookes as there be shires yn England, and shires and
greate dominions yn Wales'. His tours of England and Wales took the
best part of six years, *c.*1534–43, during which he amassed enough material
to pen, as he stated in a letter to Henry VIII, 'a description to make your
realm in writing'. Unfortunately for Leland, the achievement fell short of
the intention when illness overtook him in 1547 and he, in the words of a
fellow antiquary and friend John Bale (d.1563), 'by a most pitifull occasion
fell besides his wits'. In short, he went insane. There is, perhaps, a lesson
here for all of us who attempt the arduous task of compiling a county
history! Leland's legacy was in introducing the notion of the county or
shire as an appropriate unit for studying the history of Britain, an idea
that clearly quickly took root.

If in England the father of local history was John Leland, in Wales it
was surely that great son of Pembrokeshire George Owen (d.1613).
Historian, antiquary and genealogist, the multi-talented squire of Henllys
had, in the opinion of the late Sir Frederick Rees, 'the true concept of
local history', and was responsible for compiling the earliest 'county
history' in Wales, entitled *The Description of Pembrokeshire* (1603).
Inspired by, and owing something of its design to, Richard Carew's
(d.1620) *Survey of Cornwall* (1602), Owen's *Pembrokeshire* was possibly
intended to be published in two volumes, the 'First Booke' being a general
history of the county and the 'Second Booke', of which only a fragment

survives, a detailed history of the county parish by parish. Unfortunately, as in the case of Leland, Owen's ambition was never realized since he failed to publish the first and did not complete the second. Nevertheless, his legacy for the study of local history in Wales is no less significant than that of Leland in England. However, to dwell on the monumental achievements of Leland and Owen is to ignore the massive contribution of others in the fertile field of county history, not least in Pembrokeshire, which has been singularly fortunate in its local historians: Giraldus Cambrensis or, as he is otherwise known, Gerald of Wales (d.1223), George Owen (d.1613), Richard Fenton (d.1821), James Phillips (d.1907), Edward Laws (d.1913), Henry Owen (d.1919), Francis Green (d.1942). With the works of such a distinguished cast of historians to draw on, some of whom have themselves become firmly embedded in the stuff of history, and not forgetting the published efforts of more recent locally based researchers into the county's past, who could resist the temptation, if invited, to compose a modern, scholarly yet accessible history of Pembrokeshire? Clearly, not I, for though the thought of working in the shadow of such great historians daunts it is, nonetheless, irresistible and I can but hope that this study, though modest by comparison, will give as much pleasure and profit to as many readers as their works have done. It is to them and John Leland that I dedicate this book.

My aim has been to compose a volume that is both concise and comprehensive in its survey of Pembrokeshire history but if my achievement should fall short of the intention I can at least seek comfort in the fact that I have not, as yet, fallen 'besides my wits'. In this latter respect I have, in part, to thank my wife and fellow historian Carol for providing the support and stability necessary to complete this work. I should like to acknowledge the fine works of the many contributors who have written for the *Journal of the Pembrokeshire Historical Society* during my time as its editor and through whom I have learned a great deal of the diverse history of Pembrokeshire over the years. It is a pleasure to record my gratitude to Mrs Catrin Stevens, editor of the series, and the University of Wales Press, who kindly invited me to write the book and who gave me the encouragement and the means, unlike Leland and Owen, to realize my ambition to write a history of my adopted county.

Introduction

'Ynglond be yond Walys' or 'Little England beyond Wales'

> Perhaps, throughout the whole British Empire, there is no spot
> where the peasantry exhibit more happiness than in the northern
> parts of Pembrokeshire.
>
> (Richard Warner, *A Second Walk Through Wales*)

What is or what was Pembrokeshire? To the octogenarian minstrel from
Uzmaston, William Messenger, giving evidence in a court case in
Haverfordwest in 1518, it was 'west Walys nygh Herefford west' but to
his employer the absentee landowner James Ormond, earl of Wiltshire
(d.1461), whose conversation was recalled by the deponent, it was
'Ynglond be yond Walys'. In the period to 1536 it had been, variously, an
ancient tribal region, possibly a Roman province, a part Irish and part
Welsh kingdom, a third part of the larger kingdom of Deheubarth, a
Norman and later English earldom and Marcher shire. Between 1536 and
1974 it had been one of thirteen counties in Wales and between 1974 and
1996 a district amounting to a third part of the larger county of Dyfed, but
today it is one of twenty-two unitary authorities.

Of course, a place is more than simply a geographical expression or
political entity; it is about the people who live, work and die there. To
those who live there today it is the premier county of Wales, God's own
country in fact, to the majority of outsiders it is a pleasant place to
holiday. But what unifies both groups is not simply the wonderful
countryside, the breathtaking scenery, the lush beaches or the temperate
climate but the many monuments that dot the county and the rich history
associated with them: Iron-Age hill-forts, neolithic burial chambers, early
Christian inscribed stones and crosses, medieval castles, churches and
monasteries, gentry mansions, fine harbours, slate quarries, lime-kilns,
ruins galore in fact, though some not so ruinous! The list is endless and
so it seems is the county's capacity to generate exciting history, for
though there might not be much left to discover there remains a great
deal yet to be written.

Physiographical Background

Physiographically, Pembrokeshire is a coastal county of south-west Wales, consisting of a low coastal plateau in the south, the plain of which drains into the Milford Haven estuary, enclosed by the Preseli mountains of the north hill country which reach an elevation of 536 metres at Foel Cwmcerwyn. The county's rugged and convoluted coastline forms a peninsula with protruding headlands which, for the most part, are faced by a series of offshore islands, principally Skomer, Skokholm and Ramsey. The only other island of note is Caldy in the south-east which sits offshore from Tenby. The chief rivers of the county are the two that dissect it from north to south, namely, the Western and Eastern Cleddau with part of the latter forming the border with the neighbouring county of Carmarthen.

The oldest rocks in Pembrokeshire are the exposed and weathered igneous tuffs and granites which make up the Preseli hills. Elsewhere the main core of the county is made up of younger rocks, Ordovician grits and shales, and, younger still, the Old Red Sandstone and Carboniferous coal and limestone measures of the south. Consequently, the southern two-thirds of the county had a plentiful supply of tough stone for building and had made early use of coal as a domestic fuel. In addition, the lowland plain has one of the few areas of truly rich arable land in Wales and is blessed with a mild maritime climate which promotes vegetable and crop growth. Indeed, Pembrokeshire is still known for its early harvests. The benefits of living in Pembrokeshire were described in rather less technical terms by Emanuel Bowen in his *Britannia Depicta* (1720):

> The air is pleasant and good, and the soil in the bottom and towards the sea extraordinary fruitful. Some hills and mountains appear in the inland which are more barren yet feeding abundance of Sheep, Goats, Cattle, &c. Here is plenty of Fish, Fowl, Pit-Coal and Marl. In this County is Milford Haven, the largest and most capacious harbour in the Kingdom.

Of course, the climactic and physiological make-up of Pembrokeshire has not always been so forgiving. It has suffered its fair share of storms, one of which was recorded in a letter sent in 1702 by Grace Griffith, servant and nurse, to her mistress Hester Pakington (née Perrot):

> I hope your Ladyship was not terrified with the last storm, as we were here. I never heard the like in my life. The storm continued 3 days and 3 nights. As for thunder, lightning, rain and high wind, there was never the like known as everybody says.

The resulting damage caused to Haroldston House was recorded in another letter to Hester Pakington by William Beavans, steward of the household:

> the house is much out of order at present for your reception, the kitchen lying almost stripped, the roof besides of the house by a Hurricane, in which no less than 11 trees were blown down in the grove, two of them being oaks, one as large as will make a running beam for a mill.

In common with the rest of west Wales, the county is rather wet and subject to rainfall levels that in south-eastern Britain would be regarded with horror. Yet the rain is not so distracting as to put off potential visitors to the county since Pembrokeshire has its fair share of sun.

Boundaries and Local Divisions

The limits of modern Pembrokeshire were fixed by Acts of Parliament (1536 and 1542/3) in the reign of Henry VIII and, but for minor modifications and temporary subsumption within the greater county of Dyfed, an act of political vandalism that was thankfully short-lived (1974–96), it has remained intact to this day. Its boundaries, which are, for the most part, natural, being three-quarters bounded by the sea, enclose an area of some 616 square miles or 159,464 hectares. On its landward side to the north-east Pembrokeshire is defined by the rivers Teifi and Cuch but to the mid- and south-east its border is artificial owing its creation less to physical conditions than to war and politicking. Although the present Pembrokeshire came into existence only in the reign of Henry VIII, less than five hundred years ago, the area has a history considerably older than that. Indeed, it might fairly be argued that Pembrokeshire originated as far back as 1138 when it was created an earldom, an entity that carried with it the status, dignity and authority of a county palatinate. However, if we were to compare the known territorial and largely undefined political limits of this early county with those of the Tudor creation the differences would be considerable. Consequently, it is important to try to make some sense of a complex issue namely, the fixing, as far as we can, of Pembrokeshire's boundaries and local divisions.

The old Welsh name for the district was Dyfed or Demetia and is a title derived from the tribe of people, the Demetae, who inhabited the area the earliest reference to whom appears in the work of the Greek cartographer Ptolemy in the second century AD. The precise dimensions of Celtic and Roman Dyfed is not known but is thought to have included much of modern Carmarthenshire and Cardiganshire. Its capital, according to Ptolemy, was located at the Roman station of Moridunum, the site of modern Carmarthen. Even as the Romans left Britain Dyfed not only continued its existence but evolved into one of the four ancient kingdoms of Wales, a fact attested by the early sixth-century writer and cleric Gildas. According to his 'The Ruin and Conquest of Britain' (*De Excidio Britanniae*), composed sometime between 534 and 549, Dyfed was ruled by 'Vortipor, tyrant of the Demetae'. The extent of the kingdom ruled by Vortipor is not known but is likely to have extended far beyond the boundaries of what constitutes modern Pembrokeshire.

Although the Dyfed of his successors becomes clearer with time it is not until the tenth or eleventh century that its limits and territorial divisions acquire a degree of fixity that warrants serious description. For this the historian is almost entirely dependent on literary sources that take within their compass the prose tales known as the *Mabinogi*, some early court poetry and other exiguous evidence as survives prior to the middle of the twelfth century. According to the *Mabinogi* Dyfed was composed of seven *cantrefi*, which roughly translates as an area containing a hundred vills or townships, namely Cantref Gwarthaf, Cemais, Daugleddau, Emlyn, Pebidiog, Penfro and Rhos. By a continuing process of evolution and devolution changes occurred in which Daugleddau disappeared and the remaining six *cantrefi* were subdivided into *cymydau* or commotes. Unfortunately, the data for fixing the commotal boundaries is not so conclusive until at least the very end of the twelfth century by which time alien conquest, settlement and lordship had conspired to shape and reshape the region until much of the character of its native divisions had either been subsumed or segmented and thereby largely lost and forgotten. Even those territorial entities and divisions that managed to survive and were retained by their new Norman and later English masters, who by virtue of their frontier status became known as Marcher lords, all bore the conqueror's imprint. Thus did the *cantrefi* of Penfro and Rhos become the Marcher lordships of Pembroke and Haverford respectively, each of which was further subdivided into the baronies of Carew, Daugleddau or Wiston, Manorbier and Stackpole (subject to Pembroke), and Roch and Walwyn's Castle (subject to Haverford).

The biggest casualty of conquest, and not just at the hands of the all-conquering Normans being earlier swallowed up sometime in the tenth century to form part of the native kingdom of Deheubarth, was Dyfed itself which slipped from regular usage because it was no longer politically or administratively meaningful. Consequently, post-conquest Dyfed, which continued its existence largely in the cultural memory, gave way to Pembroke as the more apt description of the region. That Pembroke should gain greater currency than Dyfed in contemporary corridors of power is not surprising given that it was at the heart of the medieval earldom which was itself at the epicentre of a movement initiated by its ambitious earls to dominate and unify the whole region.

In spite of their best efforts, it is, perhaps, not until the fourteenth century that the region eventually came to resemble something akin to the Pembrokeshire that is familiar today. Consisting of more than a dozen independent and semi-independent lordships, the Marcher shire or earldom of Pembroke lacked the territorial, political and administrative cohesion that early characterized the development of its neighbours the royal counties of Carmarthenshire and Cardiganshire. Nevertheless, with varying degrees of success, successive earls of Pembroke did attempt to curb the independent spirit of these lesser lords and to bring under their control these lordships so as to create as compact a power base as was possible within the territorial limits of what remained of ancient Dyfed. The legacy of their work lay not so much in the real but in the notional effects of their attempt to define the territorial limits of their power as earls of Pembroke, a fact recognized in large part by the Henrician acts of parliament that fixed forever, at least in the mind, the boundaries of modern Pembrokeshire.

If politically medieval Pembrokeshire was slow to emerge, ecclesias-tically it had early developed the territorial cohesiveness that was the aim of its earls. From the time when diocesan limits became fixed in the twelfth century it lay entirely within the bounds of the diocese of St David's. As diocesan administration became heavier and more complex the bishopric was further divided into archdeaconries, four in all, with the archdeaconry of St David's centring around its cathedral and its boundaries, as far as can be determined from later evidence, largely anticipating the Pembrokeshire of today and the one aspired to by its earls. Clearly, Dyfed, in all its various forms, differed from Pembrokeshire but their ancient association can at least be said to be deeply rooted in the county that is roughly coterminous with the unitary authority of today.

Language

As the title to this introduction suggests, Pembrokeshire has features which are peculiar, if not entirely unique, to itself. One of those peculiarities is the language divide that separates north from south, being the difference between the use of English and Welsh speech. Its origin can be traced back to the beginning of the twelfth century when the region experienced an influx of alien settlers who arrived in the wake of conquest. Apparently sponsored by Henry I these colonists, mainly Flemish in nationality and speech, followed their Norman overlords in colonizing this particularly fertile corner of Wales. As they penetrated inland they drove the native Welsh north and established settlements which have left a permanent imprint on the county. The success of this colonial plantation can be gauged by the fact that George Owen, writing in 1603, was able to say that the county 'is well near equally divided into two equal parts between the English speech and the Welsh'. However, the fact that Owen was unable to trace with any confidence a language or dialect akin to either Flemish or Norman-French in the sixteenth century would suggest that there had been another more substantial immigration by English-speaking colonists which had the result of gradually displacing the languages of Flanders and Normandy. The effects of immigration and settlement on the cultural and linguistic landscape is still detectable today inasmuch as the southern half of the county has been English speaking since the Middle Ages, while the north has remained largely Welsh speaking until the present day. Although the linguistic divide remains a relatively potent characteristic of modern Pembrokeshire the racial line, thankfully, is nowhere near so hard as it was in times past. At no point today will observations and conversations take the form described by George Owen in his own time: 'the Englishmen . . . to this day . . . wonder at a Welshman coming among them, the one neighbour saying to the other, look there goes a Welshman'.

Of course, the linguistic history of Pembrokeshire is rather more complex than this short introduction might suggest since there are issues of phonology and dialect which would need to be considered but are outside the scope of this book. So too are detailed discussions on race, ethnicity and nationality, factors which have done much to excite the curiosity of both sociologists and historians not to mention linguists. Suffice to say that at the dawn of the new millennium Welsh continues to be spoken in the county by around 24 per cent or roughly 21,000 of the population, but, significantly, it is being taken up in the Anglicized south by residents willing to learn and through the national curriculum in all the schools of the area.

I

Prehistoric Pembrokeshire: From Stone Age to Iron Age

Introduction: Stone, Bronze and Iron

> Stones, the sea and the weather have moulded the look of Pembrokeshire. Man has merely scratched the surface.
>
> (V. Rees)

As with most matters archaeological and historical, they are divided into periods for ease of study and the Stone and Bronze Ages are no exception. The Stone Age can be divided into three distinct periods: the Old Stone Age or Palaeolithic, Middle Stone Age or Mesolithic and New Stone Age or Neolithic. The Bronze Age too can be divided into early, middle and late, each phase of which is normally distinguished by often subtle changes in pottery and weapon-making and in burial tradition. By the time the Iron Age is reached the periodic divisions have at least declined to two, early and late, but it is important to remember that however many 'periods' into which historians and archaeologists may wish to divide their areas of study the degree of continuity between them, particularly in terms of settlement patterns and traditions, is often quite marked. Indeed, such periodization might suggest that there is a wealth of knowledge available to the historian that requires some form of chronological cataloguing but this is not the case. As its title suggests, prehistory is very much the domain of the archaeologist and much of what is known of this time-period is derived from site excavation and the analysis of physical remains. Consequently, apart from their archaeological remains there are few traces of man's activity either in Wales or Pembrokeshire so that little is known of the earliest prehistoric periods in this corner of south-west Wales. Nevertheless, sufficient evidence exists for us to at least attempt to piece together a coherent picture of prehistoric Pembrokeshire.

Old Stone Age or Palaeolithic

Pembrokeshire has played host to people from earliest times, attracting and adapting to waves of settlers for over 50,000 years. First among them was Palaeolithic man, primitive cave-dwelling hunters who used simple stone tools and weapons. They existed in conditions very different to our own, enduring an intensely cold climate and facing an inhospitable landscape in which the islands of Ramsey and Skomer were as yet protruding headlands guarding a coastal plain. Unsurprisingly, traces of human occupation at this time occur mainly in those areas that provide man with the best shelter, such as can be found in the carboniferous limestone which runs east–west from Tenby to Pembroke, where the rock is of a type that permits of the formation of caves. Five sites in the county – Hoyle's Mouth and Little Hoyle Caves near Tenby, Priory Farm Cave at Monkton and Nanna's and Potter's Caves on Caldy Island – have yielded finds of some significance including flint blades, points and scrapers. Although few in number they are among the earliest man-made objects to have been discovered from extant sites anywhere in the whole of south-west Wales. Unfortunately, what Pembrokeshire lacks is a find as significant as Paviland on the Gower in which the skeleton of a headless young man, the renowned 'Red Lady', was discovered, in the words of Diane Williams in the Cadw guide to Gower (1998), 'amongst a rich assemblage of tools and bone'. Uncovered in Goat's Hole Cave in 1823 by William Buckland the body had been ceremonially buried with ivory bracelets and stone implements and, possibly, ritually stained in red ochre, all some 30,000 years ago.

It is noteworthy that much of what has been written about this period is usually accompanied by descriptions such as 'abysmal', 'debased', 'miserable' and 'impoverished'. Certainly, J. E. Lloyd, in his *A History of Carmarthenshire* (1935), was of the opinion that Palaeolithic, and even Mesolithic man 'eked out a debased poverty-stricken life'. It is an opinion shared by J. Graham Jones who wrote in his *Pocket Guide: The History of Wales* (1998):

> Certainly, the Palaeolithic population was thinly spread and culturally impoverished: none of the high-quality cave art which flourished in France and Spain was to be found in Wales, which remained on the very fringe of civilization.

While we may have little cause to disagree with either of them, it is important to remember that our descriptions of an earlier period, especially one so remote from our own, will almost inevitably suffer in comparison. What might seem miserable to us may not, necessarily and given the limits of their experiences, have been so to them. What is undeniable is that life was hard and dangerous. A glance at the bone-bearing deposits excavated at Palaeolithic sites in Pembrokeshire and elsewhere in Wales bears testimony to the dangers man faced from wild animals, namely, hyaena, rhinoceros, mammoth, lion, wolf and even hippopotamus. Yet, in spite of the problems facing early man he responded by adapting and so succeeded, in part, in transcending the harsh realities of his environment.

Middle Stone Age or Mesolithic

As a result of excavation and casual finds at the Wogan Cavern, Pembroke, Daylight Rock and Nanna's Cave on Caldy Island, but particularly at Nab Head, Marloes, the presence of Mesolithic culture in the county is assured. Mesolithic men were semi-nomadic hunter-gatherers who stalked their prey, elk, horse, deer, wild pig and other small mammals, which they killed by using sharp stone-tipped wooden spears and arrows. It is this development in what is termed by archaeologists the 'microlithic' character of their flint making that distinguishes Mesolithic man from his predecessors. In fact, the Mesolithic descendants of Palaeolithic man had to face entirely different conditions which were marked by an improvement in the climate, damper and less severely cold, and the spread of pine and birch forests. As the climate warmed up further sea levels rose with the result that Ramsey, Skomer and Skokholm were gradually cut off from the mainland at around which time, $c.6,000$ BC, Britain too had become cut off from continental Europe. Soon oak, elm and alder appeared to add to the afforestation of Pembrokeshire, with which an increasing human population coped by becoming more expert in its exploitation and in the management and manipulation of its environment generally. Despite Mesolithic man's increasing success in adapting to the conditions that governed daily life, it has been estimated that in Wales as a whole the population was never more than roughly 300 to 500.

New Stone Age or Neolithic

It was the advent of new, some might argue revolutionary, farming techniques that heralded the New Stone Age or Neolithic period. This is not to suggest that Neolithic man gave up the hunt, far from it, hunting, fishing and the gathering of wild fruits continued as before but as a supplement to rather than the staple means of obtaining food. There was, therefore, a change in human behaviour characterized by the introduction of domesticated plants and animals, and of advanced cultivation which required the gradual clearance of woodland and a more permanently settled way of life. Yet in spite of the resulting wholesale transformation of the landscape in which people became more tied to the land little evidence survives to reveal day-to-day aspects of Neolithic life other than a scattering of flint tools, pottery and animal bones. The only site in the county, and one of the first to be found in Wales, where anything approaching a permanent Neolithic settlement has been found is at Clegyr Boia near St David's. Successive excavations here, in 1902 and 1943, found the remains of round and rectangular huts of timber and daub, some with wall footings of stone, together with a Neolithic fire pit and rubbish dump. The importance of Clergyr Boia may well increase if it can be shown that it is among the earliest Neolithic defended hilltop sites in Britain. Long thought to be an Iron Age hill-fort because of the stone ramparts that were built on and partly over the earlier Neolithic huts, it has been suggested that these defences might, in fact, be contemporary with the later of the Neolithic houses. Although currently no more than a possibility, if the case were to be proved then Clegyr Boia would be among a select group of, as yet, rarely recognized types of monuments.

If evidence of the houses of the living are few and far between the same cannot be said of the houses of the dead. Constructed of often huge slabs and boulders, particularly the capstones, these massive stone-built 'megalithic' burial chambers still dominate the Pembrokeshire landscape. The fact that some of these capstones can weigh anything up to 40 tons and would need to have been lifted on the other equally large supporting stones suggest that Neolithic man possessed a rudimentary knowledge of engineering. Some twenty-four megalithic chambered tombs survive in Pembrokeshire with Pentre Ifan the most prominent, well known and oft visited among them. Standing isolated on the upper slopes of the Preseli hills the Pentre Ifan 'cromlech', with its curved facade and portal, reminiscent of the portal dolmens of Cornwall and Ireland, is justly celebrated as one of the most impressive megalithic monuments in Wales. No trace of burials and few artefacts were found at Pentre Ifan unlike at nearby Carreg Coetan Arthur, Newport, in which were found the tell-tale signs of human cremation: charcoal, fragments of clay urns and pieces of charred bone. These funerary monuments are suggestive of primitive deism and although little is known of the ritual that accompanied burials it is likely to have involved more than simply the family of the person or persons cremated. Indeed, such tombs bear testimony to the effort and labour that went into their construction which is itself evidence of community and of collective enterprise. It has been suggested that the erection of these tombs was as important for the living as for the dead in so far as they may have represented an overtly visual affirmation of tribal or kinship rights to territory.

Besides agriculture and engineering the Neolithic period may also be said to have borne witness to the early, if equally primitive, development of trade and industry. In 1919 archaeologists made a startling discovery at Penmaen-mawr in Gwynedd when the remains of 'a great axe factory' were uncovered. The stones quarried here and shaped into axes have been found as far afield as Wiltshire, southern Scotland and northern Ireland. It was not long before a similar axe 'manufacturing industry' was claimed for Pembrokeshire in the shape of the prized spotted dolerite used in the making of polished stone axes, the source of which is thought to have been at Carn Meini in the Preseli hills.

It is thought likely that towards the end of the Neolithic period, around 3,000 BC, some farming communities had grown to such an extent that they were able to sustain specialists in stone work and woodwork and perhaps in other crafts also. Although this is more likely to have occurred in the richer, fertile regions of southern England, southern Pembrokeshire was probably among the few areas in Wales where the conditions for agriculture were more favourable and better disposed towards diversification rather than an over-reliance on animal husbandry and pastoralism. Lest we forget, it is important to note that as Neolithic communities were attempting to eke out a miserable existence in Pembrokeshire 'the Riverine Lands of Egypt, Mesopotamia, and the Sind were', according to J. E. Lloyd (1935), 'flourishing greatly'. Indeed, as he rightly points out,

> Their inhabitants had long since built up great civilizations wherein the use of pottery, the tilling of the soil, and the building and organising of large cities had developed alongside other techniques and customs destined to remain fundamental in human economy for many centuries to come.

The contrast is not only startling but sobering also.

Bronze Age

As is the case in all transitory phases of history there was no great break or stark new beginning; one period or age simply merged into another. Therefore, the transition from stone to metal was nowhere near revolutionary but was rather unspectacularly gradual. As if to emphasize the point it is noteworthy that the first metallurgists are distinguished not so much by the metals they produced, copper initially followed by bronze, an alloy of copper and tin, but by their use of a new style of pottery. Consequently, they are often referred to as the 'Beaker People' in recognition of their highly decorated beakers, many of which have been found fragmented in burial sites across Britain. It was the makers of these distinctively 'waisted' earthenware pots that first introduced metal-working into Britain sometime around 2,500–2,000 BC. They may have done so, initially, by way of trade rather than by the large-scale movements of people though this is thought to have occurred at some point perhaps by 1,000 BC when there was an upsurge in the production and use of bronze. What seems clear is that there was a shift away from communal to personal power as evidenced by the spread of mounded round barrows which celebrated the power of a single individual. Some fine examples can still be seen at Hayscastle Cross, Pwllcrochan and, most impressive of all, Frenni Fawr Round Cairns near Crymych. Within these burial sites deposits of cremated bone and other associated objects accompanying individual deaths are suggestive of a close link between ceremonial and burial practice, the exact nature of which is not yet known.

Apart from some isolated finds such as the circular timber house at Stackpole and other peripheral evidence of settlement at Potter's Cave on Caldy, very little is known about Bronze Age habitations. Funerary and ritual sites alone offer as much as is currently known, particularly as these have become common features of our landscape. They range from simple 'ring cairns' or circular banks of stone to standing stones either singly or paired such as can be found at some seventeen different sites in the county with Foel Eryr, Maenclochog and Harold's Stone, Bosherston, prominent among them. This was also the era (c.3,500–1,500 BC) of the 'henge', stone circles (some sites were of wood as at Woodhenge) which range in size from the spectacular – Stonehenge – to the unspectacular – Gors Fawr near Mynachlog-ddu. Although comparatively large by Welsh standards and well preserved with sixteen weather-beaten stones still standing, Gors Fawr is one of a number of ritual monuments which cluster in this part of the Preseli hills. This is perhaps not surprising given the especial treatment accorded stone from this part of the country to the extent that it was the source of some of the famous bluestones of Stonehenge erected on faraway Salisbury Plain. Although there has been much speculation it is generally agreed that the purpose of these sites was to form part of the ritualistic rites associated with their beliefs as ceremonial meeting places, perhaps even to act as shrines. They may also have had a calendrical purpose related to the movement of heavenly bodies or were used to calculate the timing of seasonal festivities.

Bronze Age folk continued to farm the land but more intensively than before and at greater altitude than their predecessors. The reasons for this are twofold: a warming climate caused even high moorland to be more hospitable to farming while an increasing population encouraged greater land use. Unfortunately increasingly exhausted uplands combined with the pressure of an expanding population created competition which almost inevitably led to conflict. Unsurprisingly, in such conditions demand created supply and metal manufacturers turned their skills to making weapons, which in itself fuelled the growth of a more war-like society. As a warrior elite evolved so did a hierarchical society which became more territorially aware of itself and in which the concept of friend and foe was more readily distinguishable. Within the territoriality of a Bronze Age domain a tribal culture developed at the root of which was the all-important agricultural base for the production of food. The task of the warrior elite was to protect the tribe's agricultural resources from predators and ensure the safety of those engaged in its exploitation – the farmers. Within and between this simple twofold division of tribal society there emerged a class of craftsmen who had the freedom to produce an increasingly sophisticated range of weapons and jewellery. Soon defensive settlements emerged being deliberately sited on strategically strong hilltops or promontories. As the Bronze Age merged into the iron age these defended settlements, with their evermore elaborate banks, ditches and dry-stone ramparts, came into their own. Some six hundred such hill and promontory forts – nearly a fifth of the British total – still survive in Wales, of which a good third were raised in Pembrokeshire. The great majority of these forts were constructed during the Iron Age, a period of intense competition between increasingly recognizable tribal groups.

II

Ancient Pembrokeshire: 'Celts' and Romans

Introduction: Who were the Celts?

> Once upon a time, far back in the unfathomable long ago, there
> was a disruption of the great Aryan people who were the
> progenitors of our modern European nations . . . a section of this
> great family left their ancestral homes in Central Asia, and turning
> their heads westward sought their fortunes in the European
> continent. The Keltic race marched in the van. (E. Laws)

Such is the late Victorian view of the origin of the Celts as expressed by
Edward Laws in his introduction to the third chapter of his *History of
Little England Beyond Wales* (1888). There is no hint here of the controversy
that currently engulfs a discussion on the nature and origins of the Celts
for while Laws' geographic and demographic outlines still hold true his
ethnic label, as we shall see, does not.

Bronze gradually gave way to iron with the arrival of groups of war-
like peoples from continental Europe who began the settlement of south-
east Britain around 600 BC. Who these 'peoples' were is the subject of
intense debate. It is no longer acceptable simply to describe them as Celts
as was once the case, since it has been argued that 'Celtic' is something of
a misnomer. In the opinion of the late Gwyn A. Williams (*When Was
Wales*, 1985):

> It is used to describe a confederacy of very different peoples,
> embraced in a Europe-wide Celtic language family, probably
> originating in small warrior dynasties to the east who boasted an
> advanced iron culture and made use of the horse. This confederacy
> became a powerful civilization with a vivid art, whose peoples
> once challenged Rome, sacked Rome, and finally succumbed to
> Rome to form the human fabric of the first great European urban
> polity in the northwest.

The succinctness of Professor Williams's definition of 'Celtic' and the 'Celts' has much to recommend it and although there are issues which have been deliberately circumvented in the interests of brevity the aim was clarity. For example, how different were the peoples that made up this necessarily 'loose' confederacy and how is one to decide which of them were in and which were out? It is an issue made more complex by the often contradictory comments and observations of contemporaries. The earliest reference we have to the 'Celtic' peoples dates from the fifth century BC when they are described by the Greek ethnographers Hecataeus of Miletus and Herodotus as being one of the major ethnic groups of central and western Europe. However, in the opening passage of the *De bello Gallico*, Julius Caesar (d.44 BC) states with the authority of their conqueror that only the Gauls of central and southern Gaul (modern France) called themselves Celts. If accepted without demur, this would have the effect of disassociating the Belgae, who lived in the north of Gaul, and the Aquitani, who lived in the south-west, from this Celtic confederacy despite similarities of language and shared aspects of culture. On this basis, there are other peoples who might also qualify for membership of this 'Celtic confederacy' such as the Galatae of central Europe, a people located, before they moved east, at the headwaters of the Danube, the geographical location of the supposed 'cradle' of the Celtic civilization, and, more importantly for us, the Prettani of southern Britain.

The Prettani or Pritani first appear in the account of the voyages of the Greek explorer Pytheas of Marseilles who sailed the seas off the Pretanic Isles sometime in the late fourth century BC. Following Pytheas fellow-Greek authors like Polybius (second century BC) and Diodorus (first century BC) also wrote of the Prettani though Strabo, writing after Caesar's expeditions to the Brittanic Isles in 55 and 54 BC, called them Brettani. To Caesar and fellow-Latin authors like Catullus they were, from the first, Brittani hence the Roman name for the province, Britannia. It is significant that the people encountered by Pytheas described themselves as Pritani since this is the word, rendered *Prydain* in translation, that the Welsh use today to describe what in English, as derived from the Latin, is called Britain. Using the linguistic similarities between Welsh/Breton and Pretanic/Britonic as their base, early philologists like the Abbé Pezron in his *L'Antiquité de la nation et la langue des Celtes* (1703) and Edward Lhuyd (Llwyd) in his *Archaeologia Britannica* (1707), arrived at a definition in which a group of related languages spoken in ancient Gaul, and still surviving in parts of Brittany and Britain, namely, Breton, Cornish, Welsh, Irish, Manx and Scottish, were described as Celtic. Not content with this definition later philologists further subdivided the Celtic languages into two: Goidelic (Irish, Manx and Scottish) and Brittonic (Breton, Cornish, Welsh). It is from among the second group of 'Celts' that the Pembrokeshire tribe of the Prettani are generally thought to be descended.

'Celtic' Pembrokeshire

'Celtic' Pembrokeshire was gradually settled from the east by tribes of the Prettani who first absorbed and then displaced the few and dispersed people already living there. The Prettani were a war-like people who were as much in conflict with each other as with enemies from without, hence the need for so many hill-forts and defended settlements! Archaeological investigation of the defended settlement at Pilcornswell near Llawhaden in the early 1980s suggests that its defensive timber and earth rampart had been destroyed by fire due possibly to an enemy attack around 300 BC. Roman writers described the Celts they encountered as 'war-mad and quick to battle', and because, in their pagan belief system, the head was thought to be the seat of the soul it was usual for their warriors to collect the severed heads of their enemies. It was a society that maintained a rigid distinction between the class of elite warriors and the class of servile workers so that war was a privilege of an elite. The Prettani consisted of several tribal groups spread across southern Britain of which five settled in what is now Wales. Territorially, Wales was divided between the Ordovices in the north-west, the Deceangli in the north-east, the Cornovii in the central region, the Silures in the south-east and the Demetae in the south-west. The problem with this neat picture of 'Celtic' Pembrokeshire is that it is essentially Roman and therefore dates from the second half of the first century AD. Iron Age Pembrokeshire has a history that precedes the arrival of the 'Celts' from the east but of which little is known.

Much of what is known of Iron Age Pembrokeshire, which remains essentially prehistoric, is down to the finds and techniques of archaeology and the interpretations of archaeologists. In fact, Pembrokeshire has witnessed a two-fold development in a new technique of reconstructive archaeology in which an Iron Age settlement was not only reconstructed but peopled by volunteers in an attempt to recreate the toils of daily life. Following excavation at the inland promontory fort of Castell Henllys, Newport, Iron Age houses were reconstructed on the foundations of the prehistoric timber dwellings. Built of wattle and daub walls, reed-thatched conical roofs and central open-hearths, the houses, together with a reconstructed pottery kiln and iron smelting furnace, offer some indication of what such sites would have looked like. It has been estimated that the settlement accommodated a community somewhere in the region of a hundred people and that it might have served as the territorial centre controlling the adjacent countryside. In a more controversial recent experiment that attracted media interest, spawning both a television series and a book, a group of volunteers agreed to live on-site for a specified period in order to recreate the trials and tribulations of daily life. The success and usefulness of the venture is the subject of debate but suffice to say they found life there a great deal tougher than expected. In fact, archaeologists suggest that in comparison with the more fertile region of south-east England, life during the Iron Age in Pembrokeshire was rather poor.

Unlike, for example, Castell Henllys, Carn Ingli and Deer Park Fort, Marloes, the majority of the hundred or so most prominent hill-forts and defended enclosures in Pembrokeshire were small, sufficient only to sustain extended family groups. The difference in size between them probably indicates the development of larger regional groupings of people which contributed towards forming the basis of tribal areas within which smaller settlements came under the control of the larger hill-forts. Whatever their size and importance all depended for their survival on agriculture. The different areas of Pembrokeshire inevitably supported a variety of agricultural economic systems. The north of the county was probably largely pastoral, based on sheep-farming, particularly in the Preseli hills, while the south was more suited to a mixture of arable and pastoral. Indeed, arable field systems have been found adjacent to settlements bounded by small, square or rectangular walls the best examples of which are to be found on Skomer Island. It was the competition for land that sparked conflict and, consequently, more competitive societies came to be dominated by tribal chieftains and warrior aristocracies such as that exhibited by the Demetae. Exactly how and when the Demetae came to dominate Pembrokeshire and the south-west is not known but what can be said with some confidence is that they were certainly in control of the region when the Romans arrived. They brought with them a new culture and a Brittonic language that survives, in one of its derivative forms, as Welsh.

Henceforth, from the first century AD, we may refer to the Prettani by their Roman name, Britons, not that this should suggest they were all the same, for besides their different tribal groupings the various peoples who made up the 'Britons' of Britannia were anything but alike. They may have had a shared language and culture but the regional differences could be as acute as they are today in any modern society. Caesar considered the Britons of the south-east more civilized and of a different stock to those in the interior. The principal surviving historian of Roman Britain, Tacitus (b. c. AD 55), observed that the Britons varied widely in physical type, specifically comparing the red-haired and large limbed Caledonii of the Scottish Highlands to the swarthy and curly-haired Silures of south-east Wales. The one element that may be said to have been a unifying influence was their religion and the pagan rituals that accompanied it. They worshipped a large number of gods, such as Andate, the goddess of victory, and there were a number of widespread cult practices, such as the veneration of natural landscape features, and a significant element of ritual human sacrifice. It was the inhuman practices perpetrated in the name of their religion that earned for their priests, the white-robed druids, the scorn of Roman writers. Diodorus Siculus accused them of mass human sacrifice while he and Tacitus both claimed that they used human entrails cut from their sacrificial victims as a means of consulting their gods. Both Pliny and Dio Cassius emphasized the importance of sacred groves of oak, the use of mistletoe, golden sickles and herbal medicine in druidic religion. What is not clear is the extent to which the members of this priestly caste wielded political power or influence in British tribal society. What is certain is the prominence accorded them by Roman writers who would not have done so had they not thought them to be both influential and dangerous.

Roman Pembrokeshire

The Romans, of course, need no introduction. Their empire, their legions, their way of life, their language and their beliefs are assured a prominent place in European history. Suffice to say that it was the Romans who ushered Wales and Pembrokeshire from prehistory into recorded history. Within five years of the Roman invasion of Britain in AD 43 the tribes of southern England had been subdued. The tribes settled in Wales took a while longer, some twenty years, and considerably more effort – three legions of nearly 20,000 troops – before they too succumbed to the might of Rome. Resistance in the west was led by the Silures and the Deceangli who bore the brunt of Roman attacks until they gave way, sometime between AD 51 and AD 77, enabling the victors eventually to establish great legionary fortresses at Deva (Chester) c. AD 75, Viroconium (Wroxeter, Shropshire) c. AD 66, Burrium (Usk) and Isca (Caerleon) c. AD 75. Soon they pushed westward at which point, in south Wales, the Romans encountered the Demetae, a tribe hitherto not involved in the resistance. Indeed, at no point in the Roman conquest of Wales are they mentioned as being in conflict with Rome or its legions. This is not to suggest that there was no fighting but the absence of firm historical and archaeological evidence, apart from the lightly constructed but impressively large Roman marching camps at Y Pigwn near Llandovery, to that effect suggests a generally peaceful take-over of the south-west. What remains to be debated is not the nature of that take-over – the usual method was by the construction of roads linking a network of auxiliary forts that were permanently garrisoned – but the geographical limit of its extent. The Bishop of St David's, William Basil Jones (d.1897), dismissed the existence of Roman Pembrokeshire in his address to the British Archaeological Association held in Tenby in 1884 with the words: 'I do not know that there is any trustworthy evidence that the Romans ever got into Pembrokeshire at all.'

Thus, it has been argued that the use of the term 'Roman Pembrokeshire' is inappropriate. This is because the Romans are thought never to have penetrated far beyond Carmarthen, thus leaving Pembrokeshire clear of Rome's legions. Indeed, apart from the discovery of a number of coin hoards along with other small-scale finds and what may be the outline-remains of a Roman road running from Carmarthen to just east of Llawhaden, there is scant evidence of Roman building or occupation west of the modern boundary of Carmarthenshire. Herein lies the weakness of the argument for there was no concept of 'Pembrokeshire', no notion of modern county boundaries and to think in terms of a Roman-free Pembrokeshire is to miss the point. The Romans did not need to occupy 'Pembrokeshire' in order to dominate it since they had already subdued the tribe which controlled it, the Demetae, a large number of whom lived there. Even given the construction of the Roman fort at Moridunum (Carmarthen) and *vicus* or civil settlement outside it, the Demetae appear not to have been intensively garrisoned by the Roman army. Of the thirty-five forts constructed to hold Wales, not one, as far as is known, was established in 'Pembrokeshire'. Garrisoned by a force of auxiliary cavalry or infantry and built at 12-mile intervals – usually corresponding to a day's march – these forts were symbols of Roman power not apparently required as far west as the Pembrokeshire promontory. Therefore, outside the main network of the frontier – and it must be remembered that until the first quarter of the second century AD Wales was at the limit of the Roman Empire – it is difficult to say how far or how regularly Pembrokeshire was policed by the Romans. Although conjectural, the remains of a small, temporary Roman outpost or fortlet known as Castle Flemish near Ambleston may suggest that the despatching of mobile patrols this far west was not uncommon.

The apparent reluctance to garrison 'Pembrokeshire' may have been due to the poverty and remoteness of the area or, perhaps, due to a benign attitude towards the Romans on the part of the native population who may have felt indebted to them for defeating their enemies the Silures. Additionally, it has been argued that first contact, by way of trade, and the possible *Romanization* of the Demetae, may have begun before the legions arrived at Moridunum. Of course, domination and control take many forms and may be expressed in ways other than by military means, for example, economically, politically, socially and religiously. Politically and administratively 'Pembrokeshire' was doubtless incorporated within the *civitas* or tribal administrative district that was eventually established, when peaceful conditions permitted, and thereby becoming an integral part of the province of Britannia. Economically 'Pembrokeshire' became dependent on the *civitas*-capital, Moridunum Demetarum, that was founded at Carmarthen and served as the Romano-tribal centre for the whole of the Demetae irrespective of where they dwelt in south-west Wales.

Therefore, there can be little doubt that the impact of Roman rule was felt even in this remote corner of the empire, particularly since it lasted for some three hundred years. That said, it is evident that unlike their tribal cousins, the Britons of south-east England, who early became socially and politically sophisticated, the Britons of south-west Wales were slow to acquire a taste for things Roman. Although some Roman artefacts have been found, such as the finely decorated hand-fired red samian pottery and coins, in some of the small defended enclosures, no great villas, or other large buildings outside Carmarthen, have been discovered. In fact, it would seem that the majority of those living within 'Pembrokeshire' continued to do so within the Iron-Age hill-forts and defended settlements until comparatively late.

The *civitas* of south-west Wales was one of around fifteen self-governing tribal authorities (*civitates*) established in Britannia between AD 70 and AD 120. This system of provincial administration had the advantage of perpetuating the existing tribal framework and it is largely from among the aristocratic elite of the Demetae that the elected magistrates and council members were drawn. According to Tacitus the Britons of south-east England had, by AD 80, widely adopted Roman fashion in housing, clothing, language, and diet, even claiming that the toga was everywhere to be seen in Britain. Just how widespread the adoption of a Romanized lifestyle was in Britain is hotly debated but it is likely that the Demetae, or at least their tribal elite, were well on the way to being assimilated by at least the middle of the second century AD. Tacitus had no doubt but that the native Britons wished to emulate the lifestyle of their conquerors, as he said: 'And so the Britons were slowly introduced to the luxuries that make vice agreeable.' The benefits of *pax Romana* were obvious for all to see and by AD 220 it was decreed that Roman citizenship be extended to all upper-class Britons. It is probably the case that in some parts of the country there might have been little to distinguish between 'Roman' and 'native'. That said, to suggest that the life of the Britons of south-west Wales was completely transformed by the Romans is likely to be wide of the mark; for some, the elite, it was but for the majority of the population life probably went on much as before.

That three centuries of Roman rule and occupation had bequeathed a legacy to Wales cannot be doubted; the adoption of the Christian faith is surely to be counted among the more significant, but equally, the nature, depth and influence of that legacy probably diminishes the further west one travels. Consequently, it is reasonable to suppose that the Demetean tribespeople of 'Pembrokeshire' were less Romanized than those of their tribe who lived and traded within the orbit of Roman Carmarthen. It is probably no coincidence that towards the end of the fourth century some of the Irish sea-raiders that had plagued for some time the southern and western shores of Wales should decide to migrate and settle mainly in 'Pembrokeshire'. A lightly defended and irregularly policed territory held no terror for them and as Roman power in Britain gradually diminished these 'barbarian hordes' from Ireland became ever bolder. The dilemma and the danger facing the Britons was succinctly put by the sixth-century monk and Roman provincial Gildas who wrote: 'The barbarians drive us on to the sea and the sea drives us back on the barbarians.' Of course, without wishing to minimize the very real threat posed by such merciless raiding, to suggest that the relationship between the tribespeople of southern Ireland and south-west Wales was based purely on war and plunder is not only unreasonable but unrealistic. It is likely that for some time they had at least traded, if not mingled with each other, from which preliminary contact a host of consequences might have flowed, of which one may have been in attracting the attention of more predatory Irish clans. Indeed, it is not unreasonable to suppose that 'Pembrokeshire' and its people formed the hub of sea-borne trade routes that took in mid- and southern Ireland, mid- and south Wales and the south-west of England.

It is generally thought that the last of Rome's legions were withdrawn from Britain in AD 383 after which Roman rule lingered only for a short while longer before the citizen-nobility of the various *civitates* across the country took over. In truth, they had been encouraged to see to their own government and defence for some time, particularly as Rome's power to influence events in Britain gave way to pressures from elsewhere in a slowly disintegrating empire. Consequently, any attempt at centralization had to be abandoned and the *civitates* gradually evolved into separate states or kingdoms ruled by the most powerful of the Romano-British aristocratic elite who, in turn, founded princely dynasties. Thus, by the beginning of the fifth century, Pembrokeshire had begun a new, if turbulent, chapter in its history in which the former *civitate* of the Demetae was gradually replaced by the kingdom of Dyfed.

Early Medieval or 'Dark Age'
Pembrokeshire: An Age of Kings,
Kingdoms and Saints

Introduction: The Dark Ages

> The blank in English history which extends over the 5th and 6th
> centuries has always fascinated thinking men, for during that
> period the grandest tragedy ever played on British land was
> performed. Civilized Romano-British society was overwhelmed
> by a flood of barbarism which burst on it from north, east and
> west. Welsh pride fostered a notion that matters were very
> different in the Principality. (E. Laws)

'Dark Ages' was a term originally employed in the seventeenth and
eighteenth centuries to indicate the intellectual darkness that was
believed to have descended on Europe with the ending of the Roman
Empire and although it continues in use to this day, it is not as popular a
historical label as it once was. Nevertheless, as far as our knowledge of
the settlement, society and economy of Wales, let alone Pembrokeshire,
is concerned, the six hundred years between the collapse of Roman rule,
c. AD 400, and the arrival of the Normans, *c.* 1070, can indeed be called a
'Dark Age'. Whether or not one accepts the late Gwyn A. Williams's
assertion that 'From the fifth century the western regions of Britain drop
out of history [and] do not climb back in until the ninth century,' it is a
fact that, apart from the few references or remains, those who attempt the
study of Pembrokeshire during this period will get but scant assistance
from either history or archaeology. The paucity of material for the study
of early medieval history has best been described by Wendy Davies in
her book *Wales in the Early Middle Ages* (1982):

> There are no 'official' government or institution-sponsored
> records of the type that form the stuff of history writing of most
> parts of Western Europe from the twelfth century onwards. There
> are no censuses, no tax returns, no records of regular court
> proceedings, no estate surveys, no accounts; there are no registers

of births and deaths, of properties, of transactions; there is no written constitution, no statute book that records legislation, no statement of bye-laws, no regulations from guilds or other corporations. There is therefore scarcely any standardized procedure for written record-keeping, and no implication that the act of making the record in some sense guaranteed its veracity.

So what is left? Not much perhaps but enough that can, along with physical evidence, be pieced together to provide a working hypothesis of the early history of Pembrokeshire. Those pieces of evidence include records such as the Latin annals known as the *Annales Cambriae* and *Brut y Tywysogyon* or *Chronicle of the Princes* and the so-called Laws of Hywel Dda. Although terse in character and with the surviving copies dating only from the late eleventh century, the *Annales Cambriae* do provide a year-by-year survey of past events beginning in the fifth century and, together with references in the *Brut*, running through to the end of the thirteenth. Similarly, the law codes of Hywel Dda were copied some three hundred years after his death in *c*.949 but they do at least offer some clues about the nature of society in the early medieval period. There also exist some narrative sources (the earliest copies of which date from either the eleventh or twelfth centuries) which, when taken together, shed a little light on the history of west Wales: such as the *Life of St David* written *c*.1090s by Rhigyfarch of Llanbadarn Fawr, the ninth-century *Historia Brittonum* by Nennius, the sixth-century *De Excidio Britanniae* by Gildas and a few fragments of charters from St David's. Not to be ignored are the poems, stories, particularly the *Mabinogi*, and genealogies which, although again dating from later surviving copies, provide titbits of information, long-held beliefs and traditions.

Post-Roman Dyfed

As the Romans withdrew and the empire crumbled the kingdom of Dyfed emerged. However, the only thing that the tribe who lived there, the Demetae, bequeathed the new kingdom was its name and they were soon overrun by an Irish tribe of Goidelic Celts, traditionally thought to be the Deísi. It is almost certain that the ruling dynasty of Dyfed was drawn from among the aristocratic elite of the Deísi, the names of some of whom are known from inscribed stones dating from the time. How an Irish dynasty came to rule in this part of Wales is a matter of conjecture but there are two schools of thought, namely, that they did so by conquest or by invitation. It has been argued that as the incidence of attacks by Irish raiders increased they turned to taking territory in addition to plunder and as they did so they either enslaved or expelled the indigenous population. This had certainly happened elsewhere in Britain as the former Roman province succumbed to attacks by Angles, Jutes, Picts, Scots and Saxons.

On the other hand, it is possible to suggest that the Deísi might well have been invited by the indigenous population to settle in west Wales in order to protect it and them from further attacks by raiders such as themselves. It is perhaps no coincidence that at least one sixth-century Irish ruler of Dyfed is commemorated with the title 'protector'. This policy, whereby aggressive tribes were absorbed rather than confronted, is thought to have been initiated by the Emperor Constans (AD 337–50) in an effort to shore up the crumbling frontiers of the empire. Unable to defend themselves, the hard-pressed Romans accorded tribes such as the Deísi the status of *foederati* or mercenary force and entrusted them with the defence of the frontier. The fact that the frontier often bordered the territory given to them as a reward for their support was intended to provide them with an incentive and also ensure that in future raids they rather than the Romans would bear the brunt of the attacks. According to tradition, something similar had occurred elsewhere and later in Britain, most notably in the supposed invitation by the mid-fifth-century British king Vortigern to the Saxon chiefs Hengist and Horsa to help deliver him and his people from their enemies in return for which they were given substantial tracts of land. In Wales too there is a similar tradition in which a British chief, Cunedda Wledig and his sons, left Manaw Gododdin, a territory in southern Scotland, to settle in north Wales to help drive out the large numbers of Irish settlers who had made it their home. Clearly this was a period in which there was a great deal of tribal movement and displacement and none more so than in Demetia which offered easy access from Ireland.

If the inhabitants of Demetian 'Pembrokeshire' had to keep a wary eye on the western or seaward approaches to their land they had soon to guard against possible threats from the landward side. Although not immediately apparent, events were taking a sinister turn far to the east with the gradual erosion of Romano-British power in England at the hands of the Germanic tribes of Angles and Saxons. It is against this background of Romano-British retreat and Anglo-Saxon advance that Wales is slowly defined, emerging as a distinct entity peopled by like-minded, Celtic-speaking Christians who could more easily distinguish themselves from the pagan, alien invaders. Nevertheless, Wales was not a single political unit and the random pattern of political development within and between kingdoms is quite complex. Suffice to say that despite long-continuing conflict the independent rulers of post-Roman Wales evolved a sense of cultural identity in which they came to regard themselves as 'Cymry' or 'fellow countrymen'. To the Anglo-Saxons they were

'Welsh' or 'foreigners' whom, by the mid-seventh century, they had succeeded in pushing back to what, roughly, we would today consider the natural boundaries of Wales: the rivers Dee, Severn and Wye. By the late eighth century the distinction between the British 'Welsh' and the Anglo-Saxon 'English' was put in even sharper relief by the construction of a great earthwork or dyke running the length of Wales from the Irish Sea to the Bristol Channel. Built by the Anglo-Saxon king Offa, of the midland kingdom of Mercia, between c.784 and 795, it was intended as a boundary marker behind which he hoped to confine the Welsh. Nor was Pembrokeshire immune from the pressure exerted by the likes of Offa and his fellow Saxon kings for as he and they drove their Welsh enemies westward the native polities reacted by competing the fiercer for the diminishing land and economic resources left to them. Thus, Wales did not so much develop a refugee culture as a culturally compressed one in which the threat posed by the Anglo-Saxons gradually made for greater cultural identity if not political unity. In such pressured circumstances even bilingual and culturally bilateral 'Pembrokeshire' succumbed eventually to the power of Welsh rather than Irish influence.

The Kings and Kingdoms of Early-Medieval Dyfed

However they settled in west Wales, the fact remains that the Irish presence in Pembrokeshire was overpowering. Evidence of their settlement is provided by the memorial stones raised in honour of local notables, many of which are inscribed in Ogam (Ogham), an early Irish system of writing. Representing the oldest form of writing in Ireland, Ogam consists of an alphabet of twenty, later twenty-five, letters which were normally incised along the edge of a stone pillar. There are over 300 known Ogam stones in Ireland, the majority of which are concentrated in Munster, and nearly twenty-five in areas of south-west Wales colonized by the Irish. The genealogies too, both Welsh and Irish, bear testimony to the Irish descent of the rulers of Dyfed, the earliest of which dates to the eighth century and in which is included a reference to 'Guortepir' son of 'Aircol'. This is generally agreed to be a reference to Vortipor or Vorteporix (Gwrthefyr in Welsh), ruler of Dyfed in the first half of the sixth century, and to his father Aircol ap Triphun or Aircol Lawhir (the long-handed), who may or may not have existed. Certainly, the distinguished historian Sir J. E. Lloyd (d.1947) seems to have accepted the veracity of the pedigrees in respect of the latter's existence stating that his 'name, derived as it is from Agricola, suggests that some vestiges of the culture of Rome still survived in the land' (Dyfed). Even if he were to be but a figment of the imagination of an eighth-century genealogist, the reference bears scrutiny for the light it sheds on the mindset of contemporaries who thought it important to establish links with the Roman past for this corner of west Wales.

With Vortipor we are on more secure ground and the fact that he is commemorated in stone bearing both a Latin and Ogam inscription suggests a degree of fusion between the native Demetians and settler Irish Deísi. The social and cultural fusion that evidently took place between the Romano-British and Goidelic-Irish peoples of Dyfed may have occurred naturally over time or else was assisted, perhaps even forced, by the strong rule of its kings. It is instructive that Vortipor 'the protector', as he is styled in the anonymously inscribed sixth-century stone memorial, was known to the monk-chronicler Gildas as the 'tyrant'; both descriptions, in their own way, suggest a degree of strength and power in the nature of his rule. The memorial stone, discovered in 1895 in the Carmarthenshire churchyard of Castell Dwyran, is a significant find since its use of the title 'protector' is taken as a possible indication of the dynastic origin of the early rulers of Dyfed, that is of *foederati* employed by the Romans in the declining years of the Empire, and that its bearing by Vortipor was done hereditarily. Unfortunately, these stone memorials offer only short inscriptions giving rise to much inference on the part of historians so that information gleaned from works such as by Gildas is made more precious.

Damned for his lack of support or effort in turning the tide of barbarism that was overwhelming the last remnants of Roman civilization in Britain, almost all of what is known of this early king of Dyfed comes by way of the biased commentary of Gildas. His great work *De Excidio Britanniae* is certainly not history and nor was it intended to be; rather it is an epistle addressed to the rulers of his day, both royal and ecclesiastical, warning them of the dangers of sin. In adopting the style of the Old Testament prophets, Gildas could not help but see the evil in men and, although he admits to the existence of some good men, he only ever names one: Ambrosius Aurelianus or Emrys Wledig, whom some later writers have taken to be a reference to the mythical Arthur. The following extract is typical of his unsparing commentary the object of which, in this instance, was Vortipor, king of Dyfed:

> Your head is already whitening, as you sit upon a throne that is full of treachery and stained from top to bottom with diverse murders and adulteries, worthless son of a good king (like Manasseh son of Hezekiah): Vortipor, tyrant of the Demetae. The end of your life is gradually drawing near; why can you not be satisfied by such violent surges of sin, which you gulp down like vintage wine – or rather allow yourself to be engulfed by them?
>
> Why, to crown your crimes, do you weigh down your wretched soul with a burden you cannot shrug off, the rape of a shameless

daughter after the removal and honourable death of your own wife? (M. Winterbottom, 1978)

Whether or not the aged king of Dyfed deserved Gildas's bitter invective, and it must be remembered that his prejudices were those of a monk, it is evident that Vortipor was a ruler to be reckoned with. Nor was he alone, being one of five 'tyrant-kings' denounced by Gildas, one of whom was Maelgwn Gwynedd (d. *c*.547), so that Vortipor was clearly in good company. That he had evidently ruled his kingdom, as had the others, for some considerable time, might suggest that his very longevity betokens success.

The nature and extent of the kingdom established under Vortipor is nowhere made clear in contemporary sources. That it included Pembrokeshire is certain and was likely still, as in Roman times, to have extended at least as far as Carmarthen and into southern Ceredigion. In fact, to regard early Dyfed as a kingdom in the conventional sense of having a fixed territorial base is fraught with difficulty. Contemporaries were inconsistent in their use of the word 'kingdom' in so far as some kings were named without any reference to their kingdoms or they might be called king in, but not necessarily of, a named territory. On the other hand, some rulers, like Vortipor, were described as kings of people rather than territories. The concept and development of a fixed territorial unit belongs to a later age so that there is no hard and fast rule that can be applied to the period between the end of Roman rule to the beginning, possibly, of the tenth century. In this respect it is probably safe to assume that the power of the kings of Dyfed extended only as far they could control the dispersed communities that lay within easy reach of their war bands. After all, what was a king but the most powerful individual who could exert the greatest control over the largest population in a given geographical area? The means by which these early kings achieved this was by the employment of armed men willing to do their bidding in return for status and reward. Therefore, rulers like Vortipor were essentially soldiers, and successful ones at that, men who had earned the respect of others partly by their aristocratic pedigree, particularly those who could (or who claimed to) trace their descent back to the citizen-nobility of Roman rule, but also because they had the ability to plan and lead military campaigns. Their continued hegemony depended very much on their success in war, which was equated with virtues such as courage and honour, and their ability to bully a servile peasant-farmer population.

The royal dynasty of Dyfed lasted in the male line, i.e. as descended from Vortipor, until the death of Triphun in 814 and it continued thereafter by marriage with persons of unknown origins until Llywarch ap Hyfaidd's death in 904. Indeed, for much of the century following the death of Tryffin there was confusion and disorder in a rapidly contracting Dyfed –

territory was lost to the emerging sub-kingdoms of Ceredigion and Ystrad Tywi (roughly modern Carmarthenshire) – and it is not certainly known who ruled. According to Asser (d.909), cleric, scholar and biographer of the Saxon King Alfred (d.899), the obscure Hyfaidd ap Bleddri was King of Dyfed until his death in 892. His iron rule was stigmatized somewhat by his repressive treatment of the religious community at St David's which had appealed, unsuccessfully, through Asser, one of its number, for the aid of King Alfred whose power Hyfaidd feared. Apart from his name and the apparent loss of territory, which had once formed the easternmost region of Dyfed, to the neighbouring kingdom of Seisyllwg, nothing certain is known of Hyfaidd's son and successor Llywarch. Upon his death his daughter Elen, and her husband Hywel ap Cadell (d.949), ruler of Seisyllwg (Ceredigion and Ystrad Tywi combined), succeeded and Dyfed became part of the larger kingdom of Deheubarth. It is from roughly this point on that Pembrokeshire, in the guise of a diminished Dyfed, settles within the boundaries that equate, more or less, with the modern county.

During its heyday as an independent kingdom Dyfed had played host to countless invaders and suffered dreadfully at the hands of raiding Saxons, pillaging Vikings and conquering Cymry. Despite expansionist tendencies of its own, as witnessed by Hyfaidd's raids on the western fringes of Glywysing, Dyfed was not strong enough to resist the encroaching power of its rivals, particularly Gwynedd under Rhodri Mawr 'The Great' (d.878) and the most powerful members of its dynasty such as Rhodri's grandson, Hywel ap Cadell, otherwise known as Hywel Dda, 'The Good'. Hywel is an exceptional figure in Welsh history not simply on account of his fame having endured untarnished through more than ten centuries but because his rulership was held in such high esteem in his own day and beyond. He is the only native ruler to have acquired the epithet 'Good' which suggests that his achievements must have been somewhere near as great as those of his grandfather Rhodri. Hywel too managed to unite almost the whole of Wales under his rule but, if tradition is to be believed, his bequest to the Welsh people went far beyond political unity. It involved the codification of native law, the so-called 'Laws of Hywel Dda'. Whether or not Hywel was responsible for the laws that bear his name, the earliest copies of which date to the late twelfth century and are thought to be the work of the Lord Rhys, does not matter since it was his name, rather than that of any other Welsh king, that was thought most appropriate to be associated with such a prestigious undertaking. As far as the people of Dyfed were concerned, Hywel was their king by way of marriage rather than conquest, a fact which may have made their assimilation into the over-kingdom of Deheubarth more palatable. Until the coming of the Normans the history of the subkingdom of Dyfed would be bound up with that of Deheubarth.

The Church in Early Medieval Dyfed

The circumstances surrounding the introduction of Christianity into Britain is not certainly known but it is generally agreed that it probably has its roots in the century and a half before the end of Roman rule. True to their tradition of laissez-faire in religious matters, especially once the more dangerous elements in British druidism had been eradicated, the Romans allowed the Britons to worship their gods alongside their own. By a natural process of adoption, assimilation, diffusion and imitation the distinction between the two religions blurred sufficiently for it to gradually create a sense of unity among the people. Consequently, when the Christian faith arrived it was initially confronted by persecution which produced three early martyrs in Alban of Verulamium and Aaron and Julius of Caerleon. Once it had been given the Roman seal of approval, being encouraged by the conversion of the Emperor Constantine I (d.337), Christianity was increasingly adopted in Wales thereafter though perhaps, initially, only nominally so in the less Romanized Pembrokeshire. However, on the break-up of the Roman Empire and due to its increasing isolation, 'Celtic' Christianity developed on independent lines from 'Roman' Christianity so that it had long been established in Wales before missions from Rome were despatched, beginning in the seventh century, to convert the pagan Anglo-Saxons. In fact, the conversion of the Anglo-Saxons and the later arrival of the Normans put the Celtic and Roman churches on a collision course in which bitter conflict the latter, under its leader the Pope, would eventually emerge victorious. It is probably partly on account of this struggle for primacy between the respective church hierarchies and partly because the Normans, as we shall see later, tried to wipe it out of existence, that so little physical trace of the Celtic church survives. Indeed, early Christian stones are the only artefacts that survive in reasonable numbers, some 450 in the whole of Wales dating from the fifth to the eleventh centuries, a large proportion of which can be found in Pembrokeshire.

The church in early medieval Wales was based upon the *clas* or religious community which served as a base for worship and as a mission centre for its clergy. These communities were founded by missionary monks, some of whom were Irish, who evangelized the country during the fifth and sixth centuries. Once a *clas* had been established it functioned very much along the lines of a monastery, becoming a focus for devotion and beyond which other churches were built for the people, ensuring that the form and nature of their worship was strictly controlled by the founding community or mother church. Built originally of timber and surrounded usually by roughly circular earthen embankments which came to define a religious enclosure or *llan*, these early churches were nearly always dedicated to one or other of the most important missionary monks who came to be revered, and were later canonized, as saints. As these religious sites developed they attracted secular settlements, hence the high incidence of place names in Wales beginning with *llan* though it must be pointed out that, due largely to later alien settlement, there are fewer of these in Pembrokeshire, with the majority being located in the north of the county. It is in the northern portion of Pembrokeshire that early Christian cemeteries, a rarity in Wales as a whole, have been found. Known as cist burials, on account of their being distinctively stone-lined or slab-built graves, they have been excavated at Bayvil near Nevern and at Llanychlwydog near Fishguard. Others are known to exist at Caldy, Llanwnda and St Elvis. A relatively recent and extraordinary find took place on a burial site on Ramsey Island, a stone inscription in Anglo-Saxon dating to either the eighth or ninth century.

'Age of the Saints'

It is the activities of prominent members of the Celtic church (highlighted by the *Lives* or later biographical accounts of many of its leaders) during the fifth and sixth centuries that has earned for this period in Welsh history the label 'Age of the Saints'. It is a label that is not without its critics for although it continues to figure prominently in most surveys, both of Welsh history and of early medieval ecclesiastical history, it may not, figuratively speaking, be strictly correct. As A. H. Williams stated in his *Introduction to the History of Wales* (1941), the Age of the Saints should refer to the age of early monasticism rather than simply concentrate on the lives of a select few, since the Welsh word *sant* in this period, he argues, means only 'monk' and monks were certainly plentiful in Wales. Therefore, it is the monastic movement as a whole, characterized by the missionary zeal of its leaders, and the church that thereby became established that best describes this period in the nation's and the county's religious history. Nevertheless, the fact that the saints' lives may have been written, as Gwyn A. Williams so irreverently put it, 'in the rat-race of the Norman imposition of the Roman Church several centuries later', does not disqualify them from serious study particularly as some of the more important of them – Samson, Dyfrig, Teilo and especially David or Dewi – hailed from, or had links with, Pembrokeshire.

Who and what were these saints? In the Christian tradition saints are deceased members of the faithful believed to have already entered into heavenly glory. They provided not only a practical moral example for worshippers to follow but also a tangible bridge between the devout and the divine. This 'bridge' remained intact even in death for although the saint was no longer available in person his relics were. Until recent carbon-dating tests proved otherwise, the bones of St David were among the most precious relics held by the clergy at the cathedral of St David's. In the early medieval period saints were created by popular acclamation in response to their holiness of life and outstanding moral qualities, testified by such forms of heroic witness to the faith as miracles. For example, St David is said to have restored the sight of a blind monk and to have brought the dead back to life. Consequently, it was not long before shrines were set up, centres of pilgrimage established and cults encouraged so that they offered, for the local communities that proclaimed them, commercial and political as well as religious benefits. Indeed, by the tenth and eleventh centuries, saints could have territory, privileges and powers of protection, all of which became enshrined in and protected by law. Nevertheless, it is a fact that the majority of these saints were so localized and obscure that little or nothing is known of them. On the other hand, a select few gained a following outside their own immediate locality; St David prominent among them, he being the most frequently mentioned of the saints. Unsurprisingly, the more successful pilgrimage sites could attract countless numbers of pilgrims, all willing to pay for the privilege of worshipping at the shrine, for example Nevern. The potential power, both religious and political, of such sites was not lost on church leaders who came to monopolize their control, taking over the canonization process before it was reserved to the Holy See of Rome in the twelfth century. Thus, Welsh devotional practice, as elsewhere in Europe, became marked by the veneration of holy places, wells, and relics associated with both officially canonized and popularly proclaimed saints.

The later politicization and commercialization of these saints is a far cry from the simple and austere lives of devotion they led. True, many of them may not have actually existed but those that did devoted their lives to God and to the spiritual welfare of their contemporaries and they did so largely by means of preaching and prayer. Among the earliest of these saints was Dyfrig, dubbed by some historians as the father of the Celtic saints in Wales, who lived in the latter half of the fifth century. Although he hailed from south-east Wales he is early connected with Caldy Island which he used as a retreat, no doubt to recharge his religious batteries, and from where he sallied forth into the secular world intent on extolling the benefits of monasticism. His influence was keenly felt by Samson whom he is said to have ordained a priest and with whom he spent some time on Caldy. Samson was a man of Dyfed being the son of noble parents, Amwn and Anna of Gwent, and although not originally intended for the church he took up the religious life with relish, searching always for greater asceticism. He did not remain long in his native Pembrokeshire but travelled widely, to Cornwall, the Channel Islands and Brittany, in the last of which he settled and founded a monastery at Dol. Much of what we know of him comes from a seventh-century Breton *Life of Samson* in which the subject's contribution to the work of the church in Brittany was highly praised. According to a later tradition, Teilo too was Dyfed born, near Penally, and well educated becoming a colleague of both Samson, with whom he stayed in Brittany for a time to escape the 'yellow' plague, and David, whom he accompanied on pilgrimage to Jerusalem. Due in part to strong dedication evidence but also because of their enduring historical and religious fame, both Teilo and David are credited with causing a great revival in Celtic Christianity which was under threat from the pagan Saxons. Unlike David, who chose to head west and settle in 'Irish infested' Pembrokeshire, Teilo moved east and established a powerful monastic centre at Llandeilo Fawr in Carmarthenshire. That said, Teilo did not neglect Pembrokeshire entirely as testified by the survival of a Llandeilo near Maenclochog.

Among the more illustrious of the saintly sons of Pembrokeshire is David. Founder and abbot-bishop of St David's, and patron saint of Wales, David may have been born in neighbouring Ceredigion but it is with Pembrokeshire that he is most closely identified. Many accounts of him are based on the late eleventh-century biography (*c*.1090) by Rhigyfarch (d.1099) of Llanbadarn Fawr whose father, Sulien 'the Wise' (d.1091), had twice been bishop of St David's. It was doubtless through his father's influence that Rhigyfarch had access to, and made use of, what he himself describes as 'very old manuscripts found chiefly at St David's'. According to his clerical biographer David was born to Sant, king of Ceredigion, and the woman he ravished, a nun known as Non (Nonnita in Latin). Taking up a clerical career David is said to have travelled throughout Wales, preaching and founding monasteries before settling at Mynyw (more popularly known in its Latin form as *Menevia*) in Pembrokeshire. He was a man who revelled in the rigour of his ascetic life and though opposed by some of the Irish settlers in northern Pembrokeshire, one chieftain called Boia in particular, he overcame all obstacles to found the religious community that came eventually to bear his name. Indeed, it was not until the high Middle Ages that the original place name of Mynyw was gradually displaced by the more regular use of Tyddewi, rendered in English as St David's, though for official purposes *Menevia* continued to be used by the Latin-literate clergy to refer to the diocese that evolved around and became subject to, the cathedral and its canons.

The sixty-eight-chapter *Life of St David* has been described by historians as 'turgid' and 'its contents a hazardous mixture of the miraculous and the historical' which is both 'fanciful' and 'propaganda'. Few would argue with these opinions but that does not mean that it has no merit for even if it were a work of fiction it has much to teach us about the mindset of the author and the world, both mental and physical, in which he lived. That said, there is little doubt that though the story of his life is fraught with invention the man, be he a theologian, preacher or just simply a monk, did exist. There are, for example, references to him as early as the eighth and ninth centuries – in the so-called 'Catalogue of the Saints of Ireland' and in 'The Martyrology of Oengus' in which 1 March is recorded as the date of his festival – and he is mentioned in the early tenth-century poem *Armes Prydein*, as the spiritual leader of the Welsh against the Saxon English. More telling is the fact that his cult was well-established by the eleventh century and at least sixty churches had been dedicated to him by 1200. Whatever the truth of his identity there is no doubting the impact his legacy had on the church and although he was never canonized by Pope Calixtus II in 1123, despite repeated claims to that effect, his place as the premier saint of Wales was assured.

Pembrokeshire and the Vikings

It is not possible to study the history of a sea-going region of Wales without reference to the Vikings. An Old Norse term of disputed derivation which only came into popular usage in the nineteenth century, the so-called Vikings or Norsemen originated from Scandinavia but by the ninth century they had established strong communities elsewhere in Europe, Ireland prominent among them. From the ninth to the eleventh century the Vikings spread their terror abroad with such ferocity that their historical standing has reached epic proportions. This is not to say that their almost legendary exploits for merciless raiding are undeserved, far from it, they were every bit as fierce as they have been portrayed, but one must consider that it was as much the psychological shock that they inflicted on their hapless victims as the actuality of their attacks which bears most strikingly on their reputations. Word of mouth breeds fear and fearful exaggeration tended to characterize the tale-telling that followed their destructive raids so that the very mention of the Gentiles, as they were commonly called by contemporaries, was often by itself enough to cause uncontrollable panic. Nevertheless, it must not be thought that they were invincible for, though rare, they did find themselves at the receiving end of bloody defeats as occurred in 1042 when, according to the *Brut y Tywysogyon*, 'Hywel defeated the Gentiles who were ravaging Dyfed'.

The object of Viking attacks was, for the most part, booty, which, in addition to goods, often involved people intended for service or sale as slaves. On the other hand, they were also willing to act as mercenaries and they can frequently be found in the company of Welsh rulers who would hire them for particular campaigns. For example, in 992 Maredudd ab Owain (d.999) of Deheubarth, a kingdom which included Dyfed, 'ravaged Glamorgan by hiring Gentiles and ransoming the captives', or his great-great nephew Rhys ap Tewdwr (d.1093) who in 1088 'gave treasure to the pirates – Scots and Irish – who had come to his aid'. Nevertheless, it is clear also that they were not natural allies and that, in the long term, they were not to be trusted, being prone to turn on their former comrades-in-arms particularly if the latter were outbid by their enemies or if it simply suited their purpose. Only three years before hiring them as mercenaries Maredudd ab Owain was forced to buy off one intended raid of his kingdom and within two years of his death the Vikings had returned yet again to ravage Dyfed. That said, it is worth noting the opinion of the anonymous author of the early tenth-century Welsh poem *Armes Prydein* who considered the 'Gentiles' and the other Celtic peoples of Britain to be more trustworthy than the English:

> and there will be reconciliation between the Cymry and the men of Dublin,
> the Irish of Ireland and Anglesey and Scotland,
> the men of Cornwall and of Strathclyde will be made welcome among us.

Given the nature of their plunder it is reasonable to suppose that the areas most likely to be attacked were those with the most resources, and the regularity of their raids on particular regions might suggest that their booty was to be found in abundance. In fact, the frequency of their raids on Welsh communities was due also to their relative proximity since the majority of Viking attacks were perpetrated by freebooters who hailed from Ireland. The most fearsome were the so-called Black Gentiles of Dublin who were especially ruthless but, fortunately for Pembrokeshire, they tended to visit their wrath most frequently on Anglesey and the Llŷn peninsula. Not that Pembrokeshire escaped scot free, for it and Anglesey, no doubt on account of their respective wealth in goods, food-stuffs and people, were among the areas in Wales most troubled by Viking attacks. One of the most favoured targets was the religious community and church of St David's which was attacked no less than seven times between 878 and 1091, the last of which resulted in the total destruction by fire of the church. Nor was it only Viking 'Gentiles' that were responsible for the destructive raiding of St David's; in one year alone, 992, *Menevia* was ravaged three times by the forces of Edwin ab Einion and his Saxon ally Edylfi. As has been suggested by Wendy Davies, St David's 'must have had considerable powers of recovery, and therefore considerable resources on which to draw'. The region's wealth could occasionally be turned to its advantage as occurred in 989 when, according to *Brut y Tywysogyon,*

Dyfed was spared an attack because its ruler 'gave a penny from every person as a tribute to the Black Host'.

The Vikings were not simply pirates or mercenaries intent on plunder, they were also settlers and traders. They settled parts of Ireland in considerable numbers, even establishing a kingdom such as that centred on Dublin over which a certain King Sitriuc ruled. Ravaged by the Irish in 1000 and attacked again in 1014 by a united force of Irish kings, the Viking community did not have an easy time of it. Unlike Ireland, Wales was not extensively settled by the Vikings which might explain why they have left so little trace of their activities. Indeed, apart from their fine interlace art-style, an example of which influence can be seen in the decoration of the early Christian wheel-head cross at Carew, Scandinavian place names alone provide the most assured means of tracing their settlement activities. The fact that Pembrokeshire has more place name evidence than any other part of Wales suggests that it was heavily settled by the Vikings, but this need not be the case. The first reliable reference to the Vikings in Pembrokeshire occurs in 878 when Bishop Asser (d.909) states that a Viking force wintered in Dyfed. However, though it can be argued that Pembrokeshire, because of its location, might well have formed part of a sea-going Hiberno-Norse world there is no evidence to suggest that Viking settlements were anything but small, largely coastal and few in number. Nor did they last or else the archaeological evidence would have yielded far more than it has. In the final analysis, the Viking impact on Pembrokeshire will be remembered only so far as the islands of Skokholm, Skomer and Ramsey continue to excite the imagination of the sea-going visitors that delight in visiting their respective shores. In contrast to the fear evoked by marauding Vikings, an anonymous late ninth-century Welsh poem 'In Praise of Tenby' portrays the comradeship and merrymaking in the fortress, possibly located on Castle Hill. The former Lord, Bleiddud, of Dyfed's royal line, is mourned and extolled and the poem is a vibrant celebration of the joy of living in a safe environment during a tempestuous time:

. . . There is a fortress set above the sea,
Happy on festive days is that fair hill.
Above the ceaseless chorus of the deep
Loud are the bards mead-drenched revelry;
Safe from the grey-green ocean, stern and chill,
They leave it for then foes of old to keep.
The soaring sea-birds front the breeze pure white
As laughter echoes in the gathering night.

[trans. by Brian Price]

IV

Late Medieval Pembrokeshire: Conquests, Castles and Kings

Introduction: Medieval Pembrokeshire

> Of all the different parts of Wales, Dyfed is at once the most
> beautiful and the most productive. Of all Dyfed, the province of
> Pembroke is the most attractive; and in all Pembroke the spot
> which I have just described is most assuredly without its equal.
> It follows that in all the broad lands of Wales Manorbier is the
> most pleasant place by far. You will not be surprised to hear me
> lavish praise upon it, when I tell you that this is where my own
> family came from, this is where I myself was born. I can only ask
> you to forgive me. (Giraldus Cambrensis)

Gerald de Barri (1146–1223), better known as Gerald of Wales or Giraldus
Cambrensis, knew 'the province of Pembroke' well but he was no Welshman.
He may have been Welsh-born and he may have had a half-Welsh mother
but he was born, bred and belonged to that group of Norman and Anglo-
Norman settlers responsible for ousting the native Welsh and taking
their land. It was the settlement of families like his in southern Pembrokeshire
that helped evolve the community fondly referred to as 'Little England
beyond Wales'. Gerald represented the conquerors and the colonists
rather than the conquered natives but he was not unsympathetic to the
Welsh, some of whom were his kin, nor was he uncritical of the Anglo-
Normans, some of whom he counted among his enemies. In consequence
of his desire to be impartial, so Gerald believed, he was not accepted by
either side. It was to be a social and cultural dilemma shared down the
centuries by those born in the Anglicized half of the county in that successive
generations of 'Little Englanders' probably felt less alien but possibly
more alienated. Gerald was a Pembrokeshire patriot, proud of the county
of his birth and prouder still of being a Marcher, one of a select band of
pioneers responsible for establishing the lordships that came to form the
territories of the March or 'Frontier Wales'.

Fortunately for us, he was more than simply a contemporary commentator used to conjuring up soundbites, he was a writer of consummate skill and considerable energy who made observations and passed judgement on some of the more important figures and events of his day. Among his many works the *Journey through Wales* (1191) and *Description of Wales* (1194) are to be counted among his best, and as far as learning about Wales and Pembrokeshire is concerned, his most important. He may, as one historian suggests, have been 'incurably egotistic' but his works stand as a fitting and enduring monument to his literary talents which have withstood the test of time. A scholar, courtier and cleric who twice failed to achieve his ambition of becoming bishop of St David's, he was a widely travelled man who could boast of itineraries of Ireland, Wales, England and France. He is, therefore, an indispensable guide to understanding the turbulent period that marked the history of Wales and Pembrokeshire during his long and eventful life. Indeed, there is no one to compare with Gerald in the medieval period and with his passing historians are forced to rely on the often brief and sometimes sterile comments left us by monastic and royal scribes. Would that we had a Gerald alive in the fourteenth and fifteenth centuries who could offer an insight, complete with witty asides and gossipy titbits, into the effects on Pembrokeshire of the Black Death (1348–51), the Glyndŵr Rebellion (1400–15) and the Wars of the Roses (1455–87).

Conquest and Settlement: Normans, Flemings and English

The quarter century before the Norman conquest of England was dominated in Wales by the rise and subsequent rule of Gruffudd ap Llywelyn (d.1063). The fiercely acquisitive king of Gwynedd was determined to fulfil his ambition of uniting the whole of Wales under his rule. The chief obstacle to his ambition was the ruling dynasty of Deheubarth the chief members of whom, Hywel ab Edwin (d.1044), and his cousins, the brothers Gruffudd (d.1056) and Rhys ap Rhydderch (d.1053), were equally determined to frustrate their rival's aim of assimilating their kingdom into his rapidly expanding 'Cymric Empire'. Between 1039 and 1056 they contested no less than four battles, employed Viking mercenaries in the process and took part in as many destructive raids on each other's territory. One by one, Gruffudd killed off his foes until in 1056 he was able to claim his right to Deheubarth and thereby rule a united Wales. In the event, Gruffudd's hegemony lasted barely seven years before his Welsh kingdom was plunged into war with the Saxon English. In a closely fought campaign Gruffudd's hard-pressed forces crumbled before the advancing Saxons with the result that his men opted to murder their king for the sake of peace. Upon Gruffudd's murder his kingdom disintegrated and the royal families of its constituent parts, Gwynedd, Powys, Deheubarth and Morgannwg, resumed their kingships. Dyfed was, and remained, a substantial part of the kingdom of Deheubarth so that on Gruffudd's death there was no attempt by its ruling elites to establish a separate hegemony. After a struggle, which included victory over his Welsh enemies at the battle of Mynydd Carn (thought to have been fought somewhere in northern Pembrokeshire in 1081), power devolved to Rhys ap Tewdwr (d.1093) who succeeded in re-establishing his family's claim to Deheubarth.

However, events were to take a sinister turn for within a few years of Gruffudd's death and Rhys ap Tewdwr's ascendancy a new enemy hoved into view, the Normans. Having defeated and killed King Harold at Hastings in 1066, William the Conqueror set about the task of subduing his newly won kingdom. To him, Wales was an irritant that needed to be contained rather than conquered and he was quite content to leave the Welsh to their petty quarrels so long as they acknowledged his hegemony. At the same time, Norman barons were encouraged to ply their trade in the border regions ostensibly to protect England from attack but also to make war on the Welsh should the opportunity arise. Unlike the rest of Wales, Deheubarth, and especially Dyfed, did not encounter the Normans for some time but when they did it is likely that they did not know what to make of these French-speaking strangers. The people of Dyfed were familiar with the Irish – their king Rhys ap Tewdwr had twice fled to Ireland and twice returned bringing with him Irish mercenaries – and with the Saxons, with whom they had fought during Gruffudd's reign. It soon became clear that the Normans came as conquerors and that they were more formidable opponents than either the Irish or the Saxons. The first serious encounter occurred in 1081 when King William himself led an army through south Wales, eventually reaching his destination in deepest Dyfed at St David's cathedral. This was no idle pilgrimage but a diplomatic mission intended to overawe the Welsh and bring them to submission without the need for war. Its success can be gauged by the fact that Rhys ap Tewdwr chose to come to an understanding with the king, the nature of which is set out in the Domesday Book. This tells us that besides acknowledging the superior authority of William, Rhys had to render an annual rent of £40.

Peace at a price turned to war in 1093 when Rhys ap Tewdwr was killed in battle somewhere near Brecon. Subject to the predatory raids of Anglo-Norman adventurers, Deheubarth was defenceless and soon succumbed to piecemeal conquest. Between 1094 and 1096 a Norman settlement had been established at Pembroke under Arnulf of Montgomery but as Ifor Rowlands (1981) has stated: 'There were, however, to be no easy pickings in Dyfed and, consequently, one formative strand in the fabric of Norman colonial society there was to be its very precariousness. Periodic Welsh offensives from 1094 onwards made this province no place for the faint-hearted.' Precarious it might have been but the men who manned the walls of the hastily built earth and timber castle at Pembroke when attacked in 1096 were rugged individuals who stuck to their task with grim determination. Try as they might the Welsh could not dislodge the alien settlers, nor could they contain them and it was not long ere ambitious individuals like Gerald of Windsor ventured further east to establish himself at Carew. Here Gerald of Windsor settled and married Nest, daughter of Rhys ap Tewdwr, a move calculated to enable him, in the opinion of Gerald of Wales, 'to plant deeper roots in those areas for himself and his family'. The tentativeness that marked the colonists' early expansion in Dyfed was abandoned in the twelfth century when men such as Robert fitzMartin struck out on their own with the intention of establishing roots in the land. This they did partly by war but partly by marriage with the daughters of native rulers who saw some advantage in such familial alliances. Thus did William fitzMartin make more secure the family's hold on the cantref of Cemais by building an earth and timber castle at Nevern and by marrying one of the daughters of the powerful Lord Rhys (d.1197) whose territory bordered his own. Of course, such relationships were fragile but they were worth pursuing because the colonists knew well that their fate rested upon their own resources and the resources of their leaders. Thus did the harsh realities of life in a frontier zone encourage the rise of tough individuals who founded family dynasties, like de Barri, de Brian, de la Roche, fitzGerald, fitzMartin, fitzTancard and fitzWizo, that did much to shape the history of Pembrokeshire.

Among the more resilient settlers and for whom the Welsh seemed to have an especial hatred were the Flemings. Nor is this surprising given what the native chronicle, *Brut y Tywysogyon*, had to say in that the Flemings 'occupied the whole cantref of Rhos, near the estuary of the river called Cleddau, and drove away all the inhabitants from the land'. Today, we might fairly refer to this as a form of ethnic cleansing, a desire on the part of the colonists to live in a native-free zone. In the opinion of the half-Welsh Gerald of Wales (1194):

. . . the folk who . . . came from Flanders . . . a brave and robust people, but very hostile to the Welsh and in a perpetual state of conflict with them. They are highly skilled in the wool trade, ready to work hard and to face danger by land or sea in the pursuit of gain, and, as time and opportunity offer, prompt to turn their hand to the sword or the ploughshare.

Introduced to the county by Henry I as a deliberate act of policy to colonize the area, the first wave of Flemish settlers is thought to have arrived sometime between 1107 and 1111. They were certainly well established by 1116 when the *Brut y Tywysogyon* described the 'diverse folk' of Dyfed as including 'Flemings and French and Saxons and their own [i.e. Welsh] folk'. Why the Flemish should wish to settle in a hostile land so far from home is not difficult to fathom – they came in search of property and profit. No doubt Henry I sought to sweeten the pill by offering this Welsh land on attractive terms, as one contemporary describes it,

Whosoever shall wish for land or peace,
Horses, armour or chargers,
Gold or silver, I shall give them
Very ample pay;
Whosoever shall wish for soil and sod
Richly shall I enfeoff them. (C. W. Hollister, 2001)

Thus did the likes of Godebert, Tancard, Letard 'Litelking', William of Brabant and Wizo enter the history and folklore of Pembrokeshire. They and their ilk, be they Norman/French, Saxon/English or Welsh, did much to give shape and substance to the Pembrokeshire we know today. Indeed, it must never be forgotten that the creation of what we today regard with unconscious affection as Little England beyond Wales, was achieved by war and all its attendant evils, such as destruction and devastation, not to mention murder, plunder and rape. Once established, the alien settlers were never removed and though they suffered repeated Welsh attacks during the twelfth and thirteenth centuries, in 1115, 1136, 1147, 1189, 1193 and 1220, they remained firm and resolute. Certainly, by the mid-thirteenth century the pattern of lordships and landholdings in the county had achieved a degree of fixity that was to remain largely intact for the next two and a half centuries. In the face of such an aggressive colonial settlement the Pembrokeshire Welsh slipped slowly into oblivion, overtaken in the written record by their more thrustful neighbours with whom they learned to coexist albeit confined to their half of the county. The careers and achievements of the Lord Rhys, Llywelyn the Great (d.1240) and Llywelyn the Last (d.1282) may loom large in the pages of Welsh history but in Pembrokeshire they merit no more than a few lines of text or numbered footnotes. Indeed, if anything, William Marshal (d.1219), earl of Pembroke, had a far greater impact on the history of the county than any of the Welsh princes. He twice drove the invading Welsh out of the county, recaptured and rebuilt Cilgerran castle and is largely responsible for the magnificence that is Pembroke castle today. His sons followed their father's lead by rebuilding Tenby castle, by compelling the local

Welsh rulers to submit to them and by concluding marriage alliances with them.

'That Pembrokeshire was in ancient time a County Palatine and no part of the Principality of Wales.' Thus did the enlightened Elizabethan antiquary George Owen of Henllys begin his treatise on the origins and development of the Marcher lordship and county of Pembroke. In some respects, the term 'Pembrokeshire' is a misnomer for although the county did exist it enjoyed little of the political unity and cohesion that the use of the term might suggest. Within the bounds of the medieval county of Pembroke there existed near a dozen or so lordships and baronies, a number of ecclesiastical enclaves and seven seignorial boroughs, three of which – Haverfordwest, Pembroke and Tenby – were among the wealthiest in Wales. The territorial, racial and political divisions of medieval Pembrokeshire serve to illustrate in microcosm some of the essential features of what constituted the March in Wales. It was a frontier society, its complex structure shaped by the ebb and flow of conquest and colonization.

At the heart of the Marcher shire was the lordship of Pembroke which embraced no more than a third of the territory which constituted the county proper. This territory formed the earls' demesne, land over which they exercised direct control, and it included the manors of Castlemartin, St Florence, Coedrath, Kingswood and Gawdon and the lordship of Cilgerran. In order to reward their most faithful followers, and to make easier their rule of the county, the earls created the mesne or lesser lordships of Carew, Manorbier, Stackpole and Wiston, which were held directly of them by knights' or military service. The remaining land was granted out by the earls to their lesser military tenants to form freehold manors or knights' fees. On the other hand, the lordships of St David's, Llawhaden and Narberth were independent enclaves within the county which owed the earl of Pembroke neither loyalty nor service. The lords of the neighbouring baronies of Haverford, Walwyn's Castle and Cemais were similarly disposed towards ignoring the earl's jurisdictional power. This they accomplished with varying degrees of success for short periods during the fourteenth century. This fragmentation of the Pembrokeshsire March made for administrative chaos and local conflict. Tensions and rivalries between lordships were often fuelled by the ambitions of local officials which sometimes spilled over into violence.

To the earls of Pembroke the prime function of the administration of the earldom was to provide them with resources in men, money and power. The function of the men appointed to run the administration was primarily to facilitate this in the most efficient manner possible. Yet there was more to local government than simply the demands of administration, it was seen by the magnate as a means for reward and by the gentry as a public demonstration of their local power and influence. For those office-holders on the highest rungs of the ladder this power was real enough, for in the usual and regular absence of the lords of Pembroke the government of the county lay in the hands of those appointees drawn from the local gentry.

Politics was the lifeblood of those among the local gentry with ambition enough to risk all on the slippery ladder of promotion. Few in fourteenth-century Pembrokeshire were able or prepared to play politics on the national stage but they were willing to flex their muscles at local level. Nevertheless, there is little to suggest that the gentry indulged in serious bloodletting. If anything their collective concern was the maintenance of their political hegemony in this far-flung corner of the realm and to that end they tended to cooperate rather than quarrel. Marriage alliances, mutual business interests and service in the household of the local magnate tended to bind them into a tight-knit privileged community whose political aspirations rarely strayed beyond the borders of their county.

Such was the pattern of lordships and land-holding, together with the people who lived in the one and worked the other, by the time of the Black Death and the Glyndŵr Rebellion. Both had the potential and the capacity to tear apart the very fabric of county society but while the one was a natural disaster that struck blindly irrespective of class, wealth or race, the other was aimed deliberately at undoing the racial and territorial exclusivity that was a focus of tension between the settler and native communities.

The Black Death

Much has been said and written about the Black Death and with good reason. A bubonic plague pandemic that swept all before it as it first crossed Europe between 1347 and 1350, it is traditionally calculated to have killed at least one-third of the population on the Continent and between one-third and a half of the people of England and Wales. If one contemporary chronicler is to be believed, 'two parts of the Welsh people' succumbed to the 'Great Mortality'. Nor did it simply disappear after it had run its course, becoming an endemic feature of life, which returned no less than four times to wreak its deadly havoc in 1361–2, 1369, 1371 and 1393. Plague and pestilence were not unknown nor uncommon in the Middle Ages but the virulence, rapidity and morbidity of this particular strain of bubonic plague, a highly infectious pneumonic form spread by the ubiquitous black rat, its principal carrier, was much greater than in any previous outbreak. That it was an epidemic of catastrophic proportions is undeniable, upsetting as it did the social and economic fabric of fourteenth-century society, not to mention the personal and emotional impact which must have been traumatic. Needless to say, Pembrokeshire was not immune from its devastating effects but, regretfully, our sources are neither ample enough nor sufficiently sensitive to register with any degree of precision the extent to which the county and its people were affected. In truth, the effects of the Black Death on Wales have not been much studied. That said, there are pockets of evidence within the available source material which offer at least a snapshot of the plague's impact if not a continuous story.

The pandemic that ravaged Wales is generally assumed to have originated in central Asia in the late 1330s. It was brought to Europe aboard Genoese trading ships via the Black Sea, arriving in Genoa in 1347. From there it travelled along the principal European trade routes until it arrived in the British Isles by way of the port of Melcombe Regis in Dorset in June 1348. From here it moved rapidly across country and is traditionally thought to have reached Wales by February or March 1349, when it struck in the lordship of Abergavenny. Our knowledge of this particular outbreak of the disease is furnished by the records of an inquisition dated 17 April 1349 and held upon the death of the lord's son who is said to have died on 9 March 1349. From here the disease is thought to have moved westwards along the coast and river valleys, and northwards along the border. However, this traditional view may have to be revised in the light of evidence from contemporary records which suggest that Pembrokeshire, probably by way of its seaports, may have been among those places in Wales struck first by the plague. Certainly, as the authorities in Abergavenny were holding their inquisition, their counterparts in Pembrokeshire were similarly employed recording the deaths of no less than five members of the county's ruling elite. Between 16 March and 17 April 1349, John Perrot of Popton, Walter Scurlage of Bangeston near Pembroke, Nicholas Shirburn of Angle, William Robelyn of Cosheston and John Champagne of Llanteg met their deaths while seemingly in the prime of their lives. It is noticeable that in all but one case (the exception being Walter Scurlage who had no one but his wife to succeed him), the dead left three teenage heirs between thirteen and eighteen years old and one three-year-old toddler. That summer during the month of August and less than four months after the deaths of their neighbours, three more joined their gentle compatriots in death, namely, John Malefant of Ludchurch, Andrew Wiseman and John Cradock both of the parish of St Issells near Tenby. Again, all three left minors as heirs ranging in age from nine to seventeen years. Although it cannot be proved conclusively that these men died of the plague, there is no reason to doubt the suggestion that some, if not all of them, might have done so.

The effects of the plague on the population at large is unknown because it was probably never recorded. Not for them a coroner's inquest to determine the extent of the few trinkets they possessed in a generally miserable existence nor a burial in a predetermined family plot, but a mass grave on a suitably isolated edge of their village. It is perhaps instructive that apart from the inquisitions on the deaths of the wealthy, the most telling piece of evidence to suggest that the plague had devastated Pembrokeshire is a king's pardon for arrears of rent! In April 1350 King Edward III issued a special pardon to Richard Talbot, keeper of the Crown earldom of Pembroke, whereby a quarter of his annual rent of £320 was respited owing to the 'deadly pestilence which lately raged in those parts'. If Pembrokeshire suffered as much as the neighbouring counties of Carmarthenshire and Cardiganshire, and there is no reason not to suppose this to be so, then a few examples of the impact the plague had on the latter might make clearer the problems faced by the frightened folk of the west. In some districts of Cardiganshire, for example, local officials had to report a sharp drop in income on account of the 'pestilence' as occurred in one manor in the commote of Mefenydd where once there had been 104 tenants only 7 remained. The fact that only a fraction of the 97 tenants had actually succumbed to the plague, many had left panic-stricken never to return, shows that its impact on local communities was as much psychological as physical but that in whatever form it took the results were the same, namely, chaos and devastation. On the other hand, the plague could and often did deal a deadly blow to some communities accounting for almost the entire population in some instances, as in the Carmarthenshire village of Llanllwch. At the very least the trade of the major Pembrokeshire boroughs would have been disrupted, fairs would have been cancelled and land would have lain uncultivated. It is a bitter irony that those who survived the 'Great Pestilence' were eventually to succumb to what became known as the 'Second Pestilence in 1361–2'. Having at the age of eighteen witnessed the death of his father Nicholas in 1349, John Shirburn, his heir and successor, was himself to fall victim to the plague in 1361 when at the age of thirty-one he left a ten-year-old daughter Alice to follow him. What became of her is not certainly known but that she died childless is inferred from later evidence. Had she too fallen victim to the plague? We shall never know but suffice to say that in the half century after the first appearance of the Black Death Wales was rarely free of the virulent strains of either plague or pestilence.

The Glyndŵr Rebellion, 1400–1415

Within a year of the outbreak of the rebellion in September 1400, Adam of Usk declared that 'in these days . . . southern Wales . . . was at peace from every kind of trouble of invasion or defence'. However, if the records of an anonymous Welsh chronicler are to be believed the people of southern

Pembrokeshire would have had cause to disagree with the Welsh cleric's statement. In the summer of 1401 disaster overtook its inhabitants when they met the redoubtable Welsh rebel and his vastly inferior force, a reported 120 men, in battle at Hyddgen on the desolate moorland north of Plynlimon. An army of 1,500 royal levies, raised largely in Anglicized Pembrokeshire, were entrusted with the task of destroying the Welsh revolt. Unfortunately it failed and its defeat effectively contributed to enhancing the reputation of a Welsh guerrilla leader who had thus far met with only modest success.

Even allowing for the chronicler's probable exaggeration in underestimating the numbers who fought for Glyndŵr that day this 'outlaw' and his band of 'reckless men and robbers' had inflicted a stinging defeat on a superior Pembrokeshire force which suffered some 200 casualties in the encounter. It was the success Glyndŵr had been looking for to kick-start the rebellion. On the other hand, the effect of the defeat on the Pembrokeshire people from the Anglicized areas must have been utterly demoralizing. After this victory the seeds of insurrection spread rapidly and Glyndŵr was soon attracting support in Cardiganshire and Carmarthenshire. There is no evidence to suggest widespread support for Glyndŵr in Pembrokeshire, not even from among the Welsh squires in the northern half of the county. The alleged racial exclusivity of the royal army certainly bears out R. Rees Davies' assertion that 'Resistance to the revolt was naturally led by the English settlers in Wales', especially if Glyndŵr's reported intention to 'ruin . . . the English people and the English tongue' was believed. It is not surprising, therefore, that the substantial, though apparently ill-prepared, royal army was raised in Pembrokeshire, with additional levies from the Anglicized lowland region of southern Cardiganshire. Of course, this does not mean that the Welsh of northern Pembrokeshire were not recruited but their loyalties would most probably have been highly suspect. The defeat at Hyddgen and the spread of the rising brought King Henry IV to south Wales in October for what turned out to be an ineffectual expedition. That Pembrokeshire was not included in the royal itinerary or in the substantial confiscations of property suggests that the county was free from rebel sympathizers. In fact, two years were to pass before Pembrokeshire again came into conflict with Glyndŵr.

The year 1403 proved to be a turning point for Pembrokeshire, witnessing the defection of a number of prominent citizens to the rebel cause and the long-awaited invasion of the county by Glyndŵr. Pembrokeshire seemed fully prepared to meet the threat of a rebel incursion. Even intelligence reports were up to date, for in June 1403 a commission of array was appointed in the county on information furnished by Sir Thomas Carew that Glyndŵr, 'driven by shortage of food, was preparing . . . to waste the country'. In

July 1403 Glyndŵr duly appeared in south-west Wales with a formidable force estimated at over 8,000 men. The castles of Llandovery, Carreg Cennen and Dinefwr were closely besieged, whilst the castles of Dryslwyn, Newcastle Emlyn, Llanstephan and Carmarthen fell to the Welsh. That Glyndŵr was able to capture the centre of royal government in the south-west and dominate the region so completely points to the overwhelming failure of the commission of array issued on 16 June to provide for the defence of Carmarthenshire. It is instructive to note that the man responsible for surrendering Llanstephan castle to the rebels was Thomas Rede, steward of Pembrokeshire and deputy-justiciar of the principality of south Wales. In stark contrast, the commission issued in Pembrokeshire on the same day apparently proved successful, for when Carew assumed responsibility for the county's defence he not only refused to negotiate with Glyndŵr but, 'nothing daunted, he prepared to contest the issue in a pitched battle . . .' (J. E. Lloyd, 1931).

As constable of Narberth Carew stood directly in the path of the advancing Welsh rebels. His determination to forestall the first Welsh invasion of the county was commendable but far too optimistic; a local array could never hope to match Glyndŵr's force of 8,000 men in the field. Nevertheless, he displayed his courage and skill as a tactician when he engaged and defeated a detached force of 700 rebels somewhere – the exact location continues to elude historians – in the hill country north-west of Carmarthen. Given the disposition of Glyndŵr and Carew's forces the day before the engagement, Laugharne and Narberth respectively, it is conceivable that the encounter took place somewhere in the vicinity, quite possibly north, of St Clear's. The crushing defeat administered by Carew, almost exactly two years after the humiliation of Hyddgen, may have led Glyndŵr to revise his plans and that, in turn, saved Pembrokeshire from certain devastation. The Crown knew that it had to rely on local men like Sir Thomas Carew if it were ever to overcome the rebels since he and others like him stood to lose all should Glyndŵr's insurrection prove successful. Thus, as local magnates, Carew and his neighbours had a vested interest in securing military control of their home areas.

Relief for the besieged county came nine weeks later on 23 September, when the royal army led by the king himself entered Carmarthen. Having restored the situation to his satisfaction and leaving John Beaufort, earl of Somerset, as his lieutenant in south Wales with a substantial force at Carmarthen, King Henry returned to England without setting foot in Pembrokeshire. Although a visit to Pembrokeshire was considered unnecessary, far from neglecting the county, the king initiated a series of measures designed to protect its lucrative sea-borne trade and to restrict unlicensed trading. Suspicion of the merchant community of Tenby had led to the arrest of one of their ships at Falmouth and only an express order from the Crown released the ship and its crew from detention. Such suspicion may indeed have had some foundation, for the borough had a long tradition of piracy and privateering and, on one occasion, it had 'aided and victualled the king's enemies'. Even border communities such as Chester and Shrewsbury were suspected, and even charged, with supplying victuals to the Welsh. Although Tenby merchants helped to provision royal castles in south Wales, it is not without some significance that the most prominent defector in the county, David Perrot, was a burgess and merchant of the town. Moreover, in September 1408 some six of Tenby's leading burgesses and officials were granted a pardon for offences which hint at complicity to supply rebels. On the whole, however, up to the beginning of 1404 the merchants of the three major Pembrokeshire boroughs carried on their trade largely unhindered; in fact, they and their ports increasingly became the focus of the Crown's naval strategy in the Bristol Channel and Irish sea.

Pembrokeshire's immunity from attack came to an end towards the latter half of 1404; indeed, the county suffered its most serious and sustained rebel activity during 1404–5, culminating in the French invasion. It may have been the treaty of alliance concluded in July 1404 between Glyndŵr and Charles VI of France that finally brought Pembrokeshire to the forefront of the rebellion. The French request for a list of the 'most famous ports in Wales and the most fertile districts through which they might enter more freely' would surely, though it was not specifically mentioned, have included Milford Haven, probably the largest and safest natural harbour in Wales.

By the beginning of June 1405 it was reported that a large rebel force led by Glyndŵr himself was making its way south. In the face of rumours that the Welsh were about to invade and devastate the county large numbers of panic-stricken townspeople decided it was time to leave Haverford. There is every reason to suspect that the townsfolk of Pembroke and Tenby may also have deemed it wise to leave. Therefore, in the weeks prior to the issuing of Prince Henry's instructions this mass exodus of people from Pembrokeshire, presumably to the safety of Bristol and other ports in south-west England, led to an acute shortage of manpower. This, combined with renewed rebel activity in the south-west from mid-June onwards, hindered and, in some cases, prevented the collection of revenue and the movement of supplies. Worse was to follow. At the beginning of August, the long-awaited French invasion fleet appeared in the Haven. From their point of disembarkation on the north shore of the Haven, the 2,600 Frenchmen marched to Haverford where they most likely met the main body of Glyndŵr's reported army of 10,000 men fresh from their triumph at Cardigan. Haverford proved to be more resilient, but after a siege of some days the rebel allies managed to take the town, though the castle, defended by Sir Roland Leynthale, resisted all efforts at capture.

The allies then moved on to Tenby, no doubt pillaging the countryside as they went to augment their supplies. After a brief siege of the borough, they pressed on to Carmarthen, capturing both the town and castle.

Glyndŵr's advance to the English border – there is some dispute as to whether he actually reached Woodbury Hill, eight miles outside Worcester – brought temporary relief to the south-west. However, far from being allowed to recover during this respite, the Crown imposed its own customary demands on the community of Pembrokeshire. On 31 August, some three weeks after its capture, Carmarthen was retaken by the Crown and Thomas Roche, a king's esquire and constable of Pembroke castle since 1399, was appointed for its safe keeping. Roche's six-month appointment proved optimistic, for no sooner had he, perhaps with his Pembrokeshire levies, garrisoned the castle than he was captured. On 2 October Roche's wife Elizabeth was issued with a royal licence allowing her to negotiate a ransom and the release of rebel prisoners in return for her husband. Unfortunately for Roche, with south Wales still in the thick of rebellion, this took some time and he may well have been a captive in June 1406 when he nominated attorneys to oversee his affairs.

The return of the allied army to south Wales and the failure of the king's expedition in September no doubt encouraged local rebels to participate in a sustained campaign against those centres holding firm for the Crown. By November 'the men of Pembrokeshire, hereditary enemies of the Welsh', succumbed and sued for peace with Glyndŵr, the terms of which – a six-month truce in return for £200 in silver – were confirmed by the county court at Pembroke castle. Although such truces were expressly forbidden by the Crown, a commission was convened by the lord of Pembroke, Sir Francis de Court, charged with the task of organizing the raising of the ransom. Not surprisingly the members of the commission were drawn from a number of influential local families, men on whom de Court could rely to discharge their duties with speed and efficiency. Instructions were issued to every lordship within the county that acknowledged the authority of the county court; these would have included Carew, Cemais, Manorbier, Stackpole, Walwyn's Castle, Wiston and the demesne properties of the lord himself. Fortunately, a seventeenth-century copy of a document issued to the receivers appointed by de Court 'under the seal of the chancellor of the county' to collect the ransom is still extant for the lordship of Carew. The receivers, Stephen Perrot and John Castlemartin, were empowered 'to distrain on the goods of those who failed to pay their quota'.

The truce or agreement, which was not the first of its kind negotiated by English communities with the rebels, was denounced by the king and his council. Orders had been issued to the effect that all English residents in Wales were to resist the rebels at every opportunity; only those empowered by the king could treat with, or pardon, rebels, and they were the royal lieutenants and a few military commanders. However, royal authority in south-west Wales was at best vestigial at this time and the protestations fell on deaf ears. The nineteenth-century historian J. H. Wylie, too, reprimanded the people of Pembrokeshire for the truce, which he saw as a 'disgrace to the English government'. He reminded his readers that the county was, and still is, blessed with a 'ring of vast Norman castles, upon whose walls neither Welsh nor French could make any impression'. Nevertheless, it appears that the king did not appreciate the trauma experienced by the people of Pembrokeshire in playing host to the largest concentration of rebel forces ever to have been assembled during the rebellion. Indeed, in November 1405, a commission of inquiry with 'special letters of intendance to the county of Pembroke . . . and the lordships of Narberth, Haverford and Dewsland', was set up to investigate their actions 'being so near to the rebel country'. In fact, the truce negotiated by the Pembrokeshire gentry with Glyndŵr proved an act of foresight, for by mid-1406 (the truce was to last until May) rebel authority in the south-west had been vanquished. Except for a few isolated areas, most notably the Welshries of Narberth and Llawhaden which did not submit to the Crown until 1409, as far as Pembrokeshire was concerned the revolt was at an end and the process of reconstruction could begin.

The Medieval Gentry

At its broadest in the fourteenth and fifteenth centuries the class whom we know as the 'gentry' filled the social and economic gap between the titled nobility and the untitled mass of the peasantry. They formed a powerful elite of land-owning, and in earlier times military-trained, freemen exercising their lordship over land and men and who, in turn, were subject to the overlordship of their baronial betters. In the twelfth and thirteenth centuries they were known exclusively as knights, mounted warriors given land, the knight's fee, in return for serving their noble masters in times of war. However, by the fourteenth century Wales was becoming a more peaceful and settled country so that the demands made of the knights were becoming more civil than military. The honour of knighthood was fast acquiring a social rather than just a military distinction and it was joined by the use of other titles such as esquire and gentleman both of which evolved because of the demand by an ever-increasing number of ambitious men seeking some recognition of their status as wealthy, propertied landholders.

The problem of defining the Welsh gentry is far more of a challenge for the student of medieval Welsh history than it is for those working in the field of English history. Even the phrase 'Welsh gentry' has its critics for it seems to take little account of the fact that as a result of conquest, the country was a land of two, or more, peoples: native Welsh and mainly, though in Pembrokeshire not exclusively, English settler. In many parts of Wales the vanguard of alien colonization was led by the townsmen or burgesses who set up commercially privileged urban centres secure behind defensive pallisades which were often attached to castles. This was true of Pembrokeshire where the major plantation boroughs of Haverfordwest, Pembroke and Tenby were established, but here at least they were joined in large numbers by rural settlers drawn from the middling and lower levels of English and, in the twelfth century, Flemish society. Much of the south of the county was effectively colonized, leading to the division of Pembrokeshire on racial lines into an alien south and west, or Englishry, and native north and east, the Welshry.

It is from among the descendants of the small group of military adventurers responsible for the creation of the Pembrokeshire March in the twelfth and thirteenth centuries that the core of the early fourteenth-century 'gentry' families of the county are to be found. They were, in origin, professional soldiers intent on conquest and exploitation rather than settlement and coexistence. Chief among them was the earl of Pembroke (a creation of 1138) followed by his band of trusted retainers, the knights, together with a corps of reliable foot-soldiers and archers. Their descendants, in concert with later settler-families, were responsible for creating the pattern of feudal settlement – knights' fees and manors – established in the south of the county which was a mirror image of that to be found in any conventional English shire. It is here, south of the *landsker*, that by the fourteenth century the familiar middling ranks of knights and esquires are to be found in quantity to be served for the most part by an English peasantry largely consisting of unfree or bond tenants.

The north of the county was left to the Welsh who initially served a numerically inferior alien population but who took advantage of the opportunities that came their way to establish the means by which they could enjoy the bounty of local self-government by the mid-fifteenth century. Here the historian might have difficulty in distinguishing between the 'gentle' and 'non-gentle' in Welsh society for, as R. Rees Davies (1987) stated, 'the status definitions of Welsh law barely admitted of the existence of a noble class'. Untainted Welsh blood, good lineage and free status rather than wealth were the qualities which marked out the native gentry in earlier times. They held their lands by Welsh tenure, which included the poverty-inducing custom of partiability of inherited land, and conducted their lives largely according to Welsh laws and customs. However, native Pembrokeshire had long succumbed to conquest and alien settlement thereby becoming subject to English influence so that it is possible to detect features of English tenure and customs. For example, in the barony of Cemais tenants of both Welsh and English extraction are to be seen holding their land by knight's service. On the other hand, the native tenantry held their land according to what George Owen called 'English law and Welsh division', a curious hybrid system known as the Welsh knight's fee. Thus, Welshmen of substance had been brought within the ambit of feudal tenure without forsaking significant aspects of their native laws and customs. Although the colonial nature of settlement and administration made coexistence difficult, often leading to violent confrontation or even serious rebellion such as that led by Glyndŵr, the fact that both orthodox English and Welsh fees coexisted in the same lordship points to the fact that over time, and over the whole county, the tempo of social, racial and institutional integration increased.

It is clear that in the first half of the fourteenth century the greatest proportion of land held by the gentry consisted of knights' fees. The majority of these knights' fees or freehold carucates were located in the south of the county and they appear to have been of a standard size which suggests some evidence of planning in their creation. A single fee amounted to a manor of around ten carucates of land, a half fee some five carucates whilst a tenth equalled a single carucate in extent. Almost invariably the ten-carucate manor consisted of the manor house or, in some instances, a castle such as Roch, with attached gardens and orchards together with the farm buildings, bounded by its revenue-producing agricultural land; arable, pasture and meadow. Although many of the knights' fees never developed beyond rural farmsteads served by a small and often scattered bond population, others grew into hamlets of dependent villagers such as occurred at Popton. Indeed, according to Brian Howells (1987): 'Most of the important villages of Pembrokeshire were founded directly under the aegis of a feudal lord of the knightly class.' The growth and development of these minor tenurial units of the fourteenth century into the large and profitable estates of the sixteenth was due almost entirely to the drive and ambition of the freeholders who possessed them. As long as they discharged their obligations of service to their landlords, be it military or monetary in character, they were free to exploit their properties as they saw fit. Soldiers they may have been in origin but farmers they became for a great proportion of their income depended upon the thorough exploitation of their estates. Their main aim was to achieve a regular cash income, for as R. Hilton stated in *Peasants, Knights and Heretics: Studies in Medieval English Social History* (Cambridge, 1976): 'The demesne produce was not thought of primarily as a means of sustaining the . . . household, but as an asset realizable in cash.'

It is impossible to be precise in determining levels of gentry income in fourteenth- and fifteenth-century Pembrokeshire. The valuations given in the inquisitions *post mortem* were almost always approximate and often inaccurate while few private manorial accounts, rentals and valors survive. Therefore, the historian is forced to rely on evidence culled from scattered records for which firm conclusions are applicable in the case of only a few families and their estates. Indeed, apart from a mere handful of families, the Perrots, Bowens, Philipps, Owens of Orielton and Wogans among them, the gentry have been silent about themselves and their concerns. Happily there exists sufficient evidence at least to attempt an outline of one family's fluctuating fortunes during the later Middle Ages, namely the Perrots. In many ways a study of the Perrot family serves to illustrate the likely fortunes of a great proportion of their more successful gentle compatriots, many of whom were their friends, neighbours and associates and with whom they were connected by ties of marriage, kinship and business.

From evidence provided by the earliest extant inquisition *post mortem* on a member of the Perrots, John in 1349, we learn that they were becoming a family of some consequence with county-wide land-holdings. Although it is wise to disregard the escheator's estimate of John's annual income of £8 5s 8d we may be satisfied that the value of £26 13s 6d placed on the marriage of John's teenage heir, Peter, is closer to the truth and indicative of the family's growing prosperity. The potential to recoup this sum from the issues of the Perrot estates attracted the likes of the influential Sir John Carew, lord of Carew, who successfully bid for the right to arrange a suitable match for the teenager. Minority and wardship was an unpalatable fact of life for men of means and ambition, indeed it was a fate to be avoided if possible. As fief holders of the earl the Perrots and others like them were liable for wardship should they die when the heir was under the age of twenty-one. Minors were commodities to be bargained and sold to the highest bidder, for with them went not only temporary custody of the estates and their revenues but, if well managed, the possibility of a long-term relationship and/or social and political alliance through marriage.

Equally, a negligent or incompetent custodian could ruin a family. In one year alone (1349) eight of the county's leading gentry – Perrot, Scurlage, Shirburn, Robelyn, Champagne, Malefant, Wiseman and Cradock – experienced wardship. Some were unfortunate enough to suffer multiple minorities, the Perrots and their feudal landlords, the Hastings, earls of Pembroke, among them. The Perrots were fortunate, their custodians were generally competent and for the most part members of the extended family. It is as a result of another premature death and consequent wardship later in the fourteenth century that a firm figure can be suggested for the Perrots' annual income which was almost entirely derived from their estates. Upon the death of Peter Perrot in 1378 the Crown estimated his annual income from two-thirds of his properties to be around £40; the remaining third was held in dower by his widow Alice, the daughter of Sir Richard Harold of Haroldston. If we accept the Crown's calculations, and they were generally more accurate when calculating the value of the widow's dower, a sum approaching or more likely in excess of £60 per annum would seem a reasonably close estimate of their income so that by the standards of the time the Perrots were a family of wealthy esquires. Through a combination of lease, purchase and acquisition by marriage underpinned by careful estate management, the Perrots added considerably to their already respectable landholdings. The net result of these estate-building activities was that by the end of the fifteenth century the core of the family's landholdings amounted to some nine manors each supporting a substantial residence, the chief of which was Haroldston.

Evidence generated by death and dispute usually provide the only means of arriving at anything like a reasonable estimate of gentry income and it is to the records of one of the many disputes in which the Perrots became embroiled that we must first turn. In 1505 John Reynbot of Simpson took Owen Perrot to court citing eviction, harrassment and misappropriation of property, during which trial at the Court of Requests, it was estimated that the accused's annual income topped 500 marks and more or in excess of £334. This estimate is surely closer to the truth than the one given by the escheator in the inquisition on the death of Sir Owen Perrot in 1522 where it was decided that the Perrot family income did not exceed £185 per annum. Inquisitions post-mortem are notorious for returning underestimated values either through negligence or indifference on the part of the escheator or jury, or both, but also on account of the methods employed by testators to conceal their properties, rents and income. The higher of the two estimates of Perrot income would go some way to explaining the heavy bond of 500 marks imposed by King Henry VII in 1489 on Sir William Perrot for certain transgressions.

Since the vast majority of Pembrokeshire's gentle elite derived all or most of its income from its estates it is inevitable that estimates of the same should be based on the profits of landholding but this takes little account of salaries for service. In the case of some this may not have amounted to much and in the scheme of things it was an impermanent and fluctuating source of income, but to others it was the main source of their wealth and the means by which they clung on to, or indeed, enhanced, their gentle status. The Cradock family of Newton are a case in point, for though described by Richard Fenton in 1810 as 'the princely family of Craddock, lineally descended from Howel Dda' they were very much gentry of the second rank who were stated to have held but six bovates of land of the earls at the death of one of their number, John Cradock, in August 1350. Office-holding and public service made the Cradocks and by the time John Cradock's great-grandson Richard met his death in 1448 they had become one of the premier landholding families in Pembrokeshire and elsewhere in the West Country, principally Somerset.

It is to Richard Cradock that the credit must be given for establishing the family's fame and fortune which he achieved by means of a distinguished career in the legal profession. Cradock rose to prominence on account of his appointment as a sergeant-at-law which secured for him a place among the legal elite consisting, in the fifteenth century, of no more than 120 judges, sergeants and apprentices. Thereafter the appointments came thick and fast; in 1426 he became justice itinerant in his home county of Pembroke, in 1430 he filled the office of recorder of the courts of the city of Bristol, in 1438 he acted as deputy-justiciar of the principality of south Wales, eventually becoming lord chief justice of the Court of Common Pleas in 1439. It has been estimated that a lawyer at the top of his profession, a sergeant-at-law, could expect to earn around £300 per annum, a considerable sum by contemporary standards and more than enough to purchase substantial tracts of land, if not a whole manor or two. The capacity to earn such sums might explain how Richard Newton (having dropped the Welsh Cradock sometime during the 1420s in favour of the Anglicized name of the family seat) was able to purchase the manor of Yatton in Somerset, where he lies buried, in addition to enlarging his landholdings in Pembrokeshire.

The capacity of families like Perrot and possibly Newton (Cradock) to earn in excess of £300 per annum was not typical of the majority of Pembrokeshire's gentry in the latter half of the fifteenth century. Although firm conclusions cannot be drawn from contemporary sources, it may be conservatively estimated that by the end of the fifteenth century barely more than half a dozen families could claim membership of this emerging group of greater gentry. They included Perrot of Haroldston, Wyrriot of Orielton, Wogan of Wiston, Philips of Picton, Bowen of Pentre Ifan, White of Tenby and Henllan and Laugharne of St Bride's. Families like the Newtons and Vernons of Stackpole were also substantial landowners in the county but had become, for the most part, non-resident and thus may be omitted from the list of greater gentry. For those families that made up the greater gentry their collective aim was, as it had always been, to ensure the continuance of their hegemony, be it political, social or economic in nature. To that end they strengthened their grip on the county and in this they owed their success in large part to their outstanding wealth in land and income.

That 'the March was a land of war, interrupted on occasion by peace' was a fact not lost on the gentry of Pembrokeshire who were only too aware that their considerable landed possessions, wealth and social position came at a price. Built on the back of invasion, conquest and the profession of arms they had little option but to employ the same aggressive tactics to defend what they had won from the Welsh. During the thirteenth century this called for constant vigilance and a willingness to leave the confines of their estates to make war on an enemy with whom they shared the land that constituted Pembrokeshire but with whom they lived often at arms' length. Military service, therefore, was not only expected of the county's fiefholders but demanded as a precondition of their landed tenure. Not that the landholders of Pembrokeshire needed much persuasion to heed the call to arms since their failure to do so would at best threaten their existence and way of life but at worst lead to their total extinction. The threat of rebellion and the periodic rumours of foreign invasion were an ever-present reminder of the importance of their military duties of which active campaigning was but a small part. Castle guard was perhaps the most regular and useful aspect of feudal military service which required the county's fiefholders to serve in rotation in the garrison of the earl's castle at Pembroke. However, as the habits of peace set in, even this military obligation was converted into a cash rent payable twice yearly by the county's leading tenants.

During the fifteenth century France alone provided the war-hungry novice and the war-weary veteran with the means to pursue the profession of arms. The accession of Henry V saw a resumption of the Hundred Years' War and opportunities aplenty for the gentry of Pembrokeshire to further their military careers. Among the first to sign up for King Henry's expedition to France were those soldiers who had proved their mettle in the Glyndŵr rebellion, namely David Howell of Woodstock and Sir Thomas Carew of Carew castle, but they were joined by others from the county, most notably John Perrot of Tenby, William Wogan of Boulston and his cousin Henry Wogan of Milton. All, with the exception of David Howell, were said to have been present at the battle of Agincourt (1415), active participants in that most crushing of English victories over the French made famous by William Shakespeare. Howell joined Henry V's victorious army in France in June 1416 where he remained for the next twenty-two years serving with distinction at the battle of Verneuil in 1424 and in numerous other engagements which resulted in a knighthood and a number of land grants which made him a man of wealth and influence in those parts of northern France controlled by the English Crown. Howell was not typical of the majority of those from Wales who accompanied the king to France; not for them the life of a career soldier serving as a captain in the retinues of the cream of English nobility. Once they had discharged their obligation of service they returned home, probably richer and more wordly wise than before they left, to carve out for themselves careers in local administration and politics and no doubt investing their gains from plunder and pillage in land and estates.

Despite the service of such men, participants from among the gentle class of Pembrokeshire in the foreign wars of the fourteenth and fifteenth centuries were, generally, few and far between. This apparent reluctance to take part in the *chevauchee*, a method of campaigning so beloved of English armies abroad, was not due to any lack of military training or to a lessening of the noble or Marcher ethos which remained proudly militaristic. Indeed, from an early age the sons of the nobility and gentry were imbibed with chivalric notions of war, duty and honour, being taught that the defence of the community was in large part their *raison d'être*. For the gentle elite in Wales and the Pembrokeshire March, where friction between the races often led to violent confrontation, such notions and teaching were more than just theoretical – it was a reality that lasted well into the fifteenth century.

Dynastic Politics, Henry VII and the Wars of the Roses

In medieval Pembrokeshire most of the local gentry accepted the hegemony of the earls. Whether they were formally indentured retainers or not it seems that their lives centred on the earls' principal fortress at Pembroke with some willingness. Much of this can be explained in terms of geography. Families such as Perrot, Wyrriot, Castro, Scurlage and Beneger had little option but to cooperate since they lived within the orbit of Pembroke castle. For them an indenture would merely have added formality to the connection. Local gentry were linked to the likes of Valence and Hastings in the fourteenth century or lords Percy and Gloucester in the fifteenth not only by deeds of indenture but also by common interest. The latter's political power and influence as great magnates were connected with, and in many ways dependent on, the following they attracted among the gentry. The gentry for their part expected to benefit from the protection and patronage of the magnate to whom they gave loyal service in return for land grants, annuities and support in the promotion of their political power and influence in the locality.

Therefore, in most cases, the knights and the rich esquires would be the most substantial members of a magnate's retinue, taken in its broadest sense, and their attendance was usually only required when the lord wished to ensure a respectable following around his person. Such was the case in 1447 when Duke Humphrey of Gloucester was accompanied to Bury St Edmunds with a retinue limited by the Crown to eighty men, some two-thirds of whom were from Pembrokeshire and Carmarthenshire. Unfortunately, only the most prominent members of his retinue were named and those from Pembrokeshire included Sir Henry Wogan and five members of his immediate and extended family, Thomas Wyrriot and Owain Dwnn. It is likely that had the names of the entire retinue been recorded there would have been an additional contingent of gentry from Pembrokeshire.

Despite the perils of associating with the likes of Gloucester, the Pembrokeshire gentry were not dissuaded from seeking service in the retinues of equally ambitious and powerful magnates. Within six years of Duke Humphrey's death his former retainers had transferred their allegiance to a new lord, Jasper Tudor, created earl of Pembroke in 1452. This suggests that membership of a magnate's retinue was a prize much sought after and that there may even have been competition due to imposed limits on the size of particular retinues. The size of a magnate's retinue depended as much upon his noble status and what convention determined to be a respectable following as on the costs involved in maintaining it. Eagerness and devotion to serve drew many of Earl Jasper's newly employed retainers into the dynastic conflict known as the Wars of the Roses. These civil or dynastic wars of the latter half of the fifteenth century were characterized by political in-fighting between great lords and their factions, principally York and Lancaster, which resulted in armed clashes between the retinues of these magnates. The thirty or so years of the Wars of the Roses (1455–87) involved a fair proportion of both the aristocracy and gentry at some point and at some level from across the realm. Pembrokeshire was not spared this conflict and a number of her gentry were drawn into the domestic strife that witnessed the destruction of some noble houses, the deaths of many gentry and the murder of two kings.

Against a background of growing political tension Earl Jasper, a prime mover in the Lancastrian cause, marshalled his resources by obtaining from the Crown a commission of array in south-west Wales and thereby employing his retainers to raise an armed force. The commission included Sir William Vernon, lord of Stackpole, Sir Henry Wogan, Sir Thomas Perrot, Thomas Wyrriot, Thomas Wogan and Thomas Perrot esquires. These were men on whom Earl Jasper could rely for support and in whom he entrusted the defence and administration of his earldom. The majority repaid his trust by willingly agreeing to serve their master faithfully even if it should come to war; it was not long before their fidelity was put to the test. In February 1461 an armed force raised mainly in south-west Wales but with the addition of a motley band of French, Irish and Breton mercenaries and commanded by earls Pembroke (Jasper Tudor) and Wiltshire (James Butler), made its way north towards the border where they met an equally large contingent of Yorkists at Mortimer's Cross. The encounter was a bloody one which saw heavy casualties on both sides but which ultimately resulted in a decisive defeat for the Lancastrians. Jasper and his followers made their escape as best they could but many were captured and subsequently executed at Hereford. Following this defeat Earl Jasper and his affinity were hounded to oblivion, the former seeking refuge in exile in France, the latter trying to limit the damage their association with him had caused by coming to terms with the new regime.

The dangers resulting from the bonds of association forged between magnate and gentleman combined to cause some to become more circumspect in their dealings with the nobility. Certainly, Perrot junior took to heart the bitter lesson of his father's death after Mortimer's Cross by remaining aloof from faction politics. While others became reconciled to the new Yorkist regime under William Herbert, the newly appointed earl of Pembroke, Thomas Perrot esquire, possibly denied the opportunity to serve in the county's administration, virtually disappears from sight. Friends, neighbours, associates and even members of his extended family were not discouraged from seeking the patronage of great men irrespective of their political leanings: his cousins Jankyn Perrot of Scotsborough, John Wogan son and heir of Sir Henry Wogan of Wiston and John Eynon accompanied Earl William to Banbury in July 1469. At the ensuing battle between the largely Welsh force of the earl of Pembroke and the predominantly English army of the earl of Warwick, they and many others from south and west Wales were killed.

Bitter experience combined with self-preservation encouraged many men of influence to adopt an ambivalent attitude whereby they withdrew from politics and office-holding to concentrate on estate management. Consequently, neither they nor others who may have been deemed Lancastrian sympathizers were much troubled by the Yorkist regime at large or, closer to home, by the Yorkist rule of Earl William. Indeed, the vindictiveness evident on a national scale – witness the bitterness of the feud between the Vaughans of Tretower and the Tudors – seems not to have been repeated at a local level in Pembrokeshire. There is no evidence to suggest that the known Yorkists who accompanied Herbert to Banbury were locked in dispute with the former Lancastrian supporters of Jasper Tudor. The key to survival was flexibility, for as one contemporary observed of a defeated Lancastrian: '[he] will do as others generally do nowadays, and acclaim the victors, and though at first he sided with the others he will side with those in power' (H. T. Evans).

In August 1485 Pembrokeshire found itself at the hub of national politics when the Pembroke-born son of the late earl of Richmond, Henry Tudor, landed at Mill Bay with an armed force thought to number 2,500 men. With this motley crew of multinational mercenaries, adventurers and supporters this Lancastrian claimant hoped to make himself king of England. All that stood between him and success was King Richard III and an army estimated at anything between 10,000 and 15,000 men. Henry's hopes for success rested on the nature of his reception on landing in Wales and the use he could make of his Pembrokeshire and Welsh roots in gathering support. Although the reaction to his arrival in Pembrokeshire was far from hostile it was not particularly supportive either. Fifteen generally peaceful years of Yorkist rule had dulled the sense of loyalty former

Lancastrians once felt for their cause with the result that few of the Pembrokeshire gentry joined their erstwhile compatriot. Undaunted, Henry Tudor pressed on and after a week's march through Wales his army had swollen to double its size, mainly as a result of attracting Welsh recruits. The encounter at Bosworth Field was bitter and bloody and had it not been for the timely defection of the notoriously treacherous Stanley brothers there is every reason to suspect that Henry Tudor's prospects of winning the battle would have been much reduced. Henry Tudor never returned to the land or county of his birth, preferring instead the English countryside and the life of the court. In fairness to him and his Tudor successors, the duties of monarchy were such that they had little time or inclination to visit a part of the realm that was, even by the standards of the day, wild, remote and desolate.

The newly crowned Henry VII followed up his victory by rewarding his faithful supporters, not one of whom, as far as is known, hailed from Pembrokeshire. Given their understandable ambivalence this is neither surprising nor unexpected but once installed as King Henry VII, the Pembrokeshire gentry were not slow to demonstrate their loyalty to the new regime by offering their support and services. In the event, the only two people of note to be richly rewarded in respect of Pembrokeshire property were the king's uncle, Jasper Tudor, newly restored to his earldom, and Sir Rhys ap Thomas, a powerful potentate imported from neighbouring Carmarthenshire. Henceforth, Pembrokeshire would remain in the hands of the Crown, to be parcelled out to members of the royal family. On the death of the childless Jasper Tudor, the earldom passed to the king who granted it to his second son, Henry, duke of York. On Henry's accession as king he retained control of the county until he gifted it to his then mistress Anne Boleyn. Her interest in the county probably extended no further than the title it conferred – she became a countess – and the money it generated. It is likely she neither knew where Pembrokeshire was nor cared; the only people for whom the county meant anything were those who lived there.

V

Early Modern Pembrokeshire: Reorganization, Reformation and Revolution

Introduction: Tudor and Stuart Pembrokeshire

> In speaking in praise and worthiness of the people and of this county if I shall seem fervent therein, yet I should therefore partly deserve pardon (the love and affection of my county egging me thereunto) . . . in not being able to say herein as much as it deserves. (G. Owen)

Unlike Gerald of Wales, George Owen (1552–1613) was a Welshman who hailed from the Welsh-speaking north of the county. Owen descended from that class of native freeholders which had successfully resisted assimilation, if not conquest, by the Anglo-Normans. Interestingly, even Owen could not explain how the area had retained its Welsh character given its proximity to the aggressively expansive 'Little England'. He may not have had much in common with his compatriots from the Anglicized south, whom he says were wont to greet the northerners like himself who dared venture over the *landsker* with the derisive cry 'look there goes a Welshman', but his love of locality was no different from that felt and expressed by Gerald three centuries earlier. Owen was certainly not one of those many Welshmen his near contemporary, the humanist scholar from north Wales, William Salesbury (d.1584), accused of not knowing 'what patriotism consists of'. Deeply influenced by the great awakening in history and antiquities which marked the Elizabethan age, Owen, 'one of the finest of Welsh antiquaries', wrote much about the county and country of his birth so that even today his works remain an invaluable source to which historians turn to quarry for information. Among the more frequently used is his magisterial *The Description of Pembrokeshire* (1603) followed by the hardly less impressive *A Dialogue of the present Government of Wales* (1594).

Owen's works make clear that although remote, Pembrokeshire was not an island and that what occurred elsewhere, particularly in matters of religion and politics, had its effects upon the county and its people. The milestones of early modern Welsh and British history – the so-called

Acts of Union, the Reformation and the 'English Revolution' – were no less significant for Pembrokeshire's history. Owen wrote of one, the Union, and experienced the other, the Reformation, but what he would have made of the Civil Wars is anyone's guess. He was no political activist, he did not stand for election to parliament, nor was he a Puritan; he was conventionally pious, but he was a staunch monarchist and one who, while lamenting the death of Elizabeth, wholeheartedly welcomed the accession of James I in 1603. Of course, one might argue that he could not have been anything else since he lived in an age of deference when few questioned the actions and motives of their monarch. He did not live long enough fully to experience the popular disenchantment that marred the relationship between the Stuarts and many of their leading subjects. Doubtless he would have been staggered by the execution of Charles I (1649), the existence of the Republic (1649–60) and the experience of the Bill of Rights (1689), all of which led to a fundamental restructuring in the relationship between monarch and parliament. Every century is marked by change but the seventeenth particularly so. Certainly the world was a very different one in 1700 from what it had been in 1600, much more so than between 1500 and 1600. The period is no longer treated, as A. H. Dodd once believed, 'as a comparatively insignificant interpolation between the age of the Tudors and the stirring times of the Methodist Revival', at least not in Pembrokeshire.

The Acts of Union: Politics, Government and Administration

The Pembrokeshire we know today has its roots in the political and administrative reforms enacted during the reign of Henry VIII. The so-called Acts of Union, a twentieth-century term applied to acts of parliament passed in 1536 and 1543 in which Wales was declared 'incorporated, united and annexed' to the English realm, brought into existence the new county of Pembroke. Where once the feudal earls of Pembroke had been, in the words of George Owen, 'absolute princes of themselves', their powers to execute 'all jurisdiction', make 'all writs and process in their own names by their own officers' and pardon 'all felonies, murders and other offences', were done away with. Nor was this all, for in passing, in 1536, an 'Act for Laws and Justice to be ministered in Wales in like form as it is in this realm' the Crown effectively abolished all Marcher lordships by grouping them into new counties or by attaching them to pre-existing counties. Consequently, in Pembrokeshire, the earldom was at last united with the bishop of St David's lordships of Llawhaden and Pebidiog, and with his demesne manor of Lamphey. The lordships of Cemais, Cilgerran, Roch,

Walwyn's Castle, Narberth and Haverfordwest, over which the earls had long claimed jurisdiction, were also fused together to form the new county. On the other hand, the lordships of Laugharne, Llanddowror and Llanstephan, assigned to Pembrokeshire in 1536, were lost to the neighbouring county of Carmarthen in the Act passed in 1543. Haverfordwest too was lost to the fledgling county of Pembroke in 1543 when the Crown saw fit to recognize its unique status as a 'county in itself' as conferred by charter in 1479. According to the terms of the Act of 1543, Haverfordwest's status as a county was dependent upon 'the King's Majesty's will and pleasure' but it was to be parliament's will and pleasure that brought this privileged anomaly to an end in 1885.

The Acts of Union were part of an attempt to bring uniformity and control to provincial government, essentially laying the foundation of the 'sovereign state' by attacking franchises and associated anomalous privileges, and reflected the bureaucratic genius of the king's chief minister, Thomas Cromwell. Wales and Pembrokeshire were brought more firmly under the orbit of royal, centralist control by means of the Council in Wales and the Marches and by parliamentary representation. Although subject to the control of central government, from which it transmitted instructions to the individual shires whilst in return passing back information about conditions within them, the Ludlow-based council exercised a very real degree of control over the Welsh and English border shires that found themselves subject to its wide-ranging authority. Headed by a lord president and assisted by a twenty-member council appointed by the Crown, the success of provincial government in Wales depended upon the ready cooperation of the most powerful and influential landowners. It is partly from among this powerful group of men, with the rest being drawn largely from among the legal fraternity, that the Crown chose its council. Yet it is a fact that during the reign of Elizabeth the Welsh shires were, in the main, under-represented on the council with the majority of its members being recruited from English border shires. Of the hundred known members of the council between 1560 and 1603 twenty-one were Welsh by birth of whom eighteen represented Welsh shires. Pembrokeshire had a solitary representative on the council during this period, Sir John Perrot, who was admitted a member in 1574. Although successive Herbert earls of Pembroke served on the council, both as lord president, neither Henry Herbert (d.1601) nor his son William (d.1630) had any connection with the county from which they took their title.

If the rich and powerful monopolized membership of the council they were also to the fore in representing Welsh constituencies in parliament. For the first time Wales was bestowed parliamentary representation with each of the newly created shires given the opportunity of sending two locally elected members to Westminster, one for the county and the other for the county town. However, given Haverfordwest's especial status, this corner of the realm was able to return three MPs. The numbers able to vote were small, amounting to only a fraction of the population, and restricted to the privileged well-to-do. For example, in Haverfordwest, which had a population of somewhere between two to three thousand during the latter half of the sixteenth century, only around a 100 or 120 of the town's burgesses were eligible to vote. The knights of the shire were to be paid wages, and burgesses of the ancient boroughs were to be responsible for the wages of the borough members, thus introducing the system of contributory boroughs unique to Wales. Under this system the burgess elected to represent the shire town, Pembroke, was returned for the constituency of Pembroke Boroughs which encompassed the boroughs of Tenby, Newport, Llawhaden, Cilgerran and Wiston. Of these, only Tenby could reasonably be described as anything approaching a town, having maintained its size and prosperity by trade while the others had suffered a steep decline in both.

Once elected to parliament Welsh members of parliament were left largely to their own devices. Unless they were beholden to the patronage of greater men for their parliamentary positions, they did not have to answer to their constituents and they could participate, or not, as was often the case, in parliamentary debates and other matters as they wished. Even when it came to casting their votes within the House of Commons they could do so, within the constraints of a political system riven by faction, patronage and monarchial pressure, according to their individual consciences. Unfortunately for Wales, no less than for Pembrokeshire, its political representatives hardly distinguished themselves in parliament, being prone to absence, apathy and inaction though there were exceptions: men like Sir James Perrot (d.1637) who vigorously represented, separately, both Pembrokeshire and Haverfordwest in the Commons during the reigns of the Stuart kings James I and Charles I. As talented as he was controversial Perrot is probably to be counted among the first of any of the Welsh members of parliament who can be said to have had anything like a parliamentary career. In a career spanning over thirty years he became expert on parliamentary procedure and a leading authority of the rights and privileges of the Commons. In one session alone he made over seventy speeches and involved himself in matters of state that included war, the royal prerogative, royal marriage and, in an echo of our own time, government sleaze. If, according to the late A. H. Dodd, the period from the first Act of Union in 1536 to the outbreak of Civil War in 1642 marked 'Wales's Parliamentary Apprenticeship', then Perrot, and by virtue of his interests and representation, Pembrokeshire, may be considered to have been at its cutting edge.

Under Cromwell's reformist guidance the Lord Chancellor, Sir Thomas Audley, was empowered to convene a commission to oversee arrangements for the subdivision of the new Welsh shires into administrative units known as hundreds. Pembrokeshire was divided into seven hundreds, namely, Castlemartin, Cemais, Cilgerran, Dewisland, Daugleddau (Dungleddy), Narberth and Rhos (Roose). Consequent to this administrative reform the county was given institutions roughly corresponding to those found in any typical English shire: a sheriff, two coroners, an escheator (later to be assisted and then replaced by a ward-ship feodary) and justices of the peace. At the hundred level the administration was staffed by bailiffs and constables assisted by church-wardens who oversaw matters of religious concern in each of the parishes that made up the hundred. In fact, apart from the justices of the peace and deputy lieutenants (introduced in 1586 to oversee musters and defence) many of the offices that post-dated the Acts of Union were already familiar, as were those who filled them, to the people of Pembrokeshire. Official titles may have changed but the personnel and the power they wielded remained largely the same, so that Marcher stewards became royal justices and Marcher bailiffs royal ones. Nevertheless, change did occur not least in the evolving status and authority of the most important of these local or county offices, namely, the sheriff, justices of the peace, feodary and deputy lieutenants.

The sheriff was, in the words of George Owen, 'the chiefest man in account within the shire and the prince's lieutenant'. Certainly, the shrievalty was among the few renumerated offices within the shire administration, its post-holder being paid £5 annually for his duties. Chosen annually by the Crown from a list of names submitted by the Council in Wales, the sheriff was the nearest thing Tudor and Stuart Pembrokeshire had to a police officer since he was responsible for the arrest, custody and presentation for trial of all villains within the county. In addition to presiding over his own court, the sheriff was responsible for organizing the quarter sessions, empanelling juries and for punishing both witnesses and jurors who failed to appear. In this he was assisted by a deputy or under sheriff, bailiffs and constables all of whom in their oaths, undertook always to be at the sheriff's command. However, the sheriff was more than simply a 'police' officer – he was the fulcrum of local, regional and national administration, being the principal channel for communication between the Privy Council in London, the Council in Wales at Ludlow and the Pembrokeshire justices of the peace. Perhaps among the more significant duties exercised by the sheriff was that of returning officer in parliamentary elections. The unscrupulous sheriff could, and sometimes did, abuse his office by making false returns as happened in 1571 when one Edmund Harris, sheriff of Haverfordwest, was fined £200 for issuing threats and exerting physical force in order to prevent some of the electors from casting their votes. Indeed, if the opinion expressed in verse by Rhys Prichard (d.1644) of Llandovery, chancellor of St David's, and vicar of Llawhaden is typical then the general public had nothing but contempt for those who held the shrievalty.

Mae'r shirifaid, a'u debidion,	*The sheriff and their cormorant train*
Yn anrheithio'r bobl wirion;	*On the fleeced populace distrain*
Ac wrth rym eu braint a'u swyddau,	*And under veil of justice prey*
Yn eu 'speilio liw dydd goleu.	*Upon their wealth, in open day.*

The most innovative and important office created by the Union legislation was that of the justice of the peace (JP), whose powers and duties were derived from the commission of the peace issued annually by the Crown. They performed a wide range of administrative tasks including the maintenance of bridges, the setting of wages, the inspection of weights and measures, and the quality of goods, the licensing of alehouses, and the supervision of poor relief. As if these duties were not onerous enough they were charged, in their judicial capacity, to try and sentence a wide range of offences and offenders whom they dealt with, either sitting alone in special session as stipendiary magistrates or, more often, in concert in courts of Quarter Session held at three-monthly intervals. For this they received no wages but a paltry 4s a day allowance when attending Quarter Sessions though the means to exploit the office to make profit was ever present and an inducement for those with ambition to feather their own nests. Nor was this all, for as the office of the justice of the peace grew in importance in the sixteenth century, becoming in the opinion of one historian 'the backbone of county officialdom', ever more demanding and complex tasks were heaped upon those who occupied it. For example, in 1628 the shire's justices were expected to deal with the increased influx of Irish immigrants which threatened to erupt into violence as a resentful populace attempted to resist this unwanted incursion.

As a measure of the poverty prevalent in Wales, the rule in England whereby only men with an annual income of £20 from property could serve as justices of the peace was waived for those who dwelt across the border. Not that this opened up the office for greater competition since men of lesser means could do little to rival their wealthier gentry compatriots who coveted a role in the county's magistracy often more for its status and power than for its potential for lucre. Consequently, the potential for corruption was as legion as for that of the shrievalty as may be inferred from a report on Pembrokeshire compiled in 1575 on behalf of the Council in Wales. It is a fact that local government worked best, and was at its most efficient, when the interests of the Crown and central government coincided with those on whom they relied to govern the localities.

Those on whom the Crown relied for their diligence and discretion were the county feodary and deputy lieutenants. The county feodary was appointed by and was directly responsible to the master of the Court of Wards, a London court accorded formal recognition by statute in 1540. Acting as the court's local agent the feodary was responsible for holding inquisitions to determine the nature, extent, value – and to arrange for the disposal – of property held by the recently deceased within the shire. In all matters relating to his duties the feodary was charged with protecting and upholding the rights of the Crown. Perhaps the most successful office-holder in Pembrokeshire was Sir Thomas Canon (d.1638) who by his consummate skill, bullying and careful manipulation of the duties associated with the feodary, made the office an indispensable part of the shire's administration. In the process – at his death he had held the office for nigh on forty years – he earned himself a reputation in court circles for efficiency in increasing royal revenue, from which he too made a handsome profit, but in local circles, as one might expect, he was less than popular.

It is probably true to say that the more conscientious the official the less likely he was to be popular. There are numerous instances in the judicial records of efficient and corrupt officials – a popular resentment that was often indistinguishable in the record – being subject to assault, harrassment, malicious charges and general abuse. Thomas Phaer and John Elliot of Earwear – customs officials operating at Milford Haven and Tenby respectively – were threatened with hanging by merchants whose goods they had either seized or distrained for payment of tax. Nor were officials like the newly created deputy lieutenants immune from such threats for though they had nothing to do with the more resented duties such as the collecting of taxes, customs and fines, their responsibility for musters meant they had the unfortunate task of recruiting or impressing men for service in the defence of the county. Needless to say, service in the local militia was not universally popular. Born of fear and despair, being hastily appointed to assist the lord president in making Wales safe from an expected Spanish invasion, the deputy lieutenants became an integral part of the county's administration. The first to be appointed in Pembrokeshire, in 1587, were Sir Thomas Perrot (d.1594) and George Owen (d.1613) for the county and Henry Morton for the county-borough of Haverfordwest. Assisted by six captains and an experienced muster-master, they were to raise and train a force of 500 men, repair the town walls of Tenby and to survey Milford Sound with a view to identifying possible landing sites and strengthening its defences. However, the authority exercised by Perrot, Owen and Morton was resented by some, particularly Hugh Gwyn, a local landowner, who refused to cooperate with them saying:

'As for you, I care not for you, neither do I crave your goodwills; you have done the worst you can against me already, and that which you have done you have done without authority.'

The government and administrative structures put in place during the sixteenth century survived largely intact until the nineteenth century. The only casualty of change was the Council in Wales and the Marches which was abolished in 1689. The council's demise, and that of Ludlow as the unofficial capital of Wales, was in large part effected by the very people it was meant to govern. In the early months of 1689 William III received a petition from his Welsh subjects, including representatives from Pembrokeshire, entitled *The Grievance of their Majesties' Subjects in the Principality of Wales*, which, in the opinion of A. H. Dodd, presented the council 'as an oppressive, expensive and pettifogging anachronism, contravening the spirit of the Acts of Union themselves by depriving the Welsh of their promised privilege of common citizenship with the English'. No doubt to the gentry of Pembrokeshire, keen to see to their own affairs, the council was as distant a body and as far removed from the county's business as was the London government so that its abolition caused hardly a stir.

The Governors and the Governed

At its most basic, Tudor and Stuart society was made up of the gentle and non-gentle, those who had the power to govern and those who did not. Title, wealth, power, land and office-holding, these were some of the key determinants that separated the haves and the have-nots. In Pembrokeshire, as in every other county in the realm, the have-nots vastly outnumbered the haves but apart from the odd riot or two the poor did not seriously trouble their betters since the Church had taught them that rebellion was a sin and that they should accept what God had intended for them in his divine plan. Temporal power combined with spiritual authority ensured a social system that favoured the rich and contained the poor.

In Pembrokeshire, the nobility were rather thin on the ground so that the rich consisted of the gentry, representatives of those families who had established themselves in the medieval period. For example, the Perrots, Wyrriots, Wogans, Phillipps, Bowens, Whites and Laugharnes continued to dominate the scene though they were joined by incomers like Barlow, Owen of Orielton and Stepney. They were the elite around whom revolved the social, political, cultural and economic life of the county. It is important to remember that this gentle 'elite' was not a homogenous group but a collection of different classes within which discerning gentlemen like George Owen could and often did discriminate. For example, in 1602 he listed the names of forty-seven men, himself among them, whom he claimed to be the most important in the shire by virtue of their title. They were all either knights or esquires and were all either serving or former justices of the peace. Yet beyond this privileged group there were at least another two hundred heads of households who qualified as gentry by virtue of their lineage, wealth and occupation. Historians have paid due attention to the gentry's wealth and political influence but less has been written about what it was to be a 'gentleman' in early modern Pembrokeshire: the very essence of gentility which takes account of such fundamental issues as their attitudes to their lineage, education, learning, religious belief and social behaviour. At its core is the family, which has been defined thus:

> The early modern family existed as the primary focus of repro-
> duction, consumption and socialisation. To the principal duties
> of ensuring biological survival and economic security were added
> moral obligations to rear children with the proper religious and
> social identity. (F. Heal and C. Holmes, 1994)

The family in this context is taken to mean those members of the same kin who lived under one roof; in short, the nuclear family. This represents a significant shift of opinion by historians who once tended to think of the extended or multi-generational family as the norm and the nuclear variant as the exception. This was particularly the case in Wales where kinship and lineage were powerful elements in native Welsh society. Here Welsh law and custom reserved for the kinfolk control over essentials such as the inheritance and transmission of land and marriage. The individual landowner had no absolute rights over the land he farmed but held it in trust on behalf of the kindred or extended family. The individual proprietor could not sell, alienate or devise by will parcels of property that had descended through the family. Even in marriage the rights to arrange matches between couples lay mainly with the head of the kin rather than with the parents and certainly not with the couple themselves. Nevertheless, by the fourteenth century English law and custom was making its presence felt north of the *racial divide* which enabled the more enterprising native gentry to consolidate land and prosper.

The Pembrokeshire evidence tends to confirm the current historical thinking inasmuch as the essential core of family life in the Anglicized area of the county certainly, and in the native north probably, consisted of the conjugal pair with or without dependent children. The family was formed by marriage and, in spite of the best efforts of the Church, it continued to be regarded more as a contract rather than as a sacrament. The gentry – or at least the majority of them – did not marry for love. They married for politics, to acquire lands, or to cement social and political alliances. Many of them did not even have a say in the choice of wives. It was an accepted fact of life that, for those of sufficient social and political importance, marriage was far too serious a matter to be left to the individual bride and groom. Since the marriages of the gentry involved property it was a matter for the parents, unless they were Welsh governed by native custom, to matchmake and to negotiate the legal and financial contracts. Although office-holding, local influence and shrewd dealings in the land market contributed much to the rise of the gentry, marriage made many of them. A widow or an heiress could bring to her husband considerable landed wealth but where a wife had no land her family would normally provide a dowry in cash or goods. Few marriage settlements survive for early modern Pembrokeshire but of those that do it is clear that hard bargaining was the order of the day before any union was entered into.

Although there were love matches – the literature and poetry of the time testifies to this – with so much at stake it is probably true to say that 'the property drive could be considerably more powerful than the sex drive in forming marriages among the upper classes' (F. Heal and C. Holmes, 1994). That said, property seemed farthest from the mind of Sir John Perrot's son and heir, Thomas, when he eloped with his beloved Dorothy in July 1583. In true Shakespearean style, the thirty-year-old Perrot made off with the eighteen-year-old daughter of his father's former enemy, the late Walter Devereux (d.1576), earl of Essex, took her to the most convenient church and there encouraged a reluctant priest to marry them while armed servants stood guard over the door. Both were punished for their indiscretion, Thomas with a spell in prison and Dorothy, a lady-in-waiting to Queen Elizabeth, with banishment from court, but both lived happily together. Whether or not arranged marriages were as happy or not depended upon the temperament of the couples involved. The key to the success and longevity of the gentle marriage was duty and discretion. It was the duty of the wife to provide her husband with a son and heir as it was his duty to provide the means for their sustenance and prosperity. On the other hand, if the marriage proved loveless or unbearable it was almost inevitable that the husband would seek solace in the arms of a mistress, in which case discretion was the order of the day. Divorce was rare and in any event, due to the complications involved in the recovery of property or the dowry, it was not really an option.

Unfortunately, in the absence of such records as letters and diaries it is not possible to chronicle the daily lives of Pembrokeshire folk but if the experiences of the Pastons are typical then we may suppose that family life in this corner of Wales was no less strained and stressful. In view of the demands made on a husband in terms of estate-management, office-holding, local politics or by simply attending to the needs of those who served and depended on him and those whom he served, maintaining a meaningful relationship with his wife was fraught with difficulties. Very often wives would be left to run the household while their husbands were away, and with no one but the servants to commune with it was a solitary existence. For example, Sir John Perrot was often away from home serving in Ireland between 1571 and 1573 and again between 1584 and 1588. Some might seek comfort in play with their children but even here social custom prevailed and from an early age sons were removed by their fathers to another household in order to acquire an education or training. Daughters might remain within the household but plans were usually afoot to find them suitable husbands and to have them married by their early teens.

The setting for family life was the household, the primary purpose of which was to supply the domestic needs of the family. Yet, the household supplied more than just a gentleman's domestic needs; it was a nerve-centre of politics and administration, as well as being the symbol of local power and munificence. It is known that by the beginning of the sixteenth century powerful families like the Perrots and Wogans employed chaplains, attorneys and stewards. In the smaller, non-noble households the work of the steward was often varied and demanding, his management of the estates notwithstanding, he was usually expected to combine his function as a domestic manager with that of the family treasurer or receiver.

If the *raison d'être* of the household was in part to display the wealth and status of the family that maintained it there can be no doubt that this was the case of the buildings that housed them. The homes of the gentry provided the clearest opportunity for them to display their gentility and impress their neighbours. Indeed, by the beginning of the sixteenth century, the greater gentry of Pembrokeshire possessed a number of fine manorial houses in addition to their family seats. Besides Wiston, the senior line of the Wogan family were the proud owners of at least three fine manor houses in Pembrokeshire while their kinsmen the Perrots possessed at least nine, scattered throughout the county, many of which were either entrusted to sons or leased to members of the extended family in return for supervising the running of the attached estates. Such wealth in land and property set these families apart from the majority of their equally gentle friends and neighbours. They were joined by families responsible for the building of such grand mansions as Orielton, Picton Castle, Henllan, Tre-wern, Pentre Ifan and Carew. Between them they owned and controlled a sizeable portion of the county, employed a fair proportion of the local workforce and accounted for much of the wealth generated within the shire. Even the towns came within the orbit of gentry influence since much of what they produced on their farms found its way into the markets and shops of Haverfordwest, Pembroke, Tenby and Newport, some of which were owned, run or leased by them. In short, Pembrokeshire's social and economic life was dependent on and revolved around these gentry estates.

The so-called rise of the gentry was once thought to be a sixteenth-century phenomenon, a period that provided them with opportunities aplenty to emerge as the rulers of the county community. However, local and regional studies of the gentry allied with studies of individual families have added to the sum of our knowledge with the result that historians have come to accept the notion of gentry class already 'risen' by the sixteenth century. That the emergence or rise of the gentry spanned a period of considerably more than a single century there can be no doubt but to be precise in establishing its roots or to delineate clear lines of development for a vaguely defined class is probably asking too much. As J. C. Holt reminds us, 'the gentry are always rising; it is their habit'. Nevertheless, in Pembrokeshire at least, the sixteenth century may be regarded as the period of their apotheosis when, for historical, political, social and economic reasons, they came to occupy a pre-eminent position of leadership.

'Poverty, something experienced only by the lower classes, but defined in legislation by the ruling classes, was the major problem of the age'. Ieuan Gwynedd Jones's (1992) definition of poverty is deliciously ironic and is a truism that may be applied to any age or period in history. In Elizabethan society poverty was regarded almost as a disease, and a self-inflicted one at that, the sufferers of which needed sharp corrective treatment. The poverty-stricken masses were divided into two classes of able-bodied – physically well and active but unemployed – and impotent poor – the old, the sick, the handicapped and the young – the latter gaining a mean measure of compassion in a society not noted for its humanitarianism. Whipping, branding and virtual incarceration in a house of correction or workhouse was usually the lot of the able-bodied poor whilst their impotent brethren might look forward to some support from private charities. Self-help was promoted as a cheap and effective way of dealing with small numbers of poor; licences were issued giving the fortunate few the legal right to beg for a living. Unfortunately, Elizabethan measures to 'cure' poverty were too few, too poorly funded and too small-scale to deal with a rapidly expanding and increasingly volatile problem. Vagrancy, riot, crime and general unrest forced an increasingly perturbed government to act and it did so by legislating a series of poor laws culminating in the Poor Law Act of 1601. This Act required each parish to take responsibility for its own poor and its administration was entrusted to the parish priest and justices of the peace. In an effort to tackle vagrancy the Act of Settlement of 1662 was passed which stated that, henceforth, the 'wandering' poor would be required to return to and be supported by the ratepaying parishioners of the parishes in which they were born. Unfortunately, some parishes did not want them while others were a tad slow in raising the rate to support them.

It is probably true to say that much of the surviving evidence that deals with the poor was written not by them but by those who could write, the educated, which included the gentry. Consequently, historians are confronted with the often unsympathetic descriptions and sometimes biased opinions of one class or another. For example, George Owen, never short of an opinion on most things, described the

> common sort of people . . . being the greatest number . . . to be very mean and simple, short of growth, broad and shrubby [stunted], unacceptable in sight for their personal service howsoever they prove in action when they are put to it, so that of all the countries of Wales I find and speak by experience Pembrokeshire to be the worst mannered, and hardest to find personable and serviceable men.

In fact, Owen believed he knew why the Pembrokeshire peasant was so 'very mean and simple' because, 'although they have lost their language', they 'are the remnant and offspring of the Flemings that were sent hither . . . by Henry I and King Stephen . . . as the histories do deliver'.

However, Owen's unsubstantiated opinion aside, to label the poorest class as simply rogues and vagabonds is far from the truth and not a little misleading. In early modern Pembrokeshire, the non-gentle or peasant class made up of around 95 per cent of the population but this does not mean that all of them were poor. As in the case of the gentry, the peasant class was far from being homogenous since their economic circumstances varied widely too. Their ranks embraced, what Sir Thomas Smith (d.1583) described as 'the fourth sort of men, who do not rule', the yeoman, a more substantial landowning or land-leasing peasant-farmer, husbandmen, craftsmen, servants, labourers and the poor. In fact, it is not unknown to find some yeomen who were as wealthy, if not wealthier, than the less prosperous of their gentle neighbours but the division in class was a chasm which highlighted their social separation. Although movement between the classes was not unknown only gradually did class distinction break down sufficiently for marriages and family alliances to be concluded without attracting the disapproving writ of a contemporary commentator like Owen.

To be fair, Owen had some sympathy for the peasants he encountered, describing their often miserable existence thus:

> I have by good account numbered three thousand young people to be brought up continually in herding of cattle within this shire,

who are put to this idle education when they are first come to be ten or twelve years of age and turned to the open fields to follow their cattle, when they are forced to endure the heat of the sun in his greatest extremity to parch and burn their faces, hands, legs, feet and breasts in such sort as they seem more like tawny Moors than people of this land. And then with the cold, frost, snow, hail, rain and wind they are so tormented, having the skin of their hands, face and feet all in chinks and chaps, that poor fools, they may well hold opinion with the papists that there is a purgatory.

The working day was from dawn to dusk, summer and winter, and the rate of pay was usually set annually by the justice of the peace as allowed under the Statute of Artificers 1563, at subsistence level. Their diet was nowhere near as nutritional or as varied as that enjoyed by the yeomen and gentry, nor had it changed that much if Charles Hassall is to be believed. In 1794 he stated that in Pembrokeshire 'the labouring poor live almost entirely upon bread and cheese, milk and vegetables, except when herrings are plentiful on the coast, or in the spring of the year, when poor [quality] veal is to be got at a low rate'. They rarely ate fresh meat unless it consisted of rabbits or birds, or a poached deer or two. Their diets were such that dearth and pestilence were an ever-present danger which threatened to overtake whole communities in times of crisis.

Structurally and archaeologically the peasant class have left few remains; their homes were small simple affairs – 'dung heaps shaped into cottages' was how William Richards, author of *Wallography* (1682), described them – and their possessions few, and less durable, in number. Only the more substantial stone-built farmhouses of the yeoman and, possibly, husbandman class have survived, though, these too are comparatively few in number. Life was tough but there were lighter moments such as on holy days and religious festivals which gave the peasantry some relief from the toil of daily life; though, if George Owen is to be believed, their recreational sports were anything but playful. 'I cannot overpass a game used in one part of this shire among the Welshmen both rare to hear, troublesome to describe, and painful to practise. This game is called *cnapan* and not unfitly.' It involved teams of whole villages, together with horsemen playing hockey-style with sticks, contesting the possession of a small wooden ball-like object. It was a violent and quite dangerous sport which shocked strangers by the ferocity of its playing leaving men 'hurt and bloody', yet Owen was able to explain it thus to a stranger he met in 1588, that 'This is all play and will be taken in good part'.

From Catholicism to Protestantism: The Reformation

The shire of Pembroke lay at the very heart of the premier see in Wales, the large, sprawling diocese of St David's which extended over five of the counties created in 1536, namely, Breconshire, Carmarthenshire, Cardiganshire, Pembrokeshire and Radnorshire. Pembrokeshire accounted for over a third of the 340 parishes that made up the diocese and over a third of the monastic houses that lay within its bounds. In economic terms, a little over 30 per cent of the bishop's income came from the county while its religious houses accounted for nearly 60 per cent of all monastic revenue generated within the diocese. Large it may have been but rich it was not. In common with the other Welsh dioceses, St David's was among the poorest in the kingdom which is why many of the bishops appointed to the see, like a fair proportion of the cathedral clergy, were alien absentees. Not that this affected unduly the faith and religious experience of the people who dutifully attended church more, it might be argued, out of habit rather than any deep-seated conviction. Where once the Middle Ages might have been described by historians as an age of faith this is not now generally accepted. The people's fidelity to the Church and its doctrine was not untainted by doubt, criticism or heresy, but neither was it so base and superficial as to be almost meaningless. The simple folk of Wales and Pembrokeshire were as credulous and as superstitious as they had always been but their religious experience was marred to some extent by them being ill-served by corrupt, negligent and nepotistic clergy who cared more for their own careers than for the spiritual welfare of their flocks. On the other hand, there were many among the clergy who were honest in their endeavours to improve the quality of their parishoners' experience of religion. Consequently, to suggest, on the eve of the Reformation, that the Welsh were fanatically devoted to the Church is as inappropriate as saying that there was a crisis of faith. The Reformation was not, at least initially and contrary to its implied meaning, an attempt to reform the Church, it was an act of state that came about mainly as a result of Henry VIII's desire to divorce his wife. Any reform for the good of the Church was, arguably, incidental and unintended.

The simple folk of Pembrokeshire knew little if anything of the reasons why their king should seek a divorce from his popular wife, Katherine of Aragon, or why this should lead to a clash of wills with the Roman Pope, Clement VII. There was no understanding here of Cromwell's concept of the sovereign state nor of the reasons why the king's divorce should lead to changes in the Church. Even their betters, the educated and wealthy gentle elite, unrepresented in parliament and far from the political power base that was the royal court, may also have been largely ignorant of the issues at stake and of the likely consequences if those issues were ever resolved as Cromwell intended. As for those who had any knowledge of the 'King's Great Matter', they knew well that to voice their opinions was to invite trouble. One of the first casualties of the King's belligerence towards those who showed displeasure at the king's affair with Anne Boleyn was Rhys ap Gruffudd. Although a Carmarthenshire man by birth and inclination, he had, by way of inheritance of his grandfather Sir Rhys ap Thomas (d.1525), wide estates in Pembrokeshire so that his fate in 1531, when he was executed for treason, was not unknown to his tenants in the county.

Perhaps the first inkling the people of Pembrokeshire might have had that change was afoot was when the pre-Union Marcher earldom of Pembroke was granted in September 1532 to the king's lover Anne Boleyn. Her patronage of William Barlow (d.1568), first as prior of Haverfordwest priory (1534) and later, indirectly via Thomas Cromwell, as bishop of St David's (1536), was to have far-reaching consequences for religion in the county. In the event, the absentee marchioness of Pembroke had less than four years to enjoy her title and revenues from this remote corner of the realm before being executed for adulterous treason in May 1536. During those four years the Church in Wales no less than in Pembrokeshire had seen tremendous change: detachment from Rome and the king's assumption of power as its head (1534), the surveying of its lands and properties in the *Valor Ecclesiasticus* (1535), the appointment of William Barlow as bishop of its largest diocese and the beginning of the Crown's attack on its monasteries (1536). The scene was set for further change, not all of which would be so painless as seemed to be the case after the appointment of Barlow whose radical Protestant policies were to leave a permanent mark in Pembrokeshire.

The opening salvos of this religious change, and one with which Barlow heartily agreed, began in 1536 when parliament passed the first of two Acts. The other was in 1539, for the dissolution of the monasteries. As far as Pembrokeshire was concerned the first Act was enough to see off the county's seven religious houses inasmuch as they fell foul of the criteria imposed by the Crown which deemed institutions with an annual income of less than £200 to be religiously and economically unviable. Their combined net annual income came to a little less than £520 with just two houses, the Knights Hospitallers of Slebech and Barlow's former charge, the Augustinian priory at Haverfordwest, accounting for £217 or a shade over 40 per cent of the total. Such exact information was ascertained by Crown visitors by inspection of the financial records of each of the forty-seven monastic houses in Wales. The fruits of their accounting was included in the so-called *Valor Ecclesiasticus* which has been likened to a kind of sixteenth-century Domesday Book. Armed with such information Cromwell could better advise the king of the potential wealth available to him as head of the Church should he ever be disposed to closing the monasteries down. If the *Valor Ecclesiasticus* did for the monasteries of Pembrokeshire, what of the visitation records compiled by the inspectors separately employed by the Crown and bishop? These reports were intended to ascertain the state of the spiritual and moral condition of both the secular clergy within the diocese and the regular clergy within the monasteries. Barlow ensured that they would not make for comfortable reading since his opinion of the clergy in his diocese, both regular and secular, with few exceptions, was far from complimentary. Nor did he hold a better opinion of his parishioners, whom he considered ignorant and ill-suited to civilized ways, hence the almost missionary zeal with which he went about his business in this distant corner of the realm.

That Barlow had little love or understanding of either Pembrokeshire or its people may be gauged from his description of their religious traditions:

It has been always esteemed a delicate daughter of Rome, naturally resembling her Mother in shameless confusion and like qualified with other perverse properties and execrable malignity, as ungodly image service, abominable idolatry, and licentious liberty of dishonest living, Popish pilgrimages, disgraceful pardons, and feigned indulgences. (G. Williams, 1967)

His antagonistic attitude towards the Welsh in general and to their religious beliefs in particular bordered on the fanatical. He was a rash, if sincere, radical reformer, an iconoclast, who had early embraced the more significant aspects of Lutheranism. The 'superstitious' and 'idolatrous' religious conservatism of his flock were to him an anathema and he was determined to rid his diocese of it. One way in which he intended to stamp his authority on the diocese was to remove the cathedral and diocesan administration from Pembrokeshire altogether. The cathedral church was to be abandoned in favour of St Peter's church in Carmarthen and the bishop's palace relocated to Abergwili. His intense dislike and suspicion of both St David's and its canons is made manifest in celebrated and oft-quoted phrases in which the cathedral is described as 'being situated in such a desolate and so rare a frequented place (except by vagabond pilgrims) that evil disposed persons unwilling to do good may lurk there at liberty in secret without restraint', and its clergy of whom 'there [is] not one that sincerely preaches God's word, nor scarce any that heartily favours it, but all utter enemies there against' (G. Williams, 1967).

Despite having powerful patrons in Boleyn and Cromwell (both of whom he lost on their executions in May 1536 and July 1540 respectively), Barlow did not enjoy much success in St David's. The cathedral canons resisted him at every turn and successfully frustrated his more ambitious

The political division of Wales and Pembrokeshire since 1996, D. G. Evans,
A History of Wales, 1906–2000 (University of Wales Press, 2000).

Wales and Pembrokeshire before and after 1974, D. G. Evans,
A History of Wales, 1906–2000 (University of Wales Press, 2000).

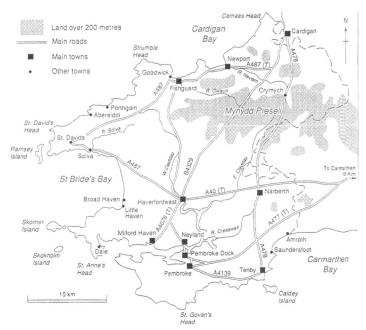

Relief and settlement, David W. Howell (ed.),
Pembrokeshire County History, vol IV (1993).

Pentre Ifan in 1905, the first protected ancient monument in Wales,
Heritage in Wales, 19 (Cadw publication, summer 2001).

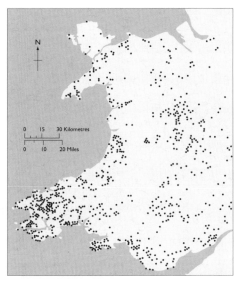

Iron Age hill-forts in south-west Wales, C. Knightly,
Chieftans and Princes (Cadw publication, 1994).

Roman forts and roads in south-west Wales, C. Knightly,
Chieftans and Princes (Cadw publication, 1994).

Administrative divisions of Dyfed, W. Rees, *An Historical Atlas of Wales*
(University of Wales Press, 1951).

The great pillar cross at Nevern, C. Knightly, *A Mirror of Medieval Wales*
(Cadw publications, 1988).

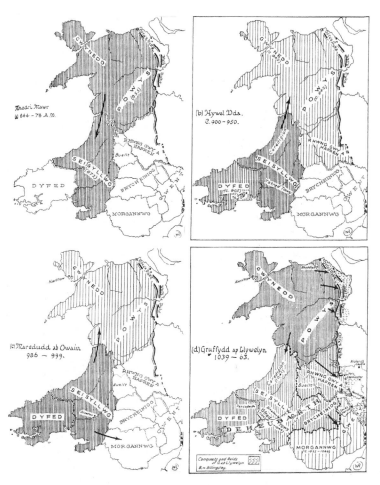

Wales and Pembrokeshire (ninth–eleventh centuries),
W. Rees, *An Historical Atlas of Wales* (University of Wales Press, 1951).

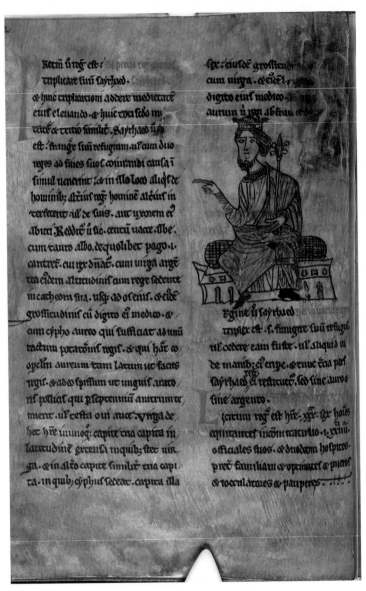

Image of the Welsh prince, Hywel Dda, as a lawgiver in a thirteenth-century copy of the Laws of Hywel Dda, Llyfrgell Genedlaethol Cymru/National Library of Wales, Peniarth MS 28 f. 1v.

The Tudor Merchant's House in Tenby, dating from the fifteenth century, the National Trust.

Early twentieth-century sculpture of Gerald of Wales in City Hall, Cardiff,
C. Knightly, *A Mirror of Medieval Wales* (Cadw publications, 1988).

Carved stone head from an effigy of a thirteenth-century knight, from the
Chapter House of Haverfordwest Priory (Cadw: Welsh Historic Monuments).

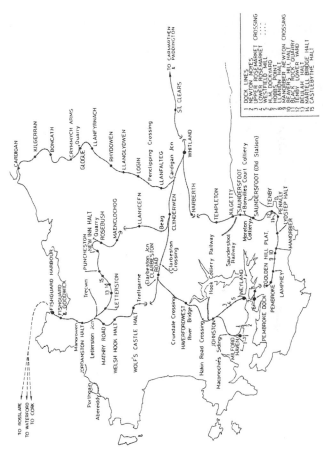

Map of Gerald of Wales's journey through Wales and Pembrokeshire, W. Rees, *An Historical Atlas of Wales* (University of Wales Press, 1951).

William Herbert (d.1469), earl of Pembroke,
British Library, MS Royal 18D II f. 6.

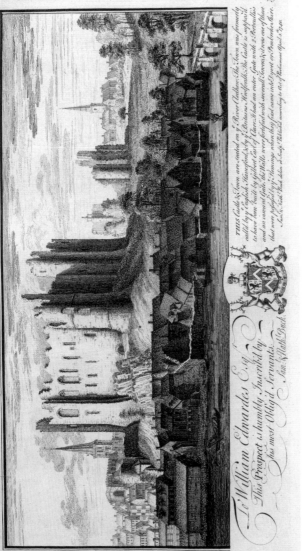

Buck print of Haverfordwest Castle from the north-east, 1740, Llyfrgell Genedlaethol Cymru/National Library of Wales.

Carew Castle, the home of Sir Rhys ap Thomas (d.1525) and Sir John Perrot (d.1592), RCAHMW.

Pembrokeshire and the Acts of Union, 1536–43,
W. Rees, *An Historical Atlas of Wales* (University of Wales Press, 1951).

ECCLESIA MENEVEN

Earliest known drawing of St David's Cathedral in the manuscripts of
George Owen of Henllys, British Library, Harleian 6077 f. 5.

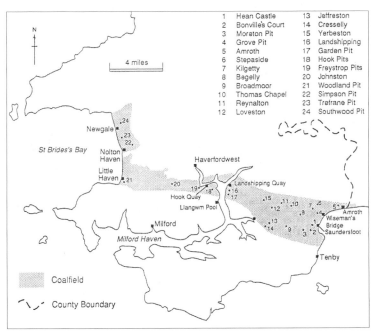

1	Hean Castle	13	Jeffreston
2	Bonville's Court	14	Cresselly
3	Moreton Pit	15	Yerbeston
4	Grove Pit	16	Landshipping
5	Amroth	17	Garden Pit
6	Stepaside	18	Hook Pits
7	Kilgetty	19	Freystrop Pits
8	Begelly	20	Johnston
9	Broadmoor	21	Woodland Pit
10	Thomas Chapel	22	Simpson Pit
11	Reynalton	23	Trefrane Pit
12	Loveston	24	Southwood Pit

Pembrokeshire coalmines, David W. Howell (ed.),
Pembrokeshire County History, vol. IV (1993).

Sir John Philipps of Picton Castle, Picton Castle Trust/B. E. Howells (ed.),
Pembrokeshire County History, vol. III (1987).

Portrait of a young Richard Fenton (d.1821), a local historian,
National Museum of Wales.

Sixteenth-century portrait of William Herbert, first Earl of Pembroke
and Montgomery, by kind permission of the eighteenth Earl of
Pembroke and Montgomery and the Trustees of the Wilton House Trust.

plans even going so far as to denounce him to the king, via Rowland Lee, as a heretic whose unorthodoxy was causing 'grave disquiet among the people of his diocese'. Barlow hit back by claiming that he had been threatened and that some among the cathedral's hierarchy were in league with pirates. Consequently, during his twelve-year episcopacy (1536–48) Barlow hardly set foot in his cathedral, preferring instead to govern his diocese either from Carmarthen or London. These bruising encounters between a tactless, reformist bishop and his conservative and stubborn senior clergy led in part to a paralysis in diocesan administration which had serious consequences for the quality of worship within the diocese. Ultimately, it was the common, largely uneducated and credulous peasant-parishoner who suffered inasmuch as he or she was an innocent bystander, ignorant of the reasons for the clerical conflict and possibly bemused, if not a little upset, by religious change such as that intended or introduced to church services by Barlow. Barlow failed to realize how unintelligible his brand of early Protestantism must have been for most of his clergy, let alone the laity. It was a lesson which his successor, an equally ardent Protestant, Bishop Robert Ferrar, also failed to heed, trying as he did to force the Protestant faith on his flock. He too had powerful patrons, the most important being the Lord Protector of England, Edward Seymour, duke of Somerset, but like Barlow his tenure as bishop was not without its problems.

Appointed by a dying Henry VIII (d.1547) to care for his young son and heir Edward VI (d.1553), Seymour took charge of a government and a nation that he determined would be Protestant in character if not in belief. Ferrar, a sincere if blunt Yorkshireman, was one of his protégés whom he willingly appointed to succeed Barlow who, incidentally, had recommended him. Having seen off Barlow, the cathedral clergy were hardly likely to yield to his successor, and so it proved, but where Ferrar erred was in taking his uncompromising Protestantism to the people whom he hoped to convert by preaching and prayer. Ferrar failed miserably but, fortunately for him, the people of Pembrokeshire did not follow the lead of their West Country compatriots who rose in rebellion in the summer of 1549. Known as the Prayer Book rising, the rebellion stemmed from the introduction of the Book of Common Prayer in English. Devonians and Cornish alike rejected the Prayer Book, complaining that the new church service was unintelligible to them because they could not, particularly the native Cornish speakers, understand the language. It was not long ere St David's became convulsed by religious bitterness and dissension which the factional nature of the conflict served only to exacerbate. It had become so bad that according to one eyewitness, the Carmarthenshire landowner Griffith Dwnn, 'if reformation be not had, and such means found that God's word may be sown among the people, and that shortly, they will think that there is no God. For how shall men think there is such a one, as is not worthy to be talked of' (G. Williams, 1967). Unfortunately for Ferrar it was he who fell foul of his detractors who conspired to ruin his reputation and charge him with various and, in most cases, spurious, crimes for which he was tried, found guilty and imprisoned in 1552. With the accession of the Roman Catholic Mary in 1553 the fate of the protestant Ferrar was sealed and in 1555 he was burned at the stake as a heretic.

His successor Henry Morgan (d.1559) was a Pembrokeshire man, born within riding distance of the cathedral. His appointment saw no major change nor was it overly controversial which was probably a blessing given the turbulence generated by both Barlow and Ferrar. Perhaps the most unpleasant duty that befell Morgan was in the persecution of Protestants within the county, one of whom, the humble William Nichol, was burnt in his home-town Haverfordwest as a heretic. Other more powerful 'heretics', such as Sir John Perrot who was known to be sheltering prominent Protestants at his home in Haroldston, were conveniently sidestepped and ignored. The only success that can be claimed by Morgan was in depriving over ninety of his clerics of their livings, thirty-eight of whom were removed from churches in Pembrokeshire, for having married during Edward VI's reign. Unfortunately for Morgan, his tenure as bishop lasted only for as long as Mary lived, being deprived of his see by Elizabeth within months of her accession on account of his 'being a devoted son of the church of Rome'. His successor Thomas Young (d.1568) was also a son of the county, hailing from Hodgeston, and was equally devout but in the Protestant faith. He served only two years in St David's before his promotion to the archbishopric of York. His successor was the gifted scholar Richard Davies (d.1581) who hailed from the Conwy valley in north Wales but who made his reputation in Pembrokeshire. Exiled during the reign of Mary, Davies returned from the Continent on the accession of Elizabeth and was by her promoted to the see of St Asaph before moving to St David's to which diocese he devoted the rest of his life (1561–81). Davies looms large in the conversion of the people of Wales, no less than the people of Pembrokeshire, to the Protestant faith but the path to that conversion was fraught with difficulties. Besides having to deal with a generally poor and ignorant parish clergy, men marked by their indifferent zeal and quality, Davies had to contend with popular conservatism, traditionalism and a vigorous recusant Catholicism which aimed to steal the initiative away from the Protestants.

Mary's reign marked the beginning of the end of Roman Catholicism in Pembrokeshire. True there remained considerable numbers of Catholics in the county and during her five-year reign they flourished but, thereafter, under Elizabeth, Protestantism gradually prevailed. Those who could not stomach Elizabeth's generally tolerant regime, and her Church Settlement of 1559, were rooted out and deprived of their livings. In Pembrokeshire a dozen clerics together with their bishop, Henry Morgan, were ejected while some of the more radical Catholics preferred exile abroad rather than accept what they regarded as a Protestant-imposed compromise. Elizabeth's religious Settlement was received in Pembrokeshire without much opposition but without much enthusiasm either. Bewildered by over two decades of change, a generally cowed and cautious people conformed partly out of fear and partly out of respect for a Church 'by law established'. It was left to the radicals on both sides, Roman Catholic and Protestant, to convert the generally indifferent mass of the people towards their version of Christianity.

Disadvantaged by legal and royal hostility, particularly after Elizabeth's excommunication by Pope Pius V in 1570, and hampered by their exile and continental affiliations, Catholic reformers and their lay followers, called recusants, had to operate covertly. Nevertheless, unlike in some parts of Wales, mainly in the border counties, recusancy was not a major factor in Pembrokeshire. Two men only have been identified as having left the county in the 1580s to train as missionary priests in the continental seminary at Douai, namely Lewis Barlow of Slebech and Erasmus Saunders of Tenby. Indeed, when ordered by the Crown in 1570 and 1576 to draw up lists of recusants in his diocese, the bishop of St David's, Richard Davies, could not readily identify anyone of any standing, certainly not in Pembrokeshire. On the other hand, that he could 'perceive a great number to be slow and cold in the service of God . . . and some that wish the Romish religion again' suggests that while the ordinary mass of the people might not knowingly be recusants they were reluctant to abandon traditional ways and habits, hence the prevalence in some remote rural areas of popish and Romish survivals. Davies was well aware, as was the Crown, that to overcome rural ignorance the Protestants had to win the hearts and minds of the people and this could only be done via prayer, the press and the pulpit.

The advantage, if not always the initiative, lay with the Protestants who had the backing of law, the Church and the state to push their message. In the Anglicized southern half of the county the people were more readily disposed to accept the Protestant message, if not the early messengers Barlow and Ferrar, with the new faith gathering an ever-increasing tide of converts. On the other hand, in the Welsh-speaking north a reformed religion based around the English Prayer Book was hardly likely to be welcomed. Here, where conservatism persisted, Protestantism was seen as an alien faith or *ffydd Saeson* which was treated with scepticism and suspicion. Only when the new faith was delivered to the people in their own language were they likely to embrace it. This was accomplished in 1588 with the publication of a translation of the Bible in Welsh. The first steps towards the translation of the Bible had been taken some twenty-five years before with the passing in 1563 of the Act for the Translation of the Scriptures in Welsh. According to the terms of this act of parliament the bishops of the four Welsh dioceses, together with the bishop of Hereford, were compelled to provide a translation into Welsh of the Bible and Book of Common Prayer. The chief architect of this act was likely the Pembrokeshire-based Bishop Richard Davies who took the lead in implementing its terms once it had passed into law. His uneasy collaboration with another gifted scholar, William Salesbury (d.1584), resulted in the translation of the New Testament and Book of Common Prayer, published in 1567, though work on the rest of the Scriptures was all but halted as a result of a quarrel which ended their partnership. It is noteworthy that the man to whom it fell to complete the translation of the Bible, William Morgan (d.1604) of Tŷ Mawr near Penmachno, was given his first appointment in the church by Richard Davies. The effect of the translation of the Bible into Welsh can be gauged by the Pembrokeshire antiquary George Owen who wrote in 1591:

> (and now not three years part), we have had the light of the gospel, yea the whole Bible, in our native tongue, which in short time must needs work great good inwardly in the hearts of the people, whereas the service and sacraments in the English tongue was as strange to many or most of the simplest sort as the mass was in the time of blindness was to the rest of England. (G. Owen, 1892–1936)

Of course, Owen spoke on behalf of his fellow Welsh speakers among whom he lived in north Pembrokeshire and it is likely that here the availability of the Bible in Welsh would have been greeted enthusiastically. However, as far as the English-speaking south was concerned the translation mattered little, if at all, and the fact that Protestantism was more readily embraced here by the gentry shows the extent to which it was, initially at least, an imported English phenomenon.

It is probably true to say that by the end of the sixteenth century there were still a fair number of clerics in the county who either did not fully understand or wholeheartedly accept the Reformation doctrines. Nor were their flocks overly disposed to abandon entirely their religous conserva-tism, the intensity of which varied from parish to parish. Nevertheless, despite themselves, the clerics would ensure that the future lay with a Protestant Pembrokeshire. Indeed, such was the strength of Protestantism in 1603 that according to a government report Wales had a mere 808 catholic recusants, of whom 145 resided within the diocese of St David's. Even allowing for considerable error on the part of the enumerators the threat of recusancy was clearly diminishing, for example, in subsequent surveys it was reported that in Pembrokeshire there were fifteen recusants listed in 1621 falling to ten in 1624. In Stuart Wales and Pembrokeshire the potential threat to religious peace and political stability came not so much from Papists as from Puritans, the consequence of which was Civil War.

A County Divided? The Civil Wars

In their quiet acceptance of Tudor rule, Welshmen did not differ fundamentally from the majority of Englishmen. Only with the accession of James I in 1603, the first of the Stuart kings, did this change. The Stuarts possessed neither the ability nor the tact of the Tudors and during the four decades following their accession they gradually alienated the more progressive elements in society which were developing a political consciousness allied to an increasing share of the nation's wealth. Where there developed in England, mainly in the prosperous south and east, a body of opinion which was not prepared to accept the unchecked exercise of royal power, in Wales, generally, there was little interest in the great constitutional and religious issues which caused the Civil War. That trading and commercial English middle class which suffered most from royal tactlessness and irresponsibility hardly existed in Wales, while Puritanism had made few converts before 1640. There was no Pembrokeshire equivalent of a Hampden or a Pym, nor was there a concerted effort either to resist Ship Money or support the Grand Remonstrance. Indeed, as the kingdom drifted almost unwittingly into Civil War between 1640 and 1642, it seemed as if Pembrokeshire would follow the example set by the rest of Wales inasmuch as a large body of its population, led by the gentry, continued to exhibit strong ties of duty towards, and affection for, their anointed monarch, Charles I. However, there existed in the county a small, cohesive and passionately active group of parliamentarians who were able to exert an influence far beyond their numerical strength. Consequently, within an almost overwhelmingly pro-royalist Wales, Pembrokeshire was to witness much of the action of the Civil War.

To suggest, as the late Sir J. E. Lloyd did in his *History of Carmarthenshire* (1935–9), that the 'Parliamentarianism of Pembrokeshire' can clearly be contrasted to the 'Royalism of Carmarthenshire' is perhaps overstating the case. The majority of the Pembrokeshire gentry were, in fact, generally supportive of the royalist cause but their allegiance to the king was of a largely tenuous or indifferent kind. For example, when hostilities broke out in late August 1642 the Pembrokeshire gentry were slow to react and few responded to Sir John Wogan (d.1644) of Wiston's parliamentary instructions for organizing the county's militia. Even when instructions were issued by far weightier personages such as the royalist marquis of

Hertford, who ordered the county's gentry to raise a regiment of men and to meet him at Carmarthen in November 1642, only the Lort brothers, Roger (d.1664) of Stackpole and Sampson (d.c.1669) of East Moor, and John Elliot of Earwear responded. On the other hand, three of the most influential men in the county, Sir Hugh Owen (d.1670) of Orielton, Sir Richard Philipps (d.1648) of Picton and Sir John Wogan, refused to do either. Not that the Lorts were diehard royalists, being prepared to trim their sails to suit the prevailing winds as they did in 1644 when they sought to make peace with parliament. Despite being prominent members of the Royalist Association of West Wales, signing several declarations on the king's side in 1642–3, by 1645 the Lorts had defected to the Parliamentary Association! Neither Lort was to be trusted, and nor were they; a contemporary said of Roger that he was interested 'in the preservation of no cause but his own'. Of his enigmatic Puritan brother Sampson, contemporaries were even less forgiving, one stating that 'he hath only the jaw of the Scriptural Sampson, yet he wrought much harm with it, he prays as long as it profits him'. Unlike their parliamentary brethren, the royalists of Pembrokeshire lacked initiative and were content to leave the leadership of their cause in the hands of their gentle compatriots from neighbouring Carmarthenshire. Thus did the earl of Carbery, Richard Vaughan of Golden Grove, assume command of the royalists in west Wales among whom the most steadfast in the service of the king in Pembrokeshire were the Catholic John Barlow of Slebech, Thomas Bowen of Trefloyne and Sir John Stepney (d.1676) of Prendergast.

The parliamentarian faction in Pembrokeshire was led by John Poyer (d.1649), a merchant and one-time mayor of Pembroke, Rowland Laugharne (d.1676) of St Bride's and Rice Powell (d.1665) of Pembroke. In contrast to Poyer, whose particular talent appears to have been in organization and propaganda, both Laugharne and Powell were experienced military men, having served in the Low Countries and in Ireland respectively. Together they formed a formidable team and in spite of their initial isolation, Poyer was in sole command of the parliamentary cause for nearly a year until joined by Laugharne and Powell in the summer of 1643; and in spite of their lack of material resources, they were able to offer the numerically superior royalist forces stout resistance. The remaining pro-parliamentarians in the county like Sir John Wogan of Wiston (unlike his son the Regicide Thomas who served the parliamentary cause with distinction in England), Sir Hugh Owen of Orielton and Griffith White (d.1664) of Henllan, tended towards equivocation so could not be relied on for active support. In fact, when confronted by royalist propaganda which aimed to scare their enemies into submission, such as that issued in 1643 which threatened to 'kill the dogs and ravish the bitches' in the county, White meekly submitted. He sent his wife to treat with Carbery at Tenby seeking protection for himself and his family of 'eight sons and eight daughters, who were virgins, and four small grandchildren'. On the other hand, Poyer was made of sterner stuff and he did not flinch when Carbery promised, on his capture, to put him 'in a barrel of nails and roll him downhill to the sea'.

Although spared the sustained battles and heavy casualties which featured in England, Pembrokeshire saw its fair share of action. First into the fray were the parliamentarians who succeeded in garrisoning, within weeks of the outbreak of hostilities, the towns and castles of Haverfordwest, Pembroke and Tenby. It was to be a year before the royalists reacted but when they did, in July 1643, they did so in considerable force. Having been persuaded to surrender by Carbery and Roger Lort respectively, by mid-September 1643 both Haverfordwest and Tenby fell almost without a shot being fired. Poyer and Pembroke Castle was all that stood between Carbery and the complete surrender of Pembrokeshire to the royalists. It was at this juncture that Poyer was joined in the besieged town and castle of Pembroke by Laugharne and Powell who brought troops and arms, thus increasing the parliamentary forces within the fortress to just over 250 men. While continuing the siege of Pembroke, Carbery set about strengthening and garrisoning the castles of Haverfordwest, Tenby, Carew, Manorbier and Roch along with smaller houses such as Stackpole Court, Trefloyne and Dale. Carbery's lack of resolve in prosecuting the siege with greater vigour enabled the parliamentarians to retain their toe-hold in the county and thereby remain a threat, while his lack of judgement in tying his forces down in garrison duty denied him the means to support and relieve his troops should they be attacked in force. It was probably thought, and with good reason, that the parliamentarians were a spent force and that their capitulation was only a matter of time.

However, as events were to prove, this belief was a serious misjudgement on the part of the royalists for within a month of the unintended arrival (23 January 1644) in Milford Haven of a fleet of eight ships serving the parliamentary cause, the balance of forces had been changed completely. Seeking shelter from the inclement weather, the commander of the naval squadron, Admiral Swanley, was persuaded by Poyer and Laugharne to release into their command 200 sailors and half a dozen cannon. Boldly, if a little recklessly, Laugharne took the offensive against royalist forces more than three times as large, but their dispersal by Carbery enabled the parliamentarian commander to pick them off one by one. First to fall were Stackpole Court and Trefloyne where garrisons of 60 and 150 men respectively surrendered after sharp exchanges of fire. Carbery's attempt to defeat Laugharne in battle between Trefloyne and Tenby ended in a miserable failure when, despite superior numbers, the royalist commander lost his nerve and retreated to the relative safety of the town's walls. His reputation in tatters and subject to bitter sniping which hinted at his cowardice, Carbery left Pembrokeshire never to return, and this despite a promise to do so with a relieving force. Laugharne now targeted a newly, if poorly, constructed fort near Milford Haven called Prix Pill, the capture of which would open up the entire Haven to parliamentary shipping. After a siege lasting no more than two days in which three men only were killed, John Barlow, commander of the fort, surrendered. Proceeding in haste to Haverfordwest, Laugharne expected a bitter contest for the town and castle but was surprised to find that the garrison commander, Sir Henry Vaughan, together with his men had fled in panic to Carmarthen. Within days the small royalist garrison at Roch surrendered which left only Carew, Manorbier and Tenby to be taken. Manorbier was soon abandoned but Tenby and Carew proved more difficult nuts to crack; here the royalists decided to make a fight of it. According to an eyewitness account, that of Simon Thelwall of Ruthin, Tenby was besieged by land and sea, and in spite of stout resistance was taken within three days; Carew Castle fell soon after. In the opinion of another contemporary eyewitness, John Vaughan of Trawscoed, the fall of Tenby was significant because it was 'absolutely the strongest hold in South Wales, and of great consequence to the King'. He even ventured to suggest why the tables had been turned so completely in parliament's favour in that as far as the royalists were concerned 'all the mischances happened for want of a moving reserve of strength to relieve the garrisons that should happen to be distressed'.

In an effort to restore their fortunes in the county, and to forestall an expected invasion of Carmarthenshire, the king's nephew, Prince Rupert, dispatched a professional soldier, Sir Charles Gerard, to assume command of the demoralized royalist forces of west Wales. According to the pro-royalist news-sheet, the *Mercurius Aulicus* (20 July 1644), Gerard had been set a most difficult task since, in its opinion, Pembrokeshire was '[t]he most seditious county in all Wales, or rather England, for the inhabitants were like English Corporations unlike loyal Welshmen'. Reinforced by battle-hardened veterans, the royalist forces descended on Pembrokeshire attacking in two columns, one out of Cardigan and the other out of Carmarthen. Within a week of their advance Roch Castle had been taken (7 July 1644) and, two weeks later, Haverfordwest (22 July 1644). Laugharne, on the other hand, had lost the support of the fleet, which had returned to London, and the sailors who had proved so effective in siege warfare, leaving him with a sizeable force of local, but largely untested, levies. Fortunately for Gerard, as Laugharne prepared to assault both Tenby and Pembroke, he was recalled to England in order to restore matters after the disastrous defeat at Marston Moor earlier in the month (2 July 1644). Reinforced by sea and supported by a large detachment of sailors, Laugharne resumed the offensive and by December the whole of Pembrokeshire was once again in the hands of parliament. Laugharne's triumph was shortlived for in January 1645 Gerard, backed by an army of 2,500 men, resumed where he had left off in the summer. However, circumstances had changed for both of them; Gerard's army was intended to cover the whole of south and mid-Wales and not just Pembrokeshire so that he was often diverted away from the county, while Laugharne had been put in charge of all parliamentary forces in south Wales. For the next three months Pembrokeshire was relatively free from conflict but in April matters took a turn for the worse when, in the most savage encounter yet to take place, near the northern fringe of the county, Gerard inflicted a crushing defeat on Laugharne. All told, over 150 were killed and nearly 500 taken prisoner, twenty of them officers, so that Laugharne was forced to retreat, in some disorder, to Haverfordwest. Within weeks of the encounter, all but Tenby and Pembroke had fallen to Gerard whose operations in the county were accompanied by unaccustomed force and brutality. According to one report in a contemporary source, *The Kingdom's Weekly Intelligencer* (23 October 1644), we read:

> That the barbarous and cruel enemy drive away our cattle, rifle our houses to the bare walls, all provision of victuals where they come carried away or destroyed. The standing corn they burn and destroy, all sexes and degrees stripped naked by the enemy, aged and unarmed persons inhumanly murdered in cold blood, and others half-hanged and afterwards stigmatized and their flesh burnt off their bodies to the bare bones, and yet suffered in great torture to live.

Even allowing for some exaggeration, the tactics employed by Gerard were brutal and designed to effect a swift submission.

Once again, as Gerard prepared to complete the campaign, fate intervened, and the king's defeat at Naseby in June resulted in his recall to England. Laugharne again took advantage of Gerard's absence to resume the offensive and in a stunning victory at Colby Moor near Llawhaden (1 August 1645) completely routed the royalist forces in the county. Outnumbered, Laugharne managed to account for 150 dead and 750 taken prisoner while the remaining royalists, some 600, escaped to Haverfordwest. Appalled at the scale of the disaster, the royalist commanders abandoned Haverfordwest and made for Carmarthen. They left a garrison of 140 men to man the castle but after a twenty-four-hour siege they too surrendered. By the middle of September Pembrokeshire had been cleared of royalist troops and every stronghold taken. As far as Pembrokeshire was concerned the Civil War was over. Elsewhere the war continued for a few months more until the king himself was forced to submit in May 1646. Raglan and Harlech alone held out for a now-imprisoned king until they too were captured in August 1646 and March 1647 respectively, thus bringing to an end the First Civil War.

'After the end of the First Civil War the most important public issue in South Wales rapidly became neither the taking of the Covenant nor the abolition of the episcopacy, but the heavy incidence of taxation.' This, according to Roland Mathias (1993b), was the chief cause of the Second Civil War. Although there is considerable truth in this it does not admit entirely to the motives of those in Pembrokeshire who felt compelled to rise in rebellion against their former parliamentary comrades. Parliament was well aware that it urgently needed to reduce its costs so as to reduce the burden of taxation which, it was hoped, would pacify an increasingly dissatisfied and vocal population. Since the military accounted for a large proportion of government expenditure the cuts would have to be made here. Accordingly, in Pembrokeshire, it was proposed that Laugharne's command be drastically reduced by 90 per cent from 2,000 to 200 men and that English officers from the New Model Army be appointed governors of the garrisons of Pembroke and Tenby. Laugharne was probably expecting the first but not the second proposition which he took as a slight on his ability to command; worse still, parliament insisted on sending down a commissioner from London to oversee the disbanding. As governor of Pembroke, Poyer too was hardly supportive of parliament's propositions and he determined to resist them, especially as his reputation had suffered somewhat in the previous few months from the constant sniping of his enemies who sought to destroy him. Summoned to London in December 1646 to answer charges of oppression, extortion and fraud, he was released from house arrest in the early summer of 1647, pending a fuller investigation, so that he returned to Pembrokeshire under a cloud of suspicion. Laugharne too was to suffer a similar fate as rumours spread which sought to undermine parliament's confidence in him. He too was summoned to London in the summer of 1647 to answer charges of excessive exactions of money and in kind, and, more seriously, of conspiring with royalist agents. He was in London when Poyer took his stand against the parliamentary commissioner Colonel Fleming who, on arriving in the county in January 1648, demanded that Pembroke Castle be handed over to him so that he might begin to pay off and disband the troops. Poyer refused to do the one or to assist in the other so that the scene was set for conflict. As one contemporary ditty amusingly put it:

Hey diddle diddle, I heard a bird sing,
The Parliament soldiers are up for the King.

It was not simply on account of losing his command that impelled Poyer to became a turncoat but his very real fear for his safety from his enemies. The Lort brothers and John Elliot especially were keen to revenge themselves on him and in spite of their previous adherence to the royalist cause their accusations were given credence; a fact which must have hurt Poyer considerably given his unstinting service in the parliamentary cause. In the least malicious of the rumours spread by Elliot about Poyer it was said that he was 'seldom or ever sober but constantly drunk in the afternoon, and a great swearer and a stiff maintainer of the Book of Common Prayer'. Sampson Lort stirred up matters further in a letter to the House of Commons by declaring that 'a new war' was inevitable, 'if care be not taken to crush this cockatrice in the egg'. Reinforced by troops sent from Gloucester, Fleming prepared to besiege Pembroke but as he did so a sizeable force of Laugharne's command, refusing to disband, joined Poyer. As news of the rising spread, royalist agents made contact with Poyer and encouraged him in his resistance, while the garrison at Tenby, under the command of Rice Powell, joined with their comrades in Pembroke. Soon Poyer felt strong enough to sally forth from the safety of his castle and in a daring raid routed a troop of parliamentarians quartered at Pwllcrochan church. If the majority of the people were indifferent to the events going on about them sufficient numbers were on hand to assist Poyer, which was the cue for Fleming and his increasingly beleagured force to retire from the county. Encouraged by letters of support and commission from the exiled Prince Charles, Poyer and Powell declared for the king and began their march eastward out of the county into Carmarthenshire. Here they recruited more men to their cause, mainly ex-royalists, and as they continued on their way to the former royalist stronghold of Glamorgan they were joined by Laugharne who took command of what had grown to be an army. Largely composed of and led by Pembrokeshire men, the 8,000-strong rebel force met the parliamentarians, led by Colonel Horton, at St Fagan's on 8 May 1648. Although the rebels outnumbered the parliamentarians by two-to-one, the latter were victorious and what began as a retreat soon turned into a rout.

Having lost his brother Thomas, a wounded Laugharne, together with Poyer and Powell, escaped back to Pembrokeshire taking shelter first in Tenby and then in Pembroke Castle. Within three weeks Horton's force had been massively reinforced by Cromwell leading a contingent of his Ironsides so that the siege of Pembroke Castle now began in earnest. Aware of Pembroke's near impregnability, Cromwell determined on starving the rebels out but as the weeks went by he became increasingly frustrated. Five weeks into the siege an over-optimistic Cromwell wrote to parliament: 'Confident I am, we shall have [Pembroke] in fourteen days by starving.' In the event, it was the arrival of heavy artillery that saw an end to the siege since even Pembroke's walls could not withstand a battering from these guns and the besieged knew it. After the walls had been breached the besieged sought terms for their surrender and on 10 July 1648 the Second Civil War came to an end in Pembrokeshire. Poyer, Powell and Laugharne were tried and found guilty of treason and insurrection and condemned to death. After a review of their case it was decided that in view of their past good service – both Laugharne and Poyer were said to have spent upwards of £38,000 and £8,000 respectively of their own money in the parliamentary cause for which they had not been compensated (being another compelling reason for their rebellion) – only one would be executed. A child was used to draw the lots and Poyer's name came out on the paper marked death. In a petition pleading for his life, Poyer stated that he had been 'wrongly proclaimed Traitor' and that he had 'surrendered to Lieut. General Cromwell, upon articles of mercy, which could not be mercy in taking away his life'. However, as Edward Laws observed, 'it was felt that the public security demanded a victim' and so Poyer was executed by firing squad in Covent Garden in April 1649. Powell and Laugharne were eventually freed from arrest, pardoned and returned to Pembrokeshire to resume their lives.

Interregnum, Restoration and a 'Glorious' Revolution?

Pembrokeshire was no Puritan stronghold, suggesting that it might suffer more than most in the post-war and post-royalist world. The Republic of the Commonwealth was dominated by Puritan beliefs and ideals and it was upon the shoulders of its zealous representatives that local government during the Interregnum devolved. It was a period (1649–60), according to historian Geraint H. Jenkins (1978), that witnessed 'A Gideon's army of armed blacksmiths, millers and tailors [who] took over local administration, expelled the old liturgy, and established a joyless Puritan regime'. Thus a class of men were empowered in local government that previously had been denied participation. In Pembrokeshire men of middling status were appointed to govern the county by committee, being led in their endeavours by James Phillips of Cardigan and Thomas Wogan, the regicide and younger son of Sir John of Wiston. The Lorts too managed to inveigle their way into local affairs and between them, Sampson, Roger and John, held the shrievalty in 1650, 1652 and 1653. In fact, Sampson Lort was to gain further prominence in that his Puritanism earned him membership of the Propagation Commission set up after the Act of 1650 for 'the Better Propagation and Preaching of the Gospel in Wales'. In short, the people were to be taught the tenets of, and thereby converted to, the Puritan faith. Part of the commission's task was to root out clerics who did not share their missionary zeal and in all some 53 incumbents, out of 278 across Wales, were ejected from Pembrokeshire livings. Approvers were then appointed to advise the commission on who should be chosen to replace those ejected but the task proved difficult and in Pembrokeshire four clerics alone are recorded. If the recruitment of clerics was a problem it did not last long for, in common with the rest of Wales, Pembrokeshire was to experience the growth of sectarian communities which was to lead to the religious pluralism of the eighteenth century. Independents, Baptists and Quakers, together with the more extreme but short-lived sects like Fifth Monarchists and Ranters, peddled their religious wares in Pembrokeshire and in the process found some willing converts to their particular brand of Christianity. Perhaps among the most willing converts were the people of Haverfordwest and adjacent districts, who had suffered terribly during an outbreak of plague in 1651. Although not as severe as was once thought, the disease nevertheless accounted for the deaths of just over 200 of the 3,000 inhabitants of the town. Its coming was, nonetheless, a timely reminder of the frailty of life and the salvation that might be had in the service and devotion to God.

Politically, Pembrokeshire was generally compliant and neither Cromwell nor his senior lieutenants had occasion to visit the county. Although the work of the sequestrators was unpopular – they collected the fines imposed on those who had opposed parliament during the Civil Wars – the gentry were generally passive and acquiescent. In fact, during the infamous rule of the major-generals (1655–7) – a scheme whereby Cromwell, for better security, entrusted regional government into the hands of military men – the appointee for Wales, James Berry, was well disposed towards the Welsh whom he found 'many dear to God amongst them' though they 'be a poor people and have suffered much'. Although deeply resented by many of the county gentry, the natural rulers of society, who attacked men like Berry as being of low birth and unworthy to govern them, there was not a whisper of complaint. All this changed after the death of Oliver Cromwell and in the parliamentary elections of 1659 old rivalries, and old adversaries, surfaced once again. Rowland Laugharne emerged from his self-imposed exile within the county to take his place among the nominees for election but he was bitterly opposed by 'the fanatic party' led by the Lorts. In the event, the Restoration of Charles II in 1660, which Pembrokeshire greeted with enthusiasm, temporarily cast a shadow over the county's petty disputes and in the new parliament called for 1661 Rowland Laugharne was elected for Pembroke Boroughs, along with two lawyers, Arthur Owen for the county and Isaac Lloyd for Haverfordwest. In calling for peace, stability and reconciliation the new regime had miscalculated the depth of bitterness and recrimination that still prevailed in some areas. Certainly in Haverfordwest, between 1660 and 1681, the lingering animosities of the Civil War and Interregnum made for some hotly contested elections. Among the many resentments held by the citizens of the borough was the infiltration of outsiders into local affairs. In 1660 Sir Robert Needham, member of parliament for Pembrokeshire, was informed that 'nothing will satisfy them but the choosing of a native of the county to be their representative'. Yet, in general, the political scene soon calmed down and in the county especially a measure of consensus emerged whereby representation in parliament, very much until the end of the century, tended to be enjoyed by the members of two families, Owen of Orielton and Owen of New Moat. Only in the boroughs was there anything like a contest in the period before the so-called Glorious Revolution of 1688 so that the representation of Pembroke changed hands no less than eight times before the accession of William and Mary.

As far as Pembrokeshire was concerned the deposition in 1688 of James II and the accession of William III was not so much 'glorious' as indifferent. It mattered not a jot to the people of the county who ruled so long as they were not called to account either financially or militarily. The ruination suffered by some county families was still palpable even after twenty-five years and they were not prepared to risk their lives in combat. Consequently, the landing of William of Orange at Torbay in November 1688 passed off without much notice or incident in Pembrokeshire. Only one among the gentry, William Barlow of Slebech and member of parliament for the county, felt compelled to join his king in exile while another, Sir Hugh Owen of Orielton, was ordered to be watched by James II in the weeks before he left the kingdom so ingloriously. The most important concern for the people of Pembrokeshire was how the deposition of a Catholic monarch by a Protestant one might affect the Irish. Pembrokeshire had long lain in the shadow of Ireland which it neighboured across the Irish Sea and with whose merchants its people traded but distrusted. The county had been plagued by large numbers of Irish refugees before and it was feared that another conflict in Ireland, as had occurred during the early 1640s, could spell further trouble. Worse was the fear that hostilities in Ireland would spill over into Pembrokeshire; twice during the Civil War Pembrokeshire had been earmarked by the royalists as a suitable embarkation point for Irish soldiers recruited to the king's cause. In the event, it was north Wales that suffered an Irish 'invasion' but the fear of the Irish still persisted even as late as the 1690s, particularly as the standard of revolt had been raised in the island by the supporters of James II only to be cruelly crushed at the battle of the Boyne.

It is probably true to say that the devotion of the people of Pembrokeshire towards the British monarchy, a devotion born with Henry Tudor's accession to the throne, survived many rude shocks in the two centuries that followed. First came the shock of the Reformation, then the substitution of a Scottish Stuart for a Welsh Tudor dynasty, and lastly the destructive energy of a Civil War which resulted in a 'world turn'd upside down' with the death of King Charles I. Their loyalty even survived the shock of a royal scandal when one of their own, Lucy Walter (d.1658), sister of Richard Walter (d.1671) of Roch, the county sheriff in 1657, became the mistress of Charles II. Not only did she bear him a love-child, James, who was subsequently ennobled as the duke of Monmouth, but rumours that they had, in fact, married were flatly denied by a king notorious for his womanizing. On being apprehended in London during Cromwell's Protectorate she was imprisoned in the Tower at which point the pro-parliamentary news-sheet, the *Mercurius Politicus* (July 1656), seized the opportunity to embarrass the exiled king: 'She passes under the character of Charles Stuart's wife, or mistress, and hath a young son whom she openly declares to be his, and it is generally believed, the boy being very like him, and the mother and child provided by him.'

At least one Pembrokian, John Evans, a husbandman from Roch, thought ill of the king, wishing Charles II to the devil upon his Restoration. Scarred by the trauma of Civil War and military dictatorship under Cromwell, the wealthy, the influential and the politically conscious, generally, adopted a more circumspect attitude towards their royal masters, putting self-preservation before self-aggrandizement in the service of the Crown. That said, when Henry, first duke of Beaufort and Lord President of Wales and the Marches, visited the county in 1684, he was most impressed by the loyalty shown by the people to their monarch. He was greeted by fireworks, the pealing of church bells and cries of 'For God and the King'. Certainly, if the politically powerful were marked by a growing ambivalence to the demands of monarchial power, which for many had lost something of its mystique, the ordinary people still held the monarchy in respect and reverence. However, that the Monmouth Rebellion of 1685 and the so-called Glorious Revolution of 1688 hardly caused a ripple in the county suggests that by the end of the seventeenth century the Crown had lost some of its prestige and, arguably, after the passing of the Bill of Rights in 1689, some of its perceived authority. The demise of the Stuarts in 1714 was not greatly lamented and nor was the accession of the Hanoverians fervently greeted. Inertia and apathy characterized an inactive gentry; even those who harboured a lingering sense of loyalty to the Old Pretender, son of the deposed Stuart King James II, did no more than toast his health in Jacobite clubs like the Society of Sea Serjeants – an act, in the opinion of Roland Thorne, that 'ritualised and trivialised their political escapism'. When the Jacobites rose in rebellion in Scotland in 1715, their Welsh compatriots remained largely silent, and no more so than in Pembrokeshire where it was clear that what mattered to the gentry was their local hegemony. Pembrokeshire was never again to play such a central role in national politics as it had done during the Civil War and it might fairly be argued that from the eighteenth century, locality rather than nationality become the dominant theme in Pembrokeshire's political history.

VI

Modern Pembrokeshire: From an 'Age of Enlightenment' to an 'Age of Reform'

Introduction: Georgian and Victorian Pembrokeshire

> We are yet, in Pembrokeshire, as to its remote antiquities only
> on the threshold of discovery; but could we once, by the aid of
> the spade and pick axe, those unerring directories of truth . . . be
> admitted into the penetralia of such treasures, I am fully
> persuaded, from the glimpse I have already had of those recesses,
> that this county would be found to justify its pretensions to the
> title it had from the earliest ages obtained, of *Gwlad yr hud*, the
> Land of Enchantment and Mystery.

Thus did Richard Fenton (1747–1821), lawyer, poet and topographical
writer, sign off his most accomplished work, *An Historical Tour through
Pembrokeshire* published in 1811. Although he hailed from Rhosson
Uchaf near St David's Fenton was, arguably, not as 'native' as George
Owen but nor was he as colonially 'alien' as Gerald of Wales; rather he
embodies the diversity of Pembrokeshire society in a transitional phase
in its social and cultural history. His love for and interest in all things
Welsh and Pembrokeshire matched that of both Gerald and Owen, both
of whom he held in high regard, especially the latter whose *The Description
of Pembrokeshire* he edited and printed in the *Cambrian Register* in
1795–6. His desire to be 'a good Welshman', which Richard Morris (d.1779),
one of the famous Morris brothers of Anglesey, was 'endeavouring to
make him' being 'deficient that way, but comes on bravely', reveals a
man of more than simply patriotic pretension.

Fenton may have been a man of literary, historical and antiquarian
pursuits but he was also rooted in the reality of the society in which he
lived and on which he held opinions and passed comment. By virtue of
his wealth and social position Fenton was one of, what Edward Laws
(d.1913) calls in his *The History of Little England Beyond Wales* (1888),
'these Pembrokeshire squires of the Georgian era'. He was also a shipping
magnate and landowner who built an impressive mansion called Glyn-y-mêl

in Lower Fishguard, so that he represents the ruling class in the county. That said, he was not unsympathetic to the plight of the poor – in 1799 he shipped grain from abroad and sold it to local people at cost price so as to alleviate the worst effects of the failure of the fish harvest – and he was not uncritical of his own class or of the civil servants and law officers whom he came across in a career spanning more than twenty years before he retired to live the life of a country gentleman. Fenton lived at a time when the vast majority of Welsh people lived, worked and earned their living on the land. Their lives were dominated by the rhythms of the seasons, by the harvest, village life and rural custom. Wales had her towns but they were few and small in comparison with their counterparts in England and the majority of them, particularly Haverfordwest in Pembrokeshire, served as markets for the agricultural produce of their rural environment. He was aware of the benefits and the problems that resulted from the so-called industrial and agrarian revolutions, a process of change which gradually, over a century and a half, transformed Wales and Britain from an agricultural to an industrial nation, so that he might not have been unduly surprised by the Rebecca Riots. It is likely that, had he lived to see them, he would have understood their grievances, if not condoning their methods, for as his philanthropic approach to the distress and poverty caused by harvest failure during the 1790s shows, he was no supporter of repressive regimes. It is worth speculating that Fenton would, most probably, have been appalled by the Poor Law (1834), outraged by the Blue Books (1847) but fascinated by the railways. As a lawyer he would probably have been aware of the deficiencies of a legal system and the inequalities of a social system that impelled men and women to flirt with or live on the edge of crime. Fortunately, Fenton was succeeded by a group of talented historians – James Phillips (d.1907), Edward Laws (d.1913), Henry Owen (d.1919) and Francis Green (d.1942) and all Victorians by birth – who can fill in the gaps, and on whose works we rely to offer an insightful guide as to the changing nature of life in Victorian Pembrokeshire.

Agriculture, Trade and Industry: The Economic Scene

According to the antiquary George Owen the chief industry in Pembrokeshire at the beginning of the seventeenth century was agriculture. And so it remained until well into the twentieth century with farming accounting for a sizeable chunk of the county's workforce and income. Indeed, as late as the 1970s it could still be said with some conviction that 'a prosperous agriculture means a prosperous Pembrokeshire'. Pembrokeshire did not escape industrialization but, unlike in large parts of south- and north-east Wales, it did not replace agriculture but rather lived alongside it in a sometimes uneasy coexistence. Thus did coal, slate and shipping take their place alongside farming and fishing but though they prospered for a time they declined and disappeared almost as rapidly as they had risen. Today, agriculture alone maintains a tenuous grip on the county's economy.

In common with much of the rest of Wales, Pembrokeshire's agriculture was, and remained until a more progressive era set in from the 1850s, primitive. That its backwardness belonged more to the pattern of previous centuries can be seen in the fact that a great deal of what George Owen had to say of it in the last decade of the sixteenth century and early years of the seventeenth was still applicable to the middle of the nineteenth century. Perhaps the most discernible change had been in the farming landscape for while Owen would have been familiar with an agrarian pattern more akin to the medieval system of open fields, by the late eighteenth century these had been largely enclosed. The often painful process of enclosure was not unknown to Owen but its acceleration and spread belonged to a later age, a fact which prompted landowner John Lewis of Manorowen to write at the beginning of the eighteenth century that 'Pembrokeshire now, though there be too much champaign (open land), still is so much altered by inclosures, that it is not liable to the same censure as it might have merited in Queen Elizabeth's days'. If the objective of enclosures had been to improve cultivation, then they were largely successful, but as an exercise in public relations they were sometimes a disaster though, to be fair, the county's landowners were, by and large, sympathetic to the plight of the small farmers and labouring poor. The substantial landlord, John Campbell of Stackpole Court, stated in 1739 that he had no intention of enriching himself 'by oppression' of his tenants. For the most part the county's landowners were progressives who attempted to improve agricultural methods by experimentation such as in the introduction of new root crops such as turnips (first grown in the county in the 1750s) and in crop rotation, but also in animal husbandry with new breeding techniques and in the development of new technology such as the threshing machine (introduced to the county in the 1790s).

Change in the eighteenth century became a byword for progress and the nature and scale of that change in agricultural terms has often been described as revolutionary. Yet if England experienced something akin to an agrarian revolution in the eighteenth century, which saw far-reaching and rapid changes in agricultural ideas, techniques and technologies, Wales, generally, did not. Given the terrain, its remoteness, poverty and problems in transport and communications, Wales unsurprisingly lagged far behind a more dynamic and progressive England. Writing in the 1790s Charles Hassall (d.1814) of Eastwood, near Narberth, was wont to lament that '[t]he slow progress of agricultural improvements in this county makes some gentlemen despair of its being carried to any considerable length during the present age, and this despite the fact that from its many harbours it is evident, no part of the kingdom of equal extent is better circumstanced for exporting its products'. In spite of Hassall's rather gloomy view, Pembrokeshire was, in fact, exceptional in so far as its farmers were in the forefront of agricultural change in Wales. Gentlemen farmers with the capital and initiative to take risks did so, landowners like John Campbell (d.1825), first Earl Cawdor of Stackpole Court, Sir Richard Philipps (d.1823), first Baron Milford of Picton Castle, William Knox of Slebech, George Bowen of Llwyn-gwair, John Colby of Ffynone and even Charles Hassall himself were among the leading agricultural improvers in Pembrokeshire. Nevertheless, for the majority of the county's small tenant-farmers subsistence rather than improvement was very much the order of the day.

George Owen had no doubt as to the importance to Pembrokeshire of the agricultural industry and for him 'corn', by which we today take to mean barley, oats and wheat, was the key to the county's prosperity. His firm belief that the county was 'more apt for tilling than for breed' suggests that arable rather than pastoral farming predominated. On the other hand, in the opinion of Charles Hassall: 'It is an undeniable fact that this is not a corn county'. A noted agriculturalist who compiled a report in 1794 on Pembrokeshire for the Board of Agriculture, Hassall's opinion is clouded by the fact that he was very much a pastoralist. Therefore, the truth of the matter lies somewhere between the two and the pattern of farming was rather more mixed than either was wont to suggest. Consequently, although farming patterns varied across the county, from the pastorally dominated highland and scrubland of the north to the agriculturally richer arable belts in the south, pasture and tillage subsisted side by side. As late as 1887 a contemporary observer, W. Barrow-Wall, noted, 'Pembrokeshire farming is mixed in the fullest sense of the word, as dairying, corn-growing, rearing of young cattle, horses, pigs, sheep and all kinds of poultry find places on most farms'.

'Coal may be numbered as one of the chief commodities of this country and is so necessary as without it the country would be in great distress.' So said George Owen who valued coal because 'it is a ready fire and very good and sweet to roast and boil meat, and void of smoke where ill chimneys are, and does not require a man's labour to cleave wood and feed the fire continually'. Coal had been mined in Pembrokeshire since at least the late fifteenth century, if not before. The early entrepreneurs in the industry were the gentry who began by exploiting the reserves of coal found on their estates. Among the earliest landowning families to see the potential for profit were the Perrots of Haroldston. As early as the middle of the sixteenth century Sir John Perrot had begun mining coal at Freystrop but in common with his gentle compatriots elsewhere in the county his entrepreneurship never developed beyond a casual interest. Consequently, by the time of his death in 1592 the mines were said to be so decayed and neglected as to be virtually valueless.

As the demand for Pembrokeshire's anthracite coal increased so did mining activity. By the middle of the eighteenth century a number of collieries had either been redeveloped or begun anew by the likes of Philipps of Picton Castle, the Barlows of Lawrenny, the Wogans of Wiston and the Owens of Orielton. Properly developed coal mining could add considerably to a family's annual income, for example in 1787 Sir Hugh Owen (d.1809) of Orielton received a net profit from his mining interests of £1,544 while the rental income from his estates in Pembrokeshire, Carmarthenshire and north Wales amounted to a little over £7,552. Nor were the great landowners alone in exploiting the coal seams found on their estates; smaller landowners too became involved in the coal industry, often combining to form mining consortia to run their own collieries or by leasing the collieries of the gentleman landowners. In spite of the profits to be made the county's landowners were apparently reluctant to invest large sums in their mining operations which is why the Pembrokeshire coal industry remained small and prone to slump, especially when competing against the larger, more profitable operations further west in Carmarthenshire and Glamorgan. In one year alone, 1828, Pembrokeshire's coal exports amounted to a mere 18,354 tons while Llanelli and Swansea were able to ship 92,144 and 339,411 tons respectively.

One reason for the county's landowners' apparent reluctance to invest may have been due in part to the fact that they could not obtain the credit facilities needed to fund coal mining properly, an issue brought to a head by the banking crisis of 1826 in which it was reported by a contemporary that 'the stopping of two banks at Swansea, one at Carmarthen, and of almost every bank in Pembrokeshire has paralysed trade'. What eventually did for the mining industry in Pembrokeshire was increased competition from cheaper foreign coal and the high cost both of extracting coal in the county and of its transportation to market. The coal owners were simply not prepared to invest in new machinery and technology, a factor that may have contributed to but did not cause the Landshipping mining disaster of 1844 in which forty miners were drowned when the river Cleddau burst through the pit walls. Incompetence and mismanagement lay at the root of the disaster, the worst ever to befall the Pembrokeshire coal industry, management traits that were to come back to haunt the industry later when a ready nerve and steady hand were required to see it through the severe economic depression of the 1870s and 1880s.

Wage cuts, short-time working, lockouts and redundancies became the preferred methods of dealing with the economic depression hence the rise in tension leading to threats of workers' strikes. Indeed, the attitude of some employers towards their workers can be described as little short of contemptuous, so that the relationship between them must have been difficult and nowhere near healthy enough to heal rifts over pay and conditions. Nor were visitors to the county any less sympathetic towards the working classes. For example, of the colliers he met in Pembrokeshire in 1847, R. R. W. Lingen, a government commissioner, had this to say: 'The average of life is very short – not above 33 years, as appears from the [parish] register. This may be accounted for by the personal dirtiness of the miners, who never wash their bodies.' As far as Pembrokeshire's coal industry was concerned the writing was already on the wall when the new century dawned, for in less than half a century the number of pits in the county had been halved. Fewer shafts were sunk, investment declined and the skilled workforce on which the industry relied for success gradually drifted away to pits further east in the south Wales valleys. It was the twentieth century that was to witness the demise of not just the Pembrokeshire but of the Welsh coal industry.

Pembrokeshire slate had been quarried since at least the twelfth century, some claim as far back as the Roman period, but the industry had to wait until the second half of the nineteenth century before its true economic potential was realized. According to George Owen, slate quarried at Cilgerran and Maenclochog was 'sent by water to Harford [Haverfordwest], Pembroke and Tenby, and to divers partes of Ireland and sold by the thousand, sometimes dear and sometimes cheap, as the plenty and scarcity in those towns do require'. This suggests that the Tudor and Stuart slate industry was operated on a casual basis and that the county's output varied enormously, depending on demand. It is likely that those who quarried the slate did so as a sideline to their main work which was on the land. However, these farmers-cum-quarrymen could not cope with the demands made on the industry when large quantities of slate were required to roof the factories and workers' houses that were the results of the industrial and urban revolutions of the eighteenth and nineteenth centuries. Consequently, the scale of development of the industry in Pembrokeshire changed markedly between the 1730s and the 1880s.

It has been estimated that at its peak in the 1890s Pembrokeshire's slate industry employed between 400 and 500 men who were responsible for an annual production of 17,500 tons. Although nowhere near as large and as vital an industry as that found in north Wales where, in the same period, production peaked at 100,000 tons of slate annually, employing some 17,000 men, Pembrokeshire slate played a significant part in the economic life of many communities in the north of the county. The villages of Rosebush, Abereiddi, Porth-gain, Llangolman, Glog, Maenclochog and Cilgerran all owed a great deal to the slate industry. The port of

Porth-gain may not have been a Porthmadog but its contribution to the export of the county's slate was no less important. If there ever was a golden age of slate in Pembrokeshire, and in spite of the continued working of the Gilfach quarries in the 1930s and 1940s, it had passed by the beginning of the twentieth century when competition from abroad, mainly north America, increasing costs and industrial tension led to a severe decline in the industry's fortunes. Although Pembrokeshire's quarries saw little of the bitterness caused by the strikes and lockouts that afflicted north Wales, there were disputes, most notably in 1878–9 when quarrymen employed in the three quarries located in the parish of Llanrhian were left without wages or work for four months. Today the Pembrokeshire slate industry is all but dead, its communities and villages having been altered out of all recognition.

Pembrokeshire being bounded on three sides by the sea and possessed of the natural harbour of Milford Haven, shipping and its associated sea trade would almost inevitably be accounted a vital factor in its economic and industrial development. Ships of all sizes, some of which had been built locally, had long been a familiar sight in the creeks and havens of the shire and the relative proximity of the West Country, Ireland and Bristol, one of the largest and busiest ports in England, ensured a constant and largely healthy seaborne trade. Indeed, as agricultural and industrial activity increased so it gave rise to a flourishing maritime commerce which involved the shipping of such commodities as butter – over 1,000 casks (over 33 metric tonnes) were shipped yearly from Fishguard and Abercastle to Bristol and Liverpool during the 1790s – and corn together with malt and oatmeal, with an estimated 160,000 bushels (nearly 6 million litres) being exported annually from Milford Haven between 1748 and 1791. As the coal and slate industries developed so too did their export by sea with the result that the sea lanes around the county were becoming clogged with vessels all vying for a suitable landfall, berth or quay. Nor were these vessels concerned simply with trade and merchandise – the county has played host to countless numbers of warships. There has been a naval presence in the county as far back as the Roman period when imperial galleys traversed the waterways seeking to protect the furthest reaches of the empire.

As befitting a maritime county fishing was, and remained until comparatively recently, an important industry. In a letter written in 1595 extolling the virtues of the Haven the bishop of St David's, Anthony Rudd (d.1615), stated that 'the sea-coasts near about it yield plenty of fish'. George Owen too was fulsome in his praise of the county's abundance in fish, being 'enclosed with a hedge of herring' which he was wont to call 'the king of fish'. Owen had no doubt as to the importance of the fishing industry inasmuch as 'the country yielded plenty for the angle, net, weel [wicker trap used for catching eels], hook or otherwise, as well in the fresh rivers as the main seas'. Fishing was a way of life for those communities that hugged the coast and its exploitation during the medieval and early modern period was almost entirely devoid of profit, being an essential means of sustaining body and soul, particularly in times of harvest failures. This is not to suggest that fishing for sale did not occur but it was on a smaller, more local scale, servicing the local markets rather than for large-scale export. Tenby alone, with its indigenous fleet, was the only fishing port of any importance in south-west Wales, boasting nineteen vessels in 1891. Unsurprisingly, the largest fish market was to be found in Tenby, 'where is a daily market thereof', a fact which impelled Owen to explain the link between the town and the industry being 'in Welsh called Denbigh y Pysgod, that is "fish Tenby", for difference between it and Denbigh in North Wales' (1892–1936). One delicacy of which Owen was fond and for which the county was famous was oyster: 'I will give place to the oyster which Milford Haven yields most delicate, and of several sorts and in great abundance, and is a commodity much uttered in many shires.' Yet for all its fame and export to various parts of the country the oyster, in common with the county's fishing industry as a whole in the period between the early seventeenth and late nineteenth centuries, remained casual and undeveloped. As late as 1817 the *Cambrian Register* expressed its opinion that 'The oyster fishery within Milford Haven would be valuable, were it properly attended to'.

Fishing on an industrial scale did not really begin until the late nineteenth century, at least not until the building of Milford Docks in 1888. Besides its safe anchorage and proximity to good fishing grounds, the existence of a rail link for the rapid transportation of fresh fish to markets as far afield as Billingsgate in London recommended Milford as a suitable place to locate an industrially proficient fishing fleet. Within two decades of its opening Milford had become one of the largest bases for trawler owners, fish buyers and proprietors of marine services in Wales. For example, in 1890 the port was used by just twelve trawlers but by 1908 this had grown to 323, consequent to which the tonnage of fish landed rose from 9,500 to nearly 44,500. By 1908 the number of fish buyers in the town had risen from one in 1889 to thirty-eight by 1908. The town's population rose also, from less than 4,000 in 1891 to nearly 6,500 in 1911, the greater part of which was due not so much to a rise in the local birth rate but to the immigration of fisher folk from elsewhere in the United Kingdom. Unfortunately for the county's fishing industry its history in the twentieth century was one of inexorable decline.

Anglicanism and Nonconformism: The Religious Scene

The Census of Religious Worship of 1851 was a truly remarkable exercise and was the first of its kind to be undertaken. Among the more significant of its findings with respect to Wales was that only 9 per cent of people who attended a place of worship went to Anglican churches while 87 per cent went to Nonconformist chapels. In addition, the census revealed that while the Church could provide 1,180 places of worship they came nowhere near rivalling the Nonconformists' 2,769. Although historians now argue over its usefulness and sometimes dispute the reliability of its statistics (it was as controversial then as now) it contains such a wealth of detail that it cannot be ignored. At the very least it serves as a convenient starting point for historians wishing to survey and study the form, nature and 'popularity' of religion in Pembrokeshire.

However, what was true of Wales as a whole was not necessarily true of Pembrokeshire since the census makes clear that here at least the Anglicans were the strongest denomination. For example, 30 per cent of worshippers were listed as Anglican followed by the Independents at 16.9 per cent, the Baptists at 15.5 per cent and the Methodists (both Wesleyan and Calvinist) at just under 15 per cent. Although not unique – the counties of Flint, Montgomery and Radnor also registered more Anglicans than any other denomination – it is the nature of the division between religious conformism and nonconformism that sets Pembrokeshire apart, in that it largely mirrored the county's ancient racial and linguistic separation. Two-thirds of the county's population lived in the English-speaking south, a region that was most strongly Anglican, while nonconformism dominated the sparsely populated Welsh-speaking north. Nor is this surprising given that Nonconformity was, in the opinion of some contemporaries, becoming more closely identified with 'Welshness' while the Church of England was seen increasingly as alien and untypically Welsh. Added to this were the divisive issues of class and linguistic distinction since Nonconformity tended to champion the Welsh-speaking lower or labouring masses while the Anglican Church was perceived as the representative of the English-speaking middle and upper classes. Of course, matters are never quite as straightforward in real life as they might appear in the pages of a book, particularly in reference to a county where English speakers were, numerically, more likely to hail from the lower than the middle or upper classes.

Although the Anglican Church took some comfort from the fact that in at least four of the thirteen Welsh counties it was the stronger denomination, it was well aware that it had serious problems, many of which long pre-dated the nineteenth century. Neglect, abuse, absenteeism, not a little corruption, class distinction and bias all combined at various times to denigrate the Church in the eyes of the faithful. There were exceptions – reforming Anglicans like Thomas Burgess and Connop Thirlwall, Bishops of St David's from 1803 to 1825 and 1840 to 1874 respectively, did much to improve matters in the diocese by encouraging their clergy to be hard-working and well-versed in the Scriptures. Sensitive to the needs of native-speaking Pembrokians, they even attempted, with some success, to supply Welsh-speaking congregations with Welsh-speaking clergy. However, through no fault of their own, the quality of religious worship was simply not good enough to meet the needs of the faithful. Both had inherited a Church that had been denied good leadership, denuded of adequate funding and in which successive bishops found themselves at the mercy of numerous private and institutional patrons, mainly local landowners, who controlled the majority of livings in the county. Private patrons tended to take advantage of their position by providing inadequate stipends so that poverty among the clergy inevitably led to the potential abuse of pluralism. For example, the impropriator of wealthy Wiston obtained an annual sum of near £275 from commuted tithes, while his hapless patronee received no more than £85.

Disillusioned and despondent clerics had also to contend with dilapidation: run-down parsonages sited alongside churches in need of repair did little to inspire the parishoners with confidence. Even bishops had to suffer the indignity of inheriting a cathedral with leaking roofs and crumbling arches; the ruined eastern portion of the cathedral was particularly dangerous, an intolerable situation which prompted Bishop Thirlwall to raise sufficient sums to initiate a rebuilding programme (1862–73) and engage the services of the renowned architect Sir George Gilbert Scott. Slowly but surely the Church responded to the challenge of righting itself while combatting the competition offered by Nonconformism. Church reform was accompanied by the recruitment of university-educated and better renumerated clergymen who were as committed to their calling as had been the dissenters of old. Nevertheless, although it might be argued that Anglicanism experienced something of a renaissance in the latter decades of the nineteenth century it took until 1919–20 and disestablishment before the ills of the Church could begin to be cured.

The extent to which Nonconformity had apparently seized the hearts and minds of the Welsh, or at least gave that impression, is illustrated by the unselfconscious way in which contemporaries like Henry Richard tended to equate the Welsh public with the Nonconformists. Even in the so-called Anglican stronghold of Pembrokeshire Nonconformity was numerically stronger than its establishment rival. According to the census of 1851 Pembrokeshire boasted a population of 84,472 souls of whom only 25,367 were registered Anglicans while the combined totals of the Nonconformist denominations could muster 40,058. Indeed, as late as

1903 one commentator, A. G. Bradley, was able to write that '[f]or South Pembrokeshire, though stronger than most Welsh regions in churchmen, is still greatly given to Nonconformity' (1984). Unencumbered by such restrictions as parish boundaries and central control the essentially decentralized Nonconformists could erect a chapel wherever the demand was greatest. The building itself did not matter, initially it might be a barn, a cottage, a farmhouse, even an inn! This flexibility, the evangelical nature of their faith, the touring preachers, meant that they were able to take religion to the people rather than, as in the case of the Anglican Church, the people coming to them. Wales had a long, and strong, tradition of dissent in matters of religious doctrine and worship dating back to at least the latter half of the seventeenth century. Although originally an imported creed from across the border the dissenters quickly established themselves in Wales; the Methodists especially found many converts among Welsh-speaking communities because they purposely associated and consciously identified themselves with things Welsh. Native culture, language and sense of 'patriotism' were taken on board and never ignored but shaped and fashioned to meet the needs of Nonconformist congregations. This they did successfully in northern Pembrokeshire whose remote rural communities willingly embraced the communality and evangelicalism of dissent.

To judge from the comments of contemporaries, the power and influence of a truly religious revival was simply breathtaking. It was an awe-inspiring experience, divinely inspired, miraculous even, which could, and frequently did, change lives. In the short term, revivalism was an almost irresistible force which tended to sweep all before it, but in the long term its effects, and the religious devotion it engendered, might wane with the passage of time. They might be local affairs or more widespread and influential like the Great Revival of 1904–5. Of course, religious revivals were nothing new, they had a history which stretched back to the medieval period and beyond, but it was the mass appeal and longevity of the 'modern', post-seventeenth-century revivals which set them apart. The Great Revival of the eighteenth century which witnessed the foundation of Methodism in England (Wesleyan Methodism, 1784) and Wales (Calvinistic and Wesleyan Methodism, 1811) had a profound effect on the people which left a lasting impression on both converted and critic.

Nor was Pembrokeshire immune from the effects of religious revivalism, being visited in the eighteenth century by the leaders of both English and Welsh Methodism, namely, John Wesley, John Whitfield and Howell Harris. Visiting Haverfordwest in August 1763, Wesley wrote in his journal: 'I have not seen so numerous a congregation since I set out from London. They are deeply attentive, surely some will bring forth fruit.' Returning the following July he wrote: 'I walked up towards the Castle and began singing a hymn. The people came together from all quarters. They have a curiosity, at least, and some I cannot doubt were moved by a nobler principle. What a harvest there might be.' The effect that Harris's preaching had on the people was reported by the Glasgow *Weekly History* (October 1742):

> Pembrokeshire hath been lately converted by means of the exhortations of Mr. Howell Harris and other Methodist exhorters . . . It is the upper part of Pembrokeshire that has been roused, and that almost universally, to a concern about religion . . . Among the clergy Mr. David Jones and Mr. Howell Davies are very eminent, especially the latter who is . . . very desirous in preaching both in churches, houses and fields.

Originally from Breconshire, Howel Davies (d.1770) had taken to wife a Pembrokian and had made Pembrokeshire his home, so that in time he became the leading Methodist in the county. Although both he and Harris were generally well received in the English-speaking south their greatest impact lay in the native-speaking north. Unsurprisingly perhaps, the folk of southern Pembrokeshire more readily embraced Wesleyan Methodism which, according to the 1851 census, was, numerically, the stronger of the two Methodist sects.

There were six more major revivals, that is, affecting more than one county or region of Wales, during the nineteenth and early part of the twentieth century – 1828–9, 1831–2, 1837–42, 1849, 1859 and 1904–5 – each of which was inspired by particular themes or problems in society such as temperance, health or poverty. The *gwerin* wanted to be comforted, they begged for answers, they wished for guidance but, above all, they hoped for security in this life and salvation in the next.

Religion acted as a focal point of social conscience where people could express their concerns, worries and fears. It might also act as a catalyst for change with religious leaders bringing pressure to bear on local and national authorities to act in the interests of the people. There was a close relationship between religion and radicalism, where the politics of dissent was making its mark in parliament. In the cultural, educational and recreational fields too religion played a more crucial part. Nevertheless, one feature of the 1851 Religious Census which should have been of great concern to both Anglican and Nonconformist was the relatively large number of people who were unaffiliated to any religious denomination and who attended no place of worship. In Pembrokeshire this amounted to a staggering 17,000 people, but such was the sectarian bickering between church and chapel, even between Nonconformist sects themselves, that this sometimes escaped their notice or did not receive the attention it deserved. On the other hand, it was not as yet an obvious or widespread problem – the number of chapels and chapel-goers in north Pembrokeshire did not reach their peak until after 1918 – but the potential remained for growth in terms either of religious apathy or atheism. Certainly by the end of the Great War the world had changed and to many people the chapels and churches seemed slow or incapable of adapting to this brave new world. The more practical issues of politics, work, wages and trade unions became far more important in daily life. As the working classes became better educated they began to question their religion and even criticize some religious ideas and teaching.

The Treason of the Blue Books

There had long existed fee-paying grammar schools in the principality, many dating back to the Elizabethan period, but they, and their rigid, classically based syllabuses, were for the wealthy and socially well-connected elite. Those with academic talent but little else had to rely on the influence and pecuniary support of patrons if they wished to enter these havens of learning. Few managed to realize their scholastic ambitions in these 'secondary' schools, settling instead for instruction in the 'elementary' sector. Indeed, elementary education was equated with mass education or, to put it another way, it was thought suitable for the education of the masses – learning by rote and subject to mechanical obedience added up to fine factory fodder. Industrialists viewed as suspicious proposals to educate the masses, believing an educated workforce was more likely to stir up trouble – they might form trade unions and challenge the power of the employer! On the other hand, they could see the value of a basic workers' education so long as it was cheap. Country landowners were more charitable than their industrial colleagues, being more readily prepared to support educational ventures without ulterior motives. Two of the more enlightened in Pembrokeshire were Sir John Philipps (d.1737) of Picton Castle who supported generously both the educational enterprise of the Society for Promoting Christian Knowledge and Griffith Jones's Circulating Schools and George Bowen (d.1810) of Llwyn-gwair.

The *Report of the Commissioners of Inquiry into the State of Education in Wales* was intended to be, and was largely completed as, an investigation into the provision (or lack of it) of educational facilities in the principality, to judge the quality of that provision and to make recommendations for its improvement. In order to assist the research and data collection process Wales was divided up between the commissioners, each of whom had the help of assistants, ten in all – Carmarthenshire, Glamorgan and Pembrokeshire was assigned to Ralph Robert Wheeler Lingen. That they may have exceeded their brief, no doubt with the best of intentions, to comment on other related social issues, which the commissioners would have defended as just and relevant, has attracted more attention and criticism than their pronouncements on education. Their findings generated debate, causing some even to hate the commissioners involved and was taken up as a cause by Welsh political and religious groups who saw within its pages an attack on the Welsh way of life. Unfortunately, all this bitterness tended to muddy the educational waters in which domain the report makes some sober judgements, making for uncomfortable reading at times, but only rarely can we impune the accuracy or integrity, if not the authority, of its findings. What the compilers lacked in sensitivity they largely made up for in objectivity which makes for an important document within which the data compiled is meat for the historian's table.

The commissioners were instructed to conduct their inquiry with reference to the social condition of the areas they investigated – 'In reporting on the number and description of schools in any district, you will not fail to keep in mind the amount, character, and condition of the population.' This they did. In fact, the commissioners took their roles very seriously, for as Symons commented: 'I conceive my province to be less that of an inspector of schools than an inquirer into education. I have deemed the mental condition of the children the primary object of my attention.' Lingen, probably the least sympathetic of the three, believed it was his mission to dig a little deeper. In Pembrokeshire, for example, he reported on Landshipping Day School (Pembrokeshire): 'On 8th January I visited the above school. It was held in a small and wretched room . . . and was kept by a person who had formerly been a shop-keeper, but had failed in business and therefore taken to school-keeping . . . The master was an old man and apparently very ignorant.' Nor was the situation any better elsewhere in the county. This was typical of what the commissioners found across Wales, badly maintained or inappropriate school rooms, poor quality teachers and teaching and an inadequate syllabus. The poverty and general social deprivation of the children, their parents and the communities at large were factors the commissioners could hardly ignore. Of course, it was not all doom and gloom, many schools, teachers and pupils were justly praised. They paid particular tribute to the work of the Sunday schools, Lingen stating that '[t]hese schools have been almost the sole, they are still the main and most congenial, centres of education'. Johnson too was impressed:

> However imperfect the results, it is impossible not to admire the
> vast number of schools which they [Dissenters] have established,
> the frequency of the attendance, the number, energy and
> devotion of the teachers, the regularity and decorum of the

proceedings, and the permanent and striking effect which they
have produced upon society. (G. T. Roberts, 1998)

They were guarded in their assessment of the educational merits of these
schools since they found that many pupils were taught to repeat by rote
verses from the Bible. That said, Johnson was sure that matters might
have been much worse if there had been no Sunday schools: 'As the influence
of the Welsh Sunday-Schools decreases the moral degradation of the
inhabitants is more apparent. This is observable on approaching the English
border.' Yet, for all their praise, the underlying bias – other historians prefer
the more emotive word prejudice – of the commissioners was always with
England and things English. Consequently, Wales and the Welsh tended
to suffer in comparison and an example may be instanced by Lingen's
comments on the system of education he found in south-west Wales:

I have no hesitation in saying that a child might pass through
the generality of these schools without learning either the limits,
capabilities, general history, or language of the empire of which
he is born a citizen, and this is the kind of knowledge which I
consider to be the province of Geography, English History, English
Grammar and English Etymology in elementary schools. (G. T.
Roberts, 1998)

This is not to suggest that schools, teachers and syllabuses were better
in comparable districts in England, they were not. In Manchester, for
instance, a government report commented on the general ignorance found
when questioning pupils on subjects taught on the curriculum, which
was put down to poor-quality teaching and the often indifferent attitudes
of parents and pupils to learning.

What is perhaps surprising is the number of schools found to be
operating in Wales, for besides the day schools founded by the National
and British Societies, there were many small, privately run institutions. In
Pembrokeshire, for example, Lingen reported on the existence of some
211 'institutions of learning' of which nearly 100 were deemed to be unfit
or unsuitable. In Symons' view the Welsh attended school because they
were eager to learn since 'they desire it to the full extent of their power to
appreciate it'. Indeed, in his view '[t]hey learn what they are even badly
taught with surprising facility' and, given the right instruction, he believed
they were capable of high achievement. His praise for the Welsh
sometimes overflowed but he was clearly impressed by what he witnessed:
'I can speak in very strong terms of the natural ability and capacity for
instruction of the Welsh people. Though they are ignorant, no people
more richly deserve to be educated.'

Fishguard and the French

The Fishguard landing of 1797 has been described, variously, as 'farcical', 'frivolous', a 'fiasco', even 'bizarre', but that it was 'a hopeless enterprise' seems certain given the outcome. In short, it was anything but a glorious episode in the military history of the county. Such pronouncements, of course, can only be made with the benefit of hind-sight and while we today have no real cause to disagree with the perceived failure of the Fishguard 'invasion', to contemporaries it was anything but 'frivolous' or 'farcical'. To the people in the front line the French landing was taken seriously and they reacted accordingly making preparations, amid panic and not a little chaos, to confront the enemy. That the invaders surrendered almost without a murmur need not detract from the courage and resourcefulness shown at the time by the local people, some of whom derived a degree of fame (Jemima Nicholas for her courage in capturing a dozen French soldiers) and notoriety (Thomas Knox who was afterwards, unfairly, accused of cowardice) in consequence of the events that transpired in the days between the landing, on 22 February, and the surrender, on 24 February. What had prompted the French government to send 1,400 troops – recruited mainly from gaols, two frigates, a corvette and lugger under the command of Colonel William Tate and Commodore Jean Castagnier respectively, to Pembrokeshire? What did they hope to accomplish and why, having landed and outnumbering the local militia, did they so soon surrender? These and other questions have been asked by historians and the answers, while generally known, do not fully resolve the circumstances surrounding an event that well merits the prefix 'bizarre'.

In truth, the Fishguard landing should never have taken place. Tate and Castagnier were meant to play a very small part of a plan which aimed at a military invasion of Ireland. While 15,000 French troops under General Hoche were to be landed in southern Ireland, and thereby hoping to rouse the rebellious Irish, two diversionary attacks would be mounted to distract the English; one led by Tate and Castagnier against Bristol and the other by General Quentin and 5,000 troops against Newcastle. The plan was a disaster; besides the foul weather, the French forces lacked coordination and discipline. Quentin, whose troops mutinied due to the rough seas, got nowhere near Newcastle while Hoche failed to land his men in a stormy Bantry Bay, and even had he done so it is doubtful the Irish would have risen in support. Tate and Castagnier too failed in their primary mission, for having been prevented by a strong offshore wind from making progress up the Bristol Channel they reverted to their alternative plan of landing somewhere in Wales, in fact, anywhere within the rim of Cardigan Bay. That Fishguard was chosen was purely by chance and the decision to land the troops was due as much to Castagnier's desire to head for home as Tate's wish to get his men on anything resembling dry land. Unfortunately for Tate, French intelligence had badly erred in believing that the Welsh were ripe for revolution and while he proceeded cautiously he nonetheless expected to be given a warm welcome. In the event, the landing proceeded almost without incident, a number of Frenchmen drowned when their boat capsized, while the native Welsh were nowhere to be seen. Having set up his headquarters in Trehowel farmhouse, Tate soon found himself in considerable difficulty. The troops fortified by liquor began to roam free and refuse orders while the disposition of the enemy was unknown; worse, Castagnier upped anchor leaving the expeditionary force to its fate. Castagnier may well have been following a prearranged plan to harrass enemy shipping in British waters before heading home, but the sense of isolation must still have been quite a profound shock to Tate and his ever-dwindling band of fighting men.

Unbeknown to Tate, the enemy were in no fitter state to contest the issue should conflict happen. Having gathered no more than 700 local militia men around him, John Campbell, Lord Cawdor with the able support of Colonels Thomas Knox of Slebech and John Colby of Ffynone, prepared to do battle. In the event, there was no battle – whatever resolve Tate had landed with he soon lost it and it was not long ere a sight presented itself that convinced the Irish-American commander to consider surrender as a serious option. Although no more than a local legend, and a colourful one at that, it is said that the French surrendered after being confronted by several hundred women wearing red cloaks which the enemy took, in the gathering gloom, to be the red tunics of regular troops. Truth or myth, it is interesting to note what Benjamin Heath Malkin had to say when he visited the county less than five years later in 1803:

> . . . it is probable that the enemy would have given some trouble to the country, had it not been for a collection of women on a distant hill, clad in red mantles peculiar to these parts, who were taken for a large reinforcement coming on to the attack. (B. H. Malkin, 1804)

Whatever the truth of the matter, Tate surrendered, explaining that he thought it 'unnecessary to attempt any military operations as they would tend only to bloodshed'. Doubtless, a relieved Cawdor took the surrender willingly and the French troops formed up on Goodwick sands to effect the handover of weapons after which they were marched to gaol in Haverfordwest. With the cessation of hostilities in 1801 the French troops were repatriated to their homeland. Although the military threat was negligible, the panic in London was enough to cause a run on the bank and to drive Britain off the gold standard. For the people of Pembrokeshire the Fishguard landing became a proud episode in their history and is unique in that the Castlemartin Yeomanry were awarded the battle honour 'Fishguard'.

The Rebecca Riots

The story of Pembrokeshire during the eighteenth and nineteenth centuries is one of transition and change. As industry rose in importance agriculture declined, populations moved and villages became towns. Beyond its borders foreigners tended to overlook Pembrokeshire believing it to be so remote, and probably backward, as hardly deserving of mention. Consequently, the problems of rural Pembrokeshire – low wages, poverty, unemployment, the general lack of opportunities and the insensitivity of some landowners – were hidden from view and sometimes too easily forgotten. However, the Rebecca Rioters and tithe agitators, sought to make known to the local authorities and national government their deep-seated discontent by refusing payments of tolls and tithes, destroying toll gates and workhouses and generally causing mayhem until their grievances were dealt with. As recent studies have shown, the Rebecca Riots were more widespread and serious than was once thought and Queen Victoria herself felt compelled to demand urgent action against them! Even the extensive and sustained presence of soldiers and professional policemen could not completely eradicate either Rebeccaism or tithe agitation. The people, it seems, were determined to be seen and to be heard.

The Rebecca Riots did not occur spontaneously but were the culmination of years of dissatisfaction and deep-seated resentment. There had been riots before Rebecca, such as at Fishguard in 1827, but their incidence had been sporadic, isolated and generally small-scale. Food, or rather the price of it, was usually the most immediate cause of protest since the hungry are understandably prone to be angry. In truth, to the outsider, the visitor, the settler and the merely curious often viewing at a distance, the Welsh were regarded as a sober, temperate folk of rustic charm and simplicity not given to tumult unless provoked or encouraged by agitators. It was this almost wholly false or patronizing impression of the Welsh that contributed to the shock at having to witness the Rebecca Riots. Indeed, if Chartism was the protest movement of industrial Wales, where a more politically conscious working population was demanding reform of the British political system, Rebecca was its rural equivalent. Landowning freeholders and land-renting leaseholders found themselves acting in concert with landless labourers, a class so near the bottom of the economic pyramid that a simple drought or wet summer could so easily tip them into the abyss of workhouse pauperism. Rebeccaism was, in large part, their answer to absentee landlords, insensitive toll-road owners and corrupt workhouse trustees.

> And they blessed Rebekah, and said unto her, Thou art our sister, be thou the mother of thousands of millions, and let thy seed possess the gates of those which hate them. (Genesis 34:60)

Rebecca was a secret movement which took the form of a sporadic guerrilla war directed mainly against toll gates but also workhouses and the properties of unpopular tithe owners. The movement originated and the first protests occurred in May 1839 on the Carmarthenshire–Pembrokeshire border. A group of some 400 men with blackened faces, dressed in women's clothes, armed with axes and sticks, and going under the name of 'Rebecca' and her 'daughters', gathered at Efail-wen where they pulled down and destroyed the toll gate. Attempts by the Whitland Turnpike Trust, which owned the gate and toll house, to replace the toll gate were met with similar destruction. When the Turnpike Trust decided to abandon the toll gate at Efail-wen the Rebecca movement too disappeared (but not before it had destroyed a further two toll gates west of Carmarthen and possibly burning the half-built Narberth workhouse). Nothing more was heard of Rebecca until mid-November 1842 when newly erected toll gates at Pwll-trap and at the Mermaid Tavern, located on either side of the village of St Clear's, were stormed and destroyed. By the beginning of January 1843 Rebecca rioters had carried out no less than six separate attacks, destroying toll gates within a fifteen-mile radius of St Clear's. By the beginning of February Rebecca had struck further west into Pembrokeshire during which campaign of sustained county-wide attacks no less than eight toll gates had been destroyed at Burton, Canaston Bridge, Fishguard, Haroldston, Narberth, Prendergast, Robeston Wathen and 'Scleddy'. Troops were rushed to the county and scattered into hastily assembled garrisons. For example, seven officers and 150 marines were sent to reinforce the naval garrison at Pembroke Dock while fifty troopers and two officers were dispatched to Haverfordwest. Narberth, Fishguard and Robeston Wathen too acquired small garrisons, no more than a platoon in strength in each, in the hope of deterring the rioters.

Turnpiking provided a focus for discontent because they were visible and tangible symbols of oppression. The toll gates and the tolls charged by the various turnpike trusts were becoming a burden to hard-pressed farmers many of whom were already suffering from severe economic pressures, partly brought on by the disastrous seasons of 1839 to 1841. The insensitivity of toll-road owners contributed to the growing discontent and one name in particular stands out, that of Thomas Bullin. His business methods were rigorous and efficient which, unsurprisingly, turned his farming 'customers' against him. Welsh farmers were particularly vulnerable to the exactions of tolls because they had no choice but to carry lime (to fertilize the soil) by cart to their farms and transport their produce to market. To make matters worse, some farmers had to pass through the toll gates of several trust companies, each of whom demanded payments in full for the service. Had the roads been of good quality and worth the expense of their upkeep then the farmers' anger might not have been as great as it was. Unfortunately, some of the trusts were in financial difficulties and their solution to the crisis was either to erect more gates and/or increase tolls. As if to add insult to injury some trusts tried to force their 'customers' to repair certain roads by cynically using an Act of 1555 which required parishoners to maintain roads in their locality! However, as a government-led commission was later to discover, this was not the only cause of the riots.

Having swept all before them without so much as a rebuff by the authorities, who, in spite of deploying special constables to protect the toll gates, seemed powerless to stop them, Rebecca and her daughters turned their attention to other perceived injustices such as tithes and the new poor law. Besides corrupt and insensitive workhouse trustees and employees, the farming communities of west Wales were particularly incensed by the so-called 'bastardy clause' of the Poor Law Amendment Act of 1834 which removed maintenance for unmarried mothers thus forcing them to starve or go into the workhouse. In February 1843 the master of the Narberth workhouse was sent three threatening letters warning him about the quality of the food given to the inmates. In June 1843 Rebecca sent a threatening letter to the master of the Haverfordwest workhouse and in one incident some 600 of Rebecca's daughters stormed the Narberth workhouse only to be thwarted in their attempt to burn down the building by a detachment of troops of the Castlemartin Yeomanry. Rebecca's Pembrokeshire 'daughters' were particularly active in adding high rents and enclosures to her list of grievances. In August 1843 a large crowd destroyed the pound of the manor of Slebech and released the animals contained therein because they had been seized by Baron de Rutzen from one of his tenants for non-payment of rent.

The plight of Welsh farmers was highlighted by Thomas Campbell Foster, correspondent for *The Times*, who came to south Wales to investigate the issue. Following exhaustive inquiries and having won the trust of the farmers, Foster sent a series of reports back to his newspaper on the unfolding events in west Wales. His reports are invaluable because they provide direct evidence of the views of Rebecca's supporters. Foster was on hand in July 1843 to witness the disastrous attack on a Pontarddulais toll gate by over a hundred Rebecca rioters which resulted in the arrest of a number of the movement's most prominent leaders. He subsequently reported (*The Times*, 20 September 1843) on the reaction of both Rebecca and the authorities to the trial in Cardiff and harsh sentences meeted out to the movement's leaders who were transported to Australia to serve terms of between seven and twenty years.

> It was fondly hoped and indeed confidently predicted by both the magistrates and the police that it would put an end to Rebeccaism and that such would be the terror felt throughout the country that the Lady Rebecca would be so struck with the terror that the outrages would at once be put to an end. The effect has, however, been precisely the reverse. The Welsh are a peculiar people and they have become completely exasperated in consequence of their countrymen having been shot, as they say, by a villainous body of police.

Rebecca, however, continued. Sporadic rioting, some serious, was reported as late as the autumn of 1844 after which the movement gradually faded away.

We shall probably never know the truth of why the movement came to acquire the name Rebecca. In the opinion of some historians the Bible may have provided the inspiration for naming the movement, but it is as likely to have been as much accident as design since the trappings of disguise, secrecy, rhyming, threats, mock trial and the pantomiming that accompanied Rebecca sprang directly from the folk traditions of rural Wales. Stemming from earlier rural protests, the *ceffyl pren* was one such custom or tradition on which wooden cock-horse the effigies of the offenders against the community were mounted and paraded to the tune of some 'rough music'. Between the violence and destruction, the disturbances were also accompanied by much mirth-making, song-singing and ballad-writing. The riots spawned a number of ballads and balladeers such as Levi Gibbon, who suggested that the founder of the movement was a Pembrokeshire farmer, Thomas Rees of Carnabwth, Mynachlog-ddu, and David Davies, alias Dai'r Cantwr. Their ballads were intended to be more than for mere entertainment for though they added to the sense of occasion they were a means of highlighting, mirroring or expressing the views of the community. Nor was this peculiar to south-west Wales since other disturbances, riots and tumults throughout Wales had their ballads and balladeers. One might even argue that these working-class balladeers were the modern successors of the bards of old. Below is an extract (in translation) of a ballad by Levi Gibbon:

> Rebecca, like myself, was born in Wales
> In the parish of Mynachlog-Ddu – a bonny child.
> She grew up to be quite tall
> And she took complete possession of the gate at Efailwen.
> Constables and policemen came there
> To try and prevent Beca stealing the old gate
> And soldiers were in power for a month
> So that every gateman could keep his livelihood.

The Rebecca Riots were, in the opinion of David Jones, 'larger than we thought and less respectable, and for a time rivalled Irish affairs as the chief topic of debate in Westminster and the country'. The prime minister at the time, Sir Robert Peel, had great difficulty in coming to terms with the fact that the riots were being carried out, to his way of thinking, by a simple rustic people who 'speaking of them generally, [are] novices in agitation and systematic outrage'. Indeed, one of the most disturbing aspects of the Rebecca movement were the threats that it issued by letter to those it wished to intimidate. This had the desired effect, serving to strike fear into the hearts of their recipients. Nor were these 'Rebecca Letters' a peculiarly Welsh phenomenon; in rural south-east England too the 'Captain Swing' movement (1830–1) had struck terror into the hearts of its victims by issuing threats by anonymous letter. An English reporter dispatched to the Pembrokeshire–Carmarthenshire border to cover the riots for the Chartist newspaper the *Northern Star*, was soon to change his biased opinion of the rioters he met: 'Any man who sets down the small farmers of south Wales as a parcel of ignorant clod-hoppers for once in his life is wide of the mark.'

One aspect of the Rebecca Riots that is generally little known or not given due recognition was the anti-tithe grievance. The largely Non-conformist farmers of south-west Wales were as dissatisfied with paying the tithe (a tenth part of a landlord's or tenant's income paid to maintain the Anglican Church) as they were with paying the toll but because the toll gates were more visible and toll payments more pressing, and their destruction more easily accomplished, the tithe issue was rarely at the forefront of either their demands or in the reporting of their activities. However, unlike the toll issue, which was largely resolved by parliament in 1844, the tithe question continued to plague and anger hard-pressed farmers but it took another severe economic depression to sting them into action. The spark that lit the fire of the anti-tithe campaign in Wales was the foundation in 1886 of the Welsh Land League by Thomas Gee. The Welsh Land League was born of frustration and though it made the tithe issue a central feature of its campaign this was just part of its aim to redress wider social, economic and political grievances. Thus, in the autumn of 1886, the Pembrokeshire Anti-Tithe League was founded which derived much of its active support from among the farmers of the Welsh-speaking and strongly Nonconformist north.

Although the nature of anti-tithe activity in Pembrokeshire nowhere near rivalled that seen in the so-called Tithe War of north-east Wales, the tithe commissioners sent to distrain on the goods of non-payers in the parishes of Llanhywel, Llangolman, Llanychlwydog, Maenclochog, Moylegrove, St Dogmael's and Whitechurch, were met with bitter resistance. According to Audrey Philpin, these parishes became the 'storm-centres of tithe riots' in the county and if the injuries, to body and soul, suffered by William Stevens, Robert Lewis and Benjamin Evans and other tithe agents is anything to go by then she is not wide of the mark. Not even police protection could prevent Narberth solicitors' clerk Benjamin Evans from being hit by 'a shower of missiles, consisting of rotten eggs, clods of earth [and] a pan containing quicklime' when he attempted 'to receive money due to one of his master's clients' from the tenants at Brynllechog farm in Maenclochog in September 1890. The issue was only partly resolved by parliamentary legislation in 1891 when The Tithe Rent Charge Recovery and Redemption Act decreed that, henceforth, landlords alone were to be responsible for the payment of tithes.

Radicalism and Reformism: The Political Scene

Following the French Revolution of 1789, which in turn led to the overthrow and execution of the king, most western European governments, Britain included, were fearful of the same happening in their country, hence the use of suppression to put down protests and demonstrations and repression to destroy workers' clubs, reform leagues and trade unions. Economic depression, social injustice, political exclusion, poverty and periodic famines made worse an already volatile situation. The formation of the National Union of the Working Classes in the 1820s shows that the working masses were slowly being organized and mobilized. Whereas the growing power and strength of the working class was feared by those in authority, mainly the propertied classes, it was celebrated elsewhere, most notably by Nonconformist radicals. During the Rebecca Riots the Baptist periodical *Seren Gomer* tried to show that the power of the ordinary people had changed history and that the rioting Welsh folk of south-west Wales were only continuing this tradition: 'Beca is the country . . . it was Beca who obtained the Charter from King John [1215], who severed the head of Charles I [1649] and who won the Independence of America [1776]; Beca executed Louis XVI [1793], Beca won the Reform Bill [1832].' The attitude and atmosphere of the time can best be summed up by the slogan adopted on behalf of the working classes in 1838 by the Revd David Rees, editor of the Independent periodical *Y Diwygiwr*, 'Cynhyrfer! Cynhyrfer! Cynhyrfer!' ('Agitate! Agitate! Agitate!').

At the beginning of the nineteenth century politics and political power were the privilege and preserve of the rich; by its end almost the entire adult male population had been enfranchised and the rich were forced to share their political power. The reasons for this apparent sea change in the political fortunes of rich and poor are many and varied but its origins can be found in the social and economic distress of the early part of the century and the religious grievances of Nonconformists which in Wales gave rise to political radicalism. Rioting, such as occurred in Pembrokeshire during the 1790s, may have been the traditional release valve for social discontent but during the nineteenth century it became ever more politicized. In this respect the reform crisis prior to 1832 was something of a turning point for it witnessed the emergence of working-class political leaders who were inspired less by native Nonconformity and more by English radicalism led by the likes of Henry 'Orator' Hunt (d.1835), William Cobbett (d.1835), Joseph Hume (d.1855) and Richard Cobden (d.1865). The result of the reform crisis and the agitation that inspired it was the passing of the 1832 Reform Act which fell well short of the radicals' demand for universal manhood suffrage. For much of the rest of the century the main political issue was reform and only after a series of parliamentary Reform Acts – 1832, 1867 and 1884 together with the Ballot Act of 1872 – was the issue largely resolved. As a result of these Acts the political initiative gradually slipped from the grasp of the rich – the aristocracy in the House of Lords and the landowning landlords in the House of Commons – into the hands of the middle class who secured the votes of the newly-enfranchised poor and working class.

Pembrokeshire was unusual in that it largely failed to respond to the political changes that were occurring elsewhere in Wales. For example, there were few, if any, Chartists in the county where a political inertia seemed to have prevailed since the mid-eighteenth century, even among the enfranchised, who tended to share out political power among a 'charmed circle' of local families. A lecture tour of the county by a leading Chartist, Henry Hetherington, in 1838, failed to move the people nor did the Liberation Society fare any better, its work being all but ignored in the county.

The ascendancy of the Liberal Party in Wales was a truly remarkable phenomenon for not only did it brush aside the challenge posed by the rival Conservative Party, represented in Pembrokeshire by the great land-owning families of Campbell of Stackpole, Scourfield of New Moat, Philipps of Picton Castle and Bowen of Llwyn-gwair, its Welsh representatives in parliament formed themselves, for a short time, into a loosely-knit 'Welsh Party' which claimed to represent the people of Wales.

In Pembrokeshire the Liberals made slow progress, winning the allegiance of the urban folk long before they won the trust of their rustic colleagues, which is not surprising given that they had to contend with the county's traditional deference to landlords which continued to prevail in elections before and after 1868. Indeed, it has been argued with some conviction that if the Welsh people were awakened in 1868 it took until 1880 before Pembrokeshire responded. In that year the Liberals won all three of the county's seats and their challenge thereafter tended to win out against stiff Conservative opposition. In the six elections held between 1880 and 1900 the Liberals won all in the traditional Tory-dominated county seats and secured the borough seat at Haverfordwest until its disenfranchisement in 1885. Only in Pembroke Boroughs did the Liberals concede three elections to the Conservatives in 1886, 1895 and 1900. It is interesting to note that in 1892 the *South Wales Daily News* could report that, in its opinion, 'South Pembrokeshire is permeated through and through with Toryism, as North Pembrokeshire is with Liberalism'. Not for the first or last time was the county to split, be it in politics, religion or culture, according to the traditional linguistic division of the shire.

By the beginning of the twentieth century the Liberals came under increasing pressure from the new Labour movement which at first it embraced but was soon to reject. The Labour Party announced its arrival on the political scene with the election in 1900 of Keir Hardie for the radical stronghold of Merthyr Tydfil. Hardie's electoral triumph was massively important in the history of the Labour movement in Wales but caused hardly a ripple of interest in Pembrokeshire. Nor did the county's folk react with any great enthusiasm to what historians tend to regard as two of the most significant issues yet to be resolved, namely, disestablishment of the Church in Wales and home rule. Unsurprisingly perhaps home rule was something to be opposed in southern Pembrokeshire – the English-speaking folk had little sympathy with the Welsh Liberals who sought self-government, fearing domination in a Welsh-speaking principality. There was little if any support for the *Cymru Fydd* movement, even among the Welsh-speaking northerners, so that the political passion of Tom Ellis and Lloyd George was largely lost on the county's folk. Nor did disestablishment make much difference to the ordinary working man or woman; only Anglicans and the politically active were excited by the prospect of setting up a Church of Wales. Nevertheless, it is probably true to say that by the end of the nineteenth century, the Welsh, including their more reticent brethren from Pembrokeshire, had found their political voice which enabled them in the next century to express themselves not just as a people but as a nation.

Grind, Grime and Crime: The Social Scene

In the period between the early decades of the eighteenth century to the twilight years of the nineteenth, it can fairly be said that Wales moved from an 'Age of Enlightenment' to an 'Age of Reform'. The ideas, hopes and ambitions of the people of one age were realized by the people of another. The social reforms envisaged by the great eighteenth-century utilitarian and social philosopher Jeremy Bentham were realized by a new generation of radical thinkers such as Edwin Chadwick. Benthamite theories of utilitarianism were a powerful legacy which influenced governments for much of the nineteenth century. Consequently, it was a period of social experimentation in which theory was put into practice though the results were not always those envisaged or expected. This was due, in part, to contemporary ignorance of social issues for which reforms were attempted by those who did not really understand either the issues or the problems. This was especially true in matters connected with health and poverty where those responsible for reforms in both generally enjoyed much the better of the first without ever really experiencing the debilitating effects of the second.

There had always been a public health problem. The plagues, sicknesses and other disease epidemics of previous centuries had long taken their toll on a people inured to suffering. Nevertheless, the reason why public health came to constitute, as one historian put it, 'a gigantic problem in Victorian Wales' was mainly on account of the higher mortality rate caused by the increasing frequency of epidemic outbreaks. True, the population was many times greater than had been the case in earlier plague-ridden centuries but the percentage number of estimated deaths per thousand had hardly declined in line with this population growth. People continued to live in appallingly unhealthy conditions but the problem was exacerbated by the rapid urbanization of Wales which was itself a consequence of the equally rapid industrialization of the country. This shift of the population away from a rural to an urban-industrialized environment is regarded by historians as fundamental to understanding the changing patterns of health in Victorian Wales. The growth of towns during the second half of the eighteenth and the first half of the nineteenth centuries occurred too quickly, was haphazard and took place without any form of building regulation. This was especially true of Haverfordwest and Tenby, both of which expanded well beyond their medieval town walls, those of the former being demolished, without any form of serious regulation. As a result, by the middle of the nineteenth century the authorities were faced with dangerously insanitary conditions caused by poor housing, overcrowding, impure water supplies and the almost total lack of means for the disposal of sewage and household refuse.

Such appalling conditions still prevailed in the countryside but here they might be better tolerated in sparsely populated villages where the volume of human refuse was inconsequential in comparison to larger populated towns like Haverfordwest. By the same token, when fatal epidemics occurred the rural death rate paled in comparison with urban mortality rates the horror of which, by the sheer number of corpses involved, was compounded by the visual impact of so many burials. This may account for the fact that contemporaries considered life in the country as being considerably healthier than in towns when in truth the benefits were, in most cases, little better than marginal. The almost total absence of proper sanitation was compounded by the equally dire consequence of ignorance. People, generally, were unaware of the health hazards that confronted them and they continued to behave in a manner calculated to perpetuate their misery. Despite the construction of a new reservoir at Portfield in the 1850s to serve the inhabitants of Haverfordwest, within a decade the *Pembrokeshire Herald* reported that it had become polluted by 'newts, leeches, decaying animals and vegetable matter'. In spite of entreaties to the contrary, it was calculated that the population of Haverfordwest was polluting its environment with upwards of 200 tons of excrement annually. In mitigation one is bound to say that though some might complain of the more obvious signs of urban decay – those that more readily offended the senses such as the smells and sights of filth – the local authorities were often reluctant to act. This was motivated in part by obscurantist views that disease was due to 'atmospheric forces' or 'divine providence' but the root cause of their apparent inertia can be found in the generally held principles of laissez-faire, the basis of which revolved around a policy of non-interference in economic and social matters. In this respect, local authorities took their lead from national governments which fully endorsed the doctrine of economic and social individualism. Unless compelled to do so – and a like-minded central government was hardly likely to force them – many local authorities were content to let matters lie in the hope that the problems would right themselves which, at the necessary expense of the poor and vulnerable, it inevitably did. Epidemics came and went, crises passed and life returned to its usual pattern until the next time.

The consequence was, of course, an ever-widening and frequent cycle of death and disease about which local and national authorities were increasingly becoming concerned. Concern turned to alarm when, in 1831–2, the country was swept by a cholera epidemic the arrival of which had been rumoured for weeks before it struck. The Pembrokeshire press was not shy of reporting the grim facts and statistics, partly by word of mouth and to the heightened state of anxiety in anticipation of the disease, which had been tracked across Europe, reaching British shores. Reaching Edinburgh in October 1848 it soon spread to Wales,

striking first in Cardiff in May 1849 where 396 victims perished. In the first
six months of the epidemic sweeping England and Wales it claimed over
53,000 lives; by its end nearly 130,000 had fallen victim to the scourge. Nor
was Pembrokeshire immune, falling victim to the disease on two further
occasions in the outbreaks of 1854 and 1865–6. As horrific as were the
number of deaths recorded they take no account of the many more who
contracted the disease, suffered its ill-effects but lived.

Cholera was a particularly frightening disease, made more so by the
often hysterical reaction to it, but it was only one of a number of endemic
killers – typhus, typhoid, dysentery and tuberculosis – which preyed on
the population at large. According to one medical historian, T. G. Davies,
typhus was

> The most persistent and devitalising fever of the first half of the
> nineteenth century. Greatly encouraged by hunger, dirt, and over-
> crowding, it is carried in the faeces of lice which dry to a light
> dust thus enabling a person to become infected by breathing in
> the dust, or by a scratch on the hand. (K. Strange, 1987)

Although typhus was a potent killer of the poor – there was a serious
outbreak of typhoid fever in Haverfordwest in 1880 – tuberculosis proved
infinitely more deadly, accounting for one in five deaths in the county
during the middle decades of the nineteenth century. Although no single
factor may be said to cause the disease, poverty, and its associated evils
of overcrowding and undernourishment, was at the root of the problem.
Poverty, poor diet and disease contributed much to the appallingly high
infant mortality rate which, as one might expect, was greater in urban than
in rural districts. Nor had conditions improved by the 1880s as evidenced
by a damning report by Dr Parson to the local government board on the
general sanitary conditions of Haverfordwest.

If, as is widely believed, the cholera outbreak of 1831–2 was largely
responsible for stimulating interest in social and sanitary conditions in
the 1830s, it took central government another decade to act decisively in
the cause of public health. According to the terms of the Public Health
Act of 1848 local authorities would be encouraged or advised rather than
compelled to comply with government directives on matters of public
health. The time taken and the expense incurred in preparing reports on
sanitary conditions by properly qualified officers acted as a disincentive
for some local authorities. Such was the case in the cathedral city of
St David's when, incredibly, the council treated as a 'joke' a request by the
inhabitants for a public water supply, and this as late as January 1910!
Public health schemes did not come cheap and it has been calculated that
between 1848 and 1875 something approaching £1.2 million was spent by

local authorities, often in partnership with private enterprise, on sewerage, drainage and piped water supplies. In local terms, public health expenditure varied from town to town and much depended on their size and the seriousness of the conditions therein. For example, in 1884 Haverfordwest town council were forced to raise a mortgage of £2,000 on the town's market house in order to fulfil the demands of the Public Health Act of 1875.

By the end of the nineteenth century the nation's health had been significantly improved yet there remained a great deal to do and the issue was certainly not resolved to the satisfaction of Chadwick's successors in the field of social reform. On the other hand, some basic lessons had yet to be learnt as a report of the chief medical officer for Haverfordwest, dated October 1910, makes clear. He complained bitterly of the casual non-observance of simple rules of hygiene by the town's inhabitants, and this from a man who was by profession a veterinary surgeon! This strikes at the heart of the issue for, in spite of half-a-century of parliamentary legislation devoted to improving the health of the nation, its success rested on the cooperation of the public in whose continued ignorance, rather than in government neglect, lay the final stumbling block to progress.

It is perhaps an indictment on a society that calls itself civilized that Victorian social reformers were faced with largely the same problems of poverty and vagrancy that had confronted their Elizabethan predecessors more than 300 years before. Equally indictable is the fact that attitudes had changed little during that period; the poor were still viewed with suspicion by those charged, by their relative wealth, to relieve them of their poverty. A culture of shame evolved where those seeking poor relief were reminded of their destitution and thereby deliberately disgraced by being 'on the parish'. At least no Pembrokeshire parish followed the example set by Cowbridge in 1770 where the poor were required to wear badges indicating that they were paupers. On the other hand, in order to discourage persons from making claims 'on the parish' in 1872 the good folk of Pembroke decided to publish a list of paupers in the local press! If reluctance and resentment tended to characterize the attitudes of the average Pembrokeshire ratepayer, upon whom fell the burden of funding initiatives for poor relief, the state and its judicial system had even less charity to spare. There was a generally held belief that poverty was a sign of bad character for which the poor ought to be punished, and punished they were, being subjected to a penal system which seemed to revel in its cruelty, which was apparently devoid of humanity but which, ultimately, had no answer to the problem it sought to eradicate. By 1822 more than 150 crimes listed in the statute book were punishable by death, some of the more absurd included the theft of a sheep and stealing articles worth more than 5 shillings (25p); even stealing a silk handkerchief might result in hanging! That crime went hand-in-hand with poverty was an acknowledged if not an established fact and in spite of the repressive measures taken to tackle the one – crime – they were almost bound to fail if the symptoms of the other – poverty – was not addressed also. For example, it has been convincingly shown that it was mainly the dire poverty suffered by the farmers and labourers in south-west Wales in the 1830s and 1840s that led to the Rebecca Riots. Consequently, fear of social unrest and possible revolution convinced the government that the Old Poor Law (1601), which had remained largely intact and only ever intended for times of crisis, required urgent amendment.

The Poor Law Amendment Act of 1834 may have signalled a change in policy but it did not herald a change in attitude; if anything attitudes towards the poor hardened. The Act required that conditions in the workhouses be made as 'less desirable' as possible so as to deter the 'indigent' poor. Consequently, in Pembrokeshire's workhouses a strict daily regime was introduced, families were split up and severe spending limits imposed; indeed, no fit or 'able-bodied' person was to receive money or other kinds of help from the Poor Law authorities except in a workhouse. The New Poor Law (1834) may be seen as a final solution to the problem of pauperism, which, it hoped, would not only reduce the cost of provision of relief, but would also improve the moral character of the poor and labouring classes. It was thought that outdoor relief undermined the labourers' will to fend for themselves and so it was intended that help should only be given inside a workhouse 'in conditions that were below the lowest standard of living outside the workhouse'. Almost inevitably, such views and the Poor Law that inspired them, attracted as much criticism as support, even praise in some quarters, as may be gauged by the reports and editorials in local newspapers more than ten years after the passing of the Act. *The Cambrian*, published in Swansea, offered its support for the Poor Law while *The Carmarthen Journal* and *The Pembrokeshire Herald* attacked it as a gross violation of people's rights.

In January 1839 a baying mob, whose motives, it has to be said, were mixed and not entirely focused on the plight of the poor, attempted to burn down the newly built workhouse at Narberth. Although the workhouse was repaired there was to be no change in the attitude of those charged with its 'efficient' administration. In 1900 the Narberth guardians took the decision to reduce spending on paupers, a policy which was still in evidence as late as 1924 when, according to a disapproving *Pembrokeshire Herald*, they turned down a suggestion for installing electric light in the workhouse being, in their view, 'the wrong time to go in for luxuries'! Nor were the Narberth guardians alone in stigmatizing the poor, in an effort to discourage persons from seeking relief. In May 1872 the Pembroke guardians published a list of paupers in the local, and very pliant, press (none other than the *Pembrokeshire Herald* in its pre-social conscience guise).

Aside from violence there was much peaceful protest against the Poor Law and in this the local gentry, particularly in rural Wales, were to the fore. Many of those elected to serve on the boards of guardians were drawn from the landowning classes, families who had a long tradition of dispensing charity to the poor, and they resented the intrusion of central government and the centralization of poor relief under the Poor Law Commission. This is not to suggest that all parish unions, their administrators and their workhouses were inefficient, deficient or inhumane; many were praised when inspected by commissioners appointed by the government to survey the workings of the Act in 1844. The Commission of Inquiry for Wales found many instances of good practice such as the provision of chaplains for religious services, gardens for inmates to grow their own food, doctors and nurses for improved medical care and teachers for instructing the children of the poor. Unlike in Cardiganshire and Carmarthenshire none of the Pembrokeshire workhouses were singled out for especial praise; rather they were criticized for their failure to provide a healthy diet for inmates.

It has been said that we can learn much about a society by the types of crimes committed. If so, then eighteenth- and nineteenth-century Britain stands condemned, for its crimes were largely caused by desperate poverty and the threat of starvation. Its criminalization of the poor and needy caused unnecessary hardship and suffering and did little to deal with the causes of crime. Unsurprisingly, it was during the nineteenth century that crime was first identified as a major social problem which required urgent remedy. Consequently, the period witnessed the origins of criminology as a scientific discipline, the introduction of local, and later national, crime statistics and the emergence of such concepts as juvenile delinquency. It was a century of change which embraced the idea of professional police forces, the humanization of the criminal code and the greater use of prisons – Pembrokeshire had one at Haverfordwest – as a form of punishment which were themselves reformed to bring them into line with proposals put forward by the Howard Association and Prison Reform League. Crime or the threat and fear of it preoccupied both government and church leaders who strove to find answers when none were forthcoming. It required a kind of radical thinking for which the Victorians were simply ill-equipped. Their belief that religion still had a major role to play as guardian of the nation's morals was ignoring the fact that the worshipping public was in steep decline.

'If the poor cannot procure employment, and are not supported, they must commit crimes or starve.' So stated Robert Owen (1816) who was of the firm opinion that poverty was a primary cause of crime. To judge from contemporary reports and judicial records the most commonly committed crimes were, in order of seriousness, drunkeness, assault, stealing, vagrancy, malicious damage to property, and, in the towns like Haverfordwest, prostitution. The list indicates a strong correlation between crime and the lower classes and so it has been proved in a number of local research studies. In her research of crime and protest in Pembrokeshire (1815–1974) Audrey Philpin (1993b) states:

> One of the most remarkable aspects of nineteenth-century crime in Pembrokeshire is the almost total absence of evidence of law-breaking amongst the middle and upper classes. In over two hundred cases of men appearing at Quarter Sessions between 1820 and 1837, only six could even remotely be judged to be men of means. Of these, five were described as 'farmer' and one as 'schoolmaster'.

The same was true with regards to middle- and upper-class females. 'Of over 3,000 cases studies between 1820 and 1900, there were sixty categories of work specified; almost all were for menial occupations such as mantua-making, domestic service, labouring, colliery work, shepherding, basket-making, quilting, brewing and the like' (A. Philpin, 1993b). Crime records have as much to teach us about Victorian morality as the occupational structure of its society.

One of the most striking aspects of crime in Wales and England during the nineteenth century was the rise in the incidence of juvenile crime. Orphaned and abandoned children had little choice but to fend for themselves and they did so, as was graphically described in Charles Dickens's novel *Oliver Twist* (1837), by turning to stealing. Even in rural Pembrokeshire children figured prominently in the gaol records of the town of Haverfordwest. Between 1820 and 1863 around 208 children, the majority with their mothers, were admitted to the town's gaol. Indeed, they seem at times to have been unwitting accomplices to crime as is shown in the case, in 1832, of ten-year-old William Michael Burns who was with his mother Mary when she broke into a house in Robeston Wathen to steal 'foodstuffs and goods'. Both were convicted and condemned to death, their sentences being commuted later to '12 calendar months of hard labour'. After serving six months the youth was removed to the town's workhouse.

In 1815 the forces of law and order were nowhere near as organized as they are today. There was no police force in the modern sense and no method of criminal detection. 'Thief-taking' was a local business, which was organized on a county basis with a high constable assisted by unpaid parish or petty constables appointed by the justices of the peace.

With the rapid increase in the incidence of crime the government was eventually moved to act and under the terms of the Municipal Corporations Act of 1835, every town in England and Wales was required to appoint watch committees who in turn were to be responsible for setting up local police forces following strictly Peel's Metropolitan Police model. Many towns in Wales, and at least four counties between 1839 and 1845 – Carmarthen, Denbigh, Montgomery and Glamorgan – did so but even those slow to react to the directive, Pembrokeshire being one, usually on account of the cost to ratepayers, were required to do so by the County and Borough Police Act of 1856. In 1857 a reluctant Pembrokeshire set up its first police force, a move which saw an initial rise in the number of people apprehended.

In 1823 James Mill submitted an article on prisons for inclusion in the *Encyclopaedia Britannica* which suggested that the purpose for imprisonment should be 'reform by industry'. It was a bold suggestion which looked towards rehabilitation rather than simply punishment. In Carmarthen and Haverfordwest, for example, the remains of their respective medieval castles were converted for use as prisons. The living conditions within them were scandalously unclean and unhealthy and no wonder when the majority of those committed to prison were themselves 'dirty' and suffering from ill health. According to the Surgeon's Record Book (1820–35) for Haverfordwest castle prison many of those convicted of vagrancy, who made up more than half of the prisoners incarcerated at any one time, suffered from malnutrition, fleas, lice, venereal disease and the 'itch', probably scabies. In line with Mill's suggestion the government encouraged local prisons to find useful employment for their inmates and by 1826 Haverfordwest was among the first gaols in Wales to install a treadmill.

Between 1821 and 1858 the register of prisoners for Haverfordwest gaol records some 8,182 convicts committed to its care: of which 1,663 were females, making up 20.3 per cent of the prison population. The ages of those serving sentences ranged from twelve to seventy-three and their crimes varied from prostitution, theft and bastardy to the desertion of children. Two examples must suffice to illustrate the types of females who might expect to be housed in the prison. The first concerns Charlotte Havard, 'a well known recidivist' according to Audrey Philpin (1993b) 'who appeared regularly before early nineteenth-century Pembrokeshire courts'. On entering Haverfordwest prison in January 1829 her list of crimes were noted down in the gaol register, she being described as 'a rogue and a vagabond, conducting herself in a riotous manner in the streets, being a prostitute, and biting the thumb of Rebecca Evans in a fight'. It is difficult to know whether she was convicted for idleness, disorderly conduct, for vagrancy, prostitution, breach of the peace or common assault. The most tragic case listed in the prison register, but by no means uncommon, was that of twelve-year-old Mary Anne Reynish. On 26 May 1826 she was given 'one month's imprisonment with hard labour, for Leaving her Service'. Those placed in domestic service by parish guardians had no choice but to work as directed; to leave without permission was tantamount to committing a criminal act. She served her time and was released on 28 June but less than three weeks later she was again apprehended for 'Leaving her Service' for which she received 'three months imprisonment with hard labour' which, in Haverfordwest, meant the treadwheel. Three days into her sentence she was punished by the prison governor Thomas Jones with solitary confinement on account of the fact that '. . . while at work on the wheel [she] made a noise by calling out to her fellow prisoners, for which offence I confined her to a dark cell for 4 hours'. Such inhumane treatment of prisoners, confirmed by the passing of the Prisons Act 1865 – 'hard labour, hard fare and a hard board' – continued until the passing of the Prisons Act of 1877 which 'nationalized' and regulated all prisons across the country.

VII

Contemporary Pembrokeshire: The Twentieth Century

Introduction: *Gwlad Hud a Lledrith* (The Land of Magic and Enchantment)

It is impossible to estimate the true value of the debt that Pembrokeshire owes to those who strove so hard in their day and generation to record the history of its past and preserve the doings of its long-forgotten sons. We may begin with Gerald de Barri, go on to the Elizabethan George Owen, include Richard Fenton, recall the devoted services of Edward Laws, and wind up with the latest, but we feel confident not the last of Pembrokeshire worthies, Henry Owen, who, as member of this Commission saw the promise of one of his most fervent longings in the start of our present undertaking, but was not permitted to share in its completion. We have had to lay the works of these men under heavy contribution without whom no study of Pembrokeshire history or archaeology can be attempted, and we would express the hope that their labours will be carried on.

(Introduction to the *The Inventory of the Ancient Monuments relating to the County of Pembrokeshire* (1925) published by the Royal Commission on Ancient Monuments in Wales and Monmouthshire)

Henry Owen, who died in 1919, did not see the publication of the *Inventory* to which he had given such excellent support. He would, doubtless, have been flattered by the kind words penned by his colleagues, none of whom were from Pembrokeshire, who valued beyond measure his intimate knowledge of Pembrokeshire's rich history. As the commissioners valued Owen so we today should pay homage to a man who did much to modernize and professionalize the study of history. Indeed, the twentieth century has seen a near revolution in most aspects of life and the scientific study of history is, in many respects, the least of them. The technological advances have truly earmarked that century above all others as one of immense change. So much has happened and there is so much evidence available that a whole book, let alone a single chapter, could be devoted to the subject. Consequently, this chapter has to take a highly selective look at the period which is still very much in the memories of those who have lived in part of it, or the rare few who have lived through all of it. Of course, one day even 'Contemporary Pembrokeshire' will succumb to the passage of time and become the stuff of long-ago history. But until then we today must continue to strive to set down and record faithfully the events of our own time, as Gerald of Wales, George Owen, Richard Fenton, Edward Laws and Henry Owen, not forgetting countless others, have done before us.

Society and Economy: Rural, Urban and Industrial Pembrokeshire

The period from the late nineteenth century to the end of the twentieth has been one of almost unremitting change. It witnessed the end of gentry rule, the political emancipation of working men and women, social advances in terms of health and education and, in the opinion of D. Gareth Evans, a 'decline of those powerful forces which once shaped Welsh life – agriculture, industry and religion'. Change is inevitable but its nature, progress and consequences vary from century to century so that it can rightly be said that the Wales at the end of one century differed from that at its beginning. Few would argue with the fact that the Wales of 2000 is very different from the Wales of 1900 but it is the sheer pace of change that marks out the century as being different from its predecessors.

Rural Wales has, arguably, seen some of the most dramatic changes and where once it was true to say in Pembrokeshire that farming was king, as opposed to south-east Wales where King Coal ruled, today it has a hollow ring. The decline in agriculture had been long in the making, having its roots in the nineteenth century, so that the first to feel its effects were the landed proprietors, most of whom descended from gentry families with pedigrees stretching back centuries. Although they had ruled with a rod of iron in the countryside for generations many did not survive the twentieth century either as landowners or as power brokers. Increasing taxation, death duties and inflation did for many large estates which were broken up and sold, usually to their land-hungry tenants. The variation in agricultural prices combined with falling rents conspired to depress estate income so that landowners tended to extend their commercial interests outside agriculture. The demise of the large estates may be said to have begun in earnest in the period after the First World

War and even those that survived did so much reduced in size. In *The Return of Owners of Land 1873*, some nineteen landlords, the 'great landowners', are listed which, if the exercise were repeated today, would yield fewer than half a dozen names, if that. Crippling financial difficulties aside, many landowners simply sold up or sold off part of their estates in order to diversify their investments. Those that have survived, such as Picton and Upton Castles, have successfully tapped into the tourist market by opening up their land and/or homes to the paying public. Other great mansions may no longer have an estate to support or be inhabited by the gentry families that built them but they survive because they have been transformed into hotels and holiday parks, like Llwyn-gwair; or field and outdoor sports centres, like Sealyham and Orielton.

The decline and break up of the great estates saw a corresponding rise in the number of smaller landholdings as greater numbers of independent farmers emerged to take the place of their landlords. Unfortunately, the depression made life difficult for what were essentially precarious, small-scale enterprises unable to bear the burden of a sustained downturn in prices. Lloyd George demonstrated his awareness of the problem by issuing the so-called 'green book', *The Land and the Nation*, in 1925 which proposed a dramatic revival of agriculture, but in order for its policies to be implemented his party, the fast-declining Liberals, had first to assume power; this they have failed to do in every election since 1918. The problems facing farmers in Pembrokeshire and in Wales generally were summed up in a government report issued by the Welsh Reconstruction Advisory Council in 1944:

> Hopes of market stability raised by the Agriculture Act, 1920, were rudely dashed by the early repeal of that legislation. Welsh farmers who had purchased their properties with borrowed monies were increasingly embarrassed by every fall in prices. In common with the prices of primary products throughout the world, the proceeds of Welsh sheep, cattle and crop sales fell steadily and with disastrous results.
>
> From the countryside the drift of population went on . . . Farm buildings were neglected through poverty, improvements went unmade, the land itself was sadly neglected; and although the family farm, which predominates in Wales offers considerable resistance to unfavourable economic conditions, it does so only by the acceptance of standards which elsewhere connote acknowledged bankruptcy. (D. W. Howell, 1993a)

Post-war governments attempted to support the agricultural industry by passing two acts, in 1947 and 1957, which guaranteed minimum prices for a variety of farm products and by paying subsidies and grants. With Britain's entry into the European Economic Community in the 1970s Welsh agriculture has been heavily influenced by European directives and subsidies, not all of which have been good for Pembrokeshire's farmers. Despite generous support in the form of EEC subsidies, tariff protection and intervention purchasing, at least until the mid 1980s, there have been drawbacks in terms of rigorous price control and ever-tightening production quotas. Farming continues and remains an important sector of the economy in Pembrokeshire but change is in the offing and the industry continues to contract. Nevertheless, Pembrokeshire's economy remains heavily dependent, but not exclusively so, on agriculture and tourism. Diversification is the key to future success, as can be seen by the remarkable development of the leisure complex Oakwood Park which has revolutionized the relationship between urban and rural Pembrokeshire.

If rural Pembrokeshire suffered during the inter-war period so did its urban and industrial equivalent. Pembroke Dock was perhaps the worst hit with the closing of the naval dockyard in 1926 which resulted in the emigration of 3,500 people from the town in the decade after 1921. In 1937 more than 55 per cent of the insured population of the town and district was listed as unemployed. Ironically, it was the advent of war which brought to an end the economic depression that had so blighted the county. In the post-war years the county has attempted to diversify in order to cope with the changing requirements of economic development. Among the more serious problems to be confronted was the closure of the long-declining coal industry in 1948 quickly followed by the fishing industry during the 1950s. The undermining of the county's industrial base continued for some time until regeneration schemes were put in place enabling investment to take place, hence the development of industrial parks attracting light industries.

Gwlad Hud a Lledrith, or 'The Land of Magic and Enchantment', is how the county was sold to potential visitors and investors by the Dyfed Official Guide and handbook issued in the late 1980s. The holiday or tourism industry is among the fastest-growing sectors in the county and is most fully developed in the Pembrokeshire Coast National Park and adjacent areas such as Tenby. Set up in 1952, the park runs for some 180 miles and is the smallest of the eleven National Parks in England and Wales but is the only one that is predominantly coastal. With its superb coastline of rugged cliffs, quiet coves and sandy beaches together with the magnificent scenery inland the county naturally attracts a large tourist population which contributes substantially to the economy of the region. During the 1960s the county outstripped all others in Wales for the sheer number of requests for holiday accommodation. By the 1970s Tenby had established itself as one of the top five tourist 'hot spots' in Wales, a distinguishing feature that holds true today. The county is also a route through which visitors reach Ireland and the investment in the rail, road and ferry terminal at Fishguard/Goodwick has paid dividends not just for tourism but for the economy generally.

Although agriculture and tourism may be regarded as the twin pillars of the county's economy, heavy industry too is of great importance, particularly on the shores of the Milford Haven waterway. In 1906 Milford Haven was the sixth largest fishing port in Britain, but the industry has declined since 1950 and the waterway now boasts several oil refineries on its shores. The Milford Haven industrial zone was created in response to the huge growth in the world demand for oil-based products and the realization by the oil companies that the haven waterway provided a natural harbour. Its development from the late 1950s did compensate, in part, for the decline of traditional industries such as fishing by providing jobs in refinery construction and in the oil industry itself. For example, the building of the Esso, Texaco, Gulf and Amoco refineries accounted for some 25 per cent of male employment in construction work. This was followed by the building of the BP Ocean Terminal, the Pembroke power station and the refinery extensions of 1978–80. This, in turn, attracted oil tankers and by the early 1990s the Haven had become the largest mainland oil port in Britain, handling close to 33,000,000 tonnes of shipping per annum. Nor were the dark days of depression in the county forgotten by those charged with supporting the development of the oil and related industries. In 1963 the local MP, Desmond Donnelly, stated: 'This is the rebirth of Pembrokeshire. I only wish the men who were discharged from Pembroke Dockyard during the dark, depressing days, were here today to see it taking place.' Unfortunately, in an ever-changing world even the oil and power industries suffered a series of setbacks with the first of a series of shocks occuring in 1983 with the closure of the Esso refinery, followed in the 1990s by the closure of the Pembroke power station after a dispute over its conversion to burn what were believed by the local population to be toxic fuels. The oil industry today may not be what it was during its heyday in the 1960s and 1970s but it is still, and will be for some time, of considerable importance to the county.

Politics and Government

In the general election of 1900, the Liberals began the new century as they had ended the old, winning twenty-eight out of the thirty-four Welsh seats among which may be included the rural constituency of Pembrokeshire. Here John Wynford Philipps, son of Sir James Erasmus Philipps of Picton Castle, maintained the Liberal hold on a county that had not fallen to the

Conservatives since 1876. After a less than distinguished career in the Commons – he contributed little to the Liberal social reforms that were being piloted through parliament by David Lloyd George – Philipps was elevated to the peerage as Baron St David's. This prompted a by-election (July 1908) which was won by a fellow Liberal and local solicitor Walter Roch but the star of the campaign was his invited guest Mrs Pankhurst, the Suffragette leader, who held a number of generally well attended meetings in the county. Roch was a radical who believed in votes for women, publicly condemning the force-feeding of imprisoned Suffragettes, disestablishment of the Church and the redistribution of wealth. In the borough election matters were slightly different; here the Liberals had a fight on their hands and the Conservative candidate, John Laurie, just edged out, by a mere fifteen votes after a recount, his opponent Thomas Terrell. In spite of an energetic career in the Commons, Laurie did not long enjoy his constituency, losing out to Owen Cosby Philipps in the Liberal landslide of 1906. The Liberals held the borough seat for the remainder of its political life, when it was disenfranchised in 1918.

As a single constituency the county was claimed by the Liberals who, in spite of their steady decline in the post-war period, managed to represent the people of Pembrokeshire almost without a break for twenty-eight years between 1918 and 1950. In various guises – National Liberal Coalition (1918), National Liberal (1922), Liberal (1923–31, 1945) and Independent Liberal (1935) – they managed to win seven out of the eight elections held between the end of two world wars, losing but once in 1924 to the Conservatives. For most of this period, 1922–4 and 1929–50, the county was represented by Gwilym Lloyd George, the younger son of the wartime prime minister who was himself a son of a Pembrokeshire farmer. His relationship with his constituency was not without its problems and he was often criticized for his apparent apathy or indifference in political affairs, especially during the difficult years of the Depression. In fact, he was known locally as 'Ask my Dad' due to the deference he showed his aged but still able politician-father whose policies he was reluctant to criticize. It has been said, perhaps unfairly, of 'Gil', as he was otherwise known, that it was only on account of his father's influence that he was given office in the wartime coalition led by Winston Churchill (1940–5). In the event, he distinguished himself by his service as minister for power and fuel and it was thought that, once the war was over, he might even be elected as Speaker. With the virtual collapse of Liberalism after the Second World War, and his own electoral defeat in 1950, Lloyd George joined the Conservatives, serving, after his re-election for Tyne and Wear in 1951, as home secretary and minister for Welsh affairs between 1954 and 1957.

The new century was to see significant change in Welsh and national politics. Where liberalism and conservatism had once dominated, socialism and, later in the century, nationalism now entered the fray to upset the traditional political balance in Welsh as well as in Pembrokeshire politics. True, the signs of change were hardly auspicious and a contemporary might have been forgiven for dismissing the new socialist challenge as presented by the Independent Labour Party as a flash in the proverbial political pan. Having won but one of the thirty-four seats in Wales in the 1900 election Labour seemed destined to remain a minority radical party existing on the fringes of serious politics. However, destiny had mapped out a different course for Labour and as Wales shifted further to the left, by 1922 it became the majority party in Wales, winning eighteen of the thirty-six seats. The party's power base was rooted firmly in the industrial valleys of the south-east so that it was the urban rather than the rural vote that counted most in Labour's rise to political prominence.

Yet, if socialism was on the march in the rest of Wales, in Pembrokeshire it had only taken a few short steps. It was not until 1918 that the party felt confident enough to field a candidate in the largely rural Pembrokeshire constituency. The Labour candidate, Ivor Gwynne, was soundly beaten by his National Liberal Coalition rival, Sir Evan Davies Jones, but in polling a respectable 7,712 votes he had won a 25 per cent share of the popular vote. Thereafter, the party contested every election bar one (1931) between the wars where it invariably came in third behind the Liberals and Conservatives. The county had to wait until 1950 before it fell under the spell of Labour and as it did so it largely rid itself of the last vestiges of Liberalism. Henceforth, the political contest would be fought between the Conservatives and Labour.

The man to whom the county electorate turned, rather reluctantly at first given the winning margin of 129 votes, was Desmond Donnelly. The son of a tea-planter in the Indian province of Assam, Donnelly had been a journalist, editor of *Town and Country Planning*, before he turned his hand to politics. He was a radical who supported Aneurin Bevan and was the youngest member of parliament to be elected in 1950. However, his radicalism, occasional lack of judgement and quarrelsome nature – he split from the Bevanite group in 1954 – conspired to deny him high office so that his potential was never realized. Having represented Pembrokeshire for twenty years, winning six straight election victories between 1950 and 1970, he resigned the party whip in 1968 and set up the Democratic Party. In spite of his being a good constituency MP, the voters failed to re-elect him in 1970, preferring instead to have the Conservative Nicholas Edwards as their representative. Had Donnelly remained with Labour the party would undoubtedly have won the election, but once he had secured the seat Edwards did not intend to let it go, representing Pembrokeshire well into the Thatcher era. Only in the post-Thatcher 1990s, when the Pembrokeshire constituency had been subdivided into two, namely,

Carmarthen West and South Pembrokeshire and Preseli did the county
return to Labour which represents it still.

As post-war Pembrokeshire warmed to socialism it also, tentatively,
opened itself up to nationalism. In 1959 the Welsh nationalist party
Plaid Cymru fielded its first candidate, the noted Pembrokeshire poet
Waldo Williams, in the general election for that year polling just 2,253
votes out of a total cast of 52,077. In spite of their poor showing then
and in subsequent elections, the nationalists continue to contest the
seat hoping to fulfil a political mission that might see them emulate the
remarkable rise of Labour earlier in the century. Thus far it has not
happened, certainly not in Pembrokeshire, though the signs of a revival
in the fortunes of political nationalism in the rest of Wales might give
the nationalists cause for optimism. Certainly the political make-up of
the recently established National Assembly (1997), in which the
nationalists have secured official opposition party status, suggests
that the pendulum may yet swing Plaid Cymru's way though the strength
of Labour's support in the county should not be underestimated. It is
interesting to note that in largely Welsh-speaking Pembrokeshire,
represented by the Preseli constituency, a swing of 10 per cent from
Labour to Plaid Cymru was recorded in the 1999 Assembly elections. In
South Pembrokeshire too, the nationalist vote held up firmly with the
party polling 8,399 votes, second only to Labour's 9,891. What the
future holds for Plaid Cymru in Pembrokeshire remains to be seen but
since it secured victories in such Labour strongholds as the Rhondda,
Islwyn and Llanelli the county may yet fall under the spell of Welsh
nationalism in the twenty-first century.

The National Assembly is but one of a number of fundamental changes
that have occurred in the restructuring of Welsh political life. In
Pembrokeshire such restructuring began early when, in 1885, Haverfordwest
lost its representative status being submerged within Pembroke Boroughs
until it too was disenfranchised in 1918. Henceforth, Pembrokeshire was
reduced to a single constituency until further reconstructive surgery in
the 1980s and 90s saw parts of the old county farmed out to form larger
constituencies. In fact the 'old' county found itself under pressure to
change in the early 1970s when it was eventually metamorphosed into a
smaller constituent of the cumbersome 'super' county of Dyfed. In an
echo of its past, Pembrokian Dyfed re-emerged to take its place once
again on the political map of the day. Unfortunately, the political
boundaries of late-twentieth-century Dyfed bore no relation to that of its
ancient predecessor and, if anything, the new county created in 1974
should rightly have been called Deheubarth. Doubtless, Dyfed was
considered far easier to pronounce and spell than Deheubarth, not that
this stopped the English media, particularly its newsreaders and journalists,

from getting it wrong! Nor was Pembrokeshire allowed to retain its integrity within the new Dyfed since it, in common with Carmarthenshire, was further divided into districts – Preseli and South Pembrokeshire – in which local government operated. Dyfed was not popular, not least in Carmarthenshire but especially not in Pembrokeshire where a campaign was launched to revive the old county. The people responsible for the creation of Dyfed – the politicians, civil servants and planners – failed to take account of the strength of local loyalty and identity in Wales. As the drover and poet Edward Morris (d.1689) of Cerrigydrudion wrote: 'Wherever the Welshman is raised, therein he chooses to tarry.' Although not as strong today as it had been in Morris's time, the power of 'localism' still prevails even in a world where the revolutionary influence of globalization seemingly sweeps all before it.

Pembrokeshire at War: From The South African War to the Second World War

As the new century dawned, Britain was already at war. Since 1899 the Boers of South Africa had not only dared to challenge the might of the British Empire, they appeared to be winning! It was a vicious war in which Boer civilians found themselves in the front line and suffered as much as their armed and belligerent brethren, providing a foretaste of conflicts to come. It was a war, moreover, that was to drag on for a further two years until 1902 when the struggling Boer farmers were finally defeated by the mightily relieved British. Its impact on British public opinion was massive, partly as a result of extensive newspaper coverage but partly also as a result of it being dragged into the political domain. The 'Khaki' election of October 1900 whipped up 'war fever' and those politicians who dared speak out against the war, most notably David Lloyd George, were denounced as traitors. In Pembrokeshire too there was dissent in so far as the sitting member for the county, the Liberal John Philipps, turned from reluctantly supporting the war to criticizing the Conservative government's conduct of it. Not that it harmed his political career for his change of opinion coincided with that of the British public, especially as the military seemed unable to crush the Boer farmers. As far as the people of Pembrokeshire were concerned this was no distant war in a remote part of the Empire, it touched them personally because of the service of the Pembrokeshire Yeomanry. Serving abroad for the first time in its long history – the Yeomanry had confronted the French at Fishguard (1797) and the Rebecca rioters (1839–44) prior to their deployment to South Africa – the troops were led by a local officer, Lt Col Frederick Meyrick of Bush near Pembroke. Although their war service was anything but spectacular they did contribute to wearing down the enemy and were granted the battle honour 'South Africa 1901' to which was added 'Fishguard' in 1904.

In common with the rest of Wales and the United Kingdom, Pembrokeshire responded with enthusiasm to the call to arms in August 1914. Men enlisted in their hundreds and the Pembrokeshire Yeomanry was again made ready for active service. The Yeomanry served for two years against Turkey (1916–18), receiving battle honours for Gaza, Jerusalem, Tel Asur and Jericho, before being shipped to the Western Front for the last few months of the war. Here they distinguished themselves in the Somme and Bapaume before their involvement in the pursuit of the Germans towards Mons as the enemy front line cracked. Soldiers from the county also formed part of the Welsh Division created by the Prime Minister Lloyd George, which saw action on the Somme under the command of Sir Ivor Philipps of Picton Castle. Pembrokeshire's casualty rates were every bit as high as those suffered by the rest of Wales where in all some 40,000 Welshmen were either killed or wounded. As a result of its maritime connection the county found itself in the forefront of the sea war against Germany. Naval activity in the Haven was stepped up and ships were deployed to deal with the U-boat menace. Some 250 men from the Milford naval base were honoured for their part in the war against the U-boats. The devastating effect of the war was brought home to the people of Milford Haven and Fishguard in particular, since they carried the burden of accommodating the large numbers of survivors from ships sunk by German submarines. In Milford Haven alone over 4,000 survivors from nearly 150 ships sunk by enemy action were given shelter after their harrowing ordeal. Perhaps the biggest casualty of the war, or rather its ending, was the naval dockyard at Pembroke Dock which was gradually scaled down. One visitor in 1918 who had been impressed by what he had seen there was the future president of the United States, Franklin D. Roosevelt:

> It has been expanded since the War from 1,000 to nearly 4,000 employees, and does mostly repair work to patrol vessels and is also building four submarines. I was particularly interested to see over 500 women employed in various capacities, some of them even acting as moulders' helpers in the foundry, and all of them doing excellent work. (L. Phillips, 1993)

Their 'excellent work' notwithstanding, the dockyard was eventually closed in 1926 prompting the *Telegraph Almanack* to report a year later that Pembroke Dock had become 'almost entirely a town of unemployed and pensioners'.

In 1939 war broke out again. As in the first, the Pembrokeshire people rallied, though perhaps not with the same degree of enthusiasm, to the cause in the second. Men and women enlisted or were conscripted for the various armed services and the military bases in the county were again put on alert. Besides quartering British troops, a role it had fulfilled since the Civil War, the county played host to foreign soldiers for the first time when American GIs of the 110th US Infantry Regiment arrived at the Llanion Barracks at Pembroke Dock. There they trained and prepared for the invasion of Europe using the beaches at Amroth and Wiseman's Bridge for this purpose. The war brought distinguished guests to the county, such as General Eisenhower following in the footsteps of Roosevelt, and the prime minister, Winston Churchill. Unfortunately, as is the nature of war, there were some uninvited guests also, primarily the Luftwaffe. The German air force raided the county on several occasions between the first attack in July 1940 and the last in July 1942. The oil storage tanks, the dropping of magnetic mines to block the Haven sea-way and any vulnerable shipping anchored in the area were the main targets of the bombing offensives but the proximity of Pembroke Dock to the military bases meant that it too was severely hit. These bases accom-modated planes of the Fleet Air Arm and Coastal Command, each of which was given the task of hunting out enemy submarines and surface shipping in the Atlantic. Recognition of the county's contribution to the war effort was given in a speech by Vice-Admiral Fairburn in which Milford Haven's role was praised having 'made a not unimportant contri-bution to the D-Day operations'.

The year 1945 may have spelt the end of war for Pembrokeshire but it did not mean the end of her involvement in military matters. The Brawdy airbase and the naval presence in the Haven continued until well into the second half of the twentieth century and they were joined by a more controversial military decision when men of the West German Armed Forces were invited to train on the Castlemartin firing range. Their coming to the county in the 1960s was met with some apprehension, though not with outright hostility but they soon made their presence felt becoming a part of the community and their leaving in the 1990s was met with a great deal of sadness. Brawdy and the Admiralty armaments depot at Trecŵn too succumbed to the change in government policy and the ending of the Cold War. The latter half of the twentieth century has been a haven of peace for the county compared to the first half though the military have not yet done with Pembrokeshire, as the late 1990s deployment of Welsh troops to the former Brawdy airbase testifies.

Pembrokeshire at Peace: Leisure and Recreation

The twentieth century has seen something approaching a revolution in leisure and recreation due in large part to the advent of new technology, widening access, availability and opportunity but also because it became an industry. True, traditional forms of entertainment continued much as they had done during Victorian times, such as eisteddfodau, fairs and other locally organized musical and variety type events but they did have to compete against new media like the cinema, television and participatory team sports like rugby. It is in respect of the latter that the real revolution in leisure and recreation took place. Nor was this 'recreational revolution' confined, as one might have expected, being always the first to experience new media, to the towns; the countryside too saw changes. Perhaps the biggest casualties of change in the twentieth century were those forms of recreation and entertainment organized by or associated with religious groups, the Church and Nonconformist denominations. Society, generally, has become less religious, or certainly less disposed to participate in religious observance if attendance figures are considered, so that the social and recreational life that once revolved so vibrantly around the local church and chapel has been much reduced. Change in the recreational activities of the people did not meet with the approval of all, for as the *Pembrokeshire Herald* reported in May 1900:

> As a generation we have lost much by letting go many of the idyllic and pastoral customs which in days past marked the circling year in this land of ours. Would it be to us of this latest generation a harm or a humiliation were we to bring back the dance and frolic of the may pole?

Clearly, even in the days before the advent of cinema, and long before the appearance of either radio or television, the recreational habits of the people were changing markedly. Not only were the key events in the trad-itional rustic calendar being forgotten, but life generally was changing, a process noted by the *Pembrokeshire County Guardian* in February 1926:

> The rusticity that formerly marked the 'country cousin' is nowadays little noticeable to town dwellers. Rural life is becoming more and more urbanised, thanks to the motor bus, the telephone, cinema, wireless, entertainments, and the penetration of newspapers and fashion news into every home. These modern developments have filled the countryside with a new mentality. The village has its whist drives and dances like the rest of the world.

What the mid 1920s reporters and readers of the *Pembrokeshire County Guardian* would have made of television, let alone the home computer, is anyone's guess!

Technologically, perhaps the most dramatic development came in the form of moving pictures via the cinema which gradually supplanted live theatre. The cinema became a vital source of entertainment that was both cheap and engaging, though it has to be said that the authorities in some urban centres were not altogether happy with the opening of permanent cinemas, the first of which was established at Milford Haven in the spring of 1913. For example, the opening of the Palace Cinema in Haverfordwest in the summer of 1913 was met with apprehension by some on the town council because they feared that 'the morality of the inhabitants would be corrupted'. Far from corrupting their audiences the movies provided an escape from the toils and trials of daily life. The heyday of cinema was probably during the 1920s and 1930s for although audiences reached their peak during the late 1950s and by the early 1960s it was already in decline. As David Howell (1993b) has pointed out: 'just as the live theatre succumbed to the cinema so in the long run was the cinema to lose out to television.' It was the fate of many cinemas either to be closed down or converted to bingo halls which, as events in the late 1980s and 1990s have suggested, may have been short-sighted since audience numbers have picked up considerably.

The transformation in leisure and recreation activities was particularly evident in sport, especially in team sports such as association football and rugby union which became massively popular. Today, Welsh culture is often shallowly equated with being a rugby culture but if there is any truth in the observation then the people of Pembrokeshire were as 'Welsh' as any of their compatriots outside the county. Rugby clubs were established as early as the 1870s in Pembrokeshire, as elsewhere in the principality most notably at Haverfordwest and Narberth being followed in the 1880s by Fishguard, Llangwm, Neyland, Pembroke Dock, St David's and Tenby. Played with passion and supported by equally passionate spectators, the bitterest contests were usually reserved for 'derby' matches between rival towns and villages. By the 1890s teams from Pembrokeshire were competing against teams from neighbouring Carmarthenshire and further afield. For example, the *Pembrokeshire Herald* reported on a keenly contested match, held on Boxing Day 1894, between Haverfordwest and Ammanford – 'the finest game ever witnessed' – which was won by the visitors.

The county turned out a crop of fine Welsh internationals in the inter-war period but the allure of playing for the 'big clubs' further east such as Llanelli and Swansea tended to take away local talent. In fact, Pembrokeshire has always occupied the fringes of Welsh rugby, even more so in the professional era ushered in during the 1990s, but the county's commitment to the sport is as total and passionate as may be found anywhere else in south Wales. Initially, football came second to rugby and the first teams were not properly established until the 1890s at Milford, Pembroke Dock and Tenby. If Haverfordwest was the home of Pembrokeshire rugby then Milford was its football equivalent, entering the Welsh league in the 1930s. Soon other teams joined and Pembrokeshire's representation in the league was exceptionally strong. However, just as in rugby, Pembrokeshire tended to lose its most gifted football players to the professional clubs in south-east Wales – Cardiff and Swansea – and England, for example Simon Davies of Solva.

Parochialism, Patriotism and Nationalism: Cultural and National Identity

It may be fairly argued that this is a subject that might better have been discussed in the previous chapter, but if modern notions of nationalism and cultural identity have their roots in the nineteenth century it took until the twentieth before they could be properly and more freely expressed. Indeed, Pembrokeshire's cultural diversity defies simple definition, being much more of a complex subject than might be the case in the other counties of Wales, with the exception of those areas that border England. For example, in 1896 the *Pembrokeshire Herald* published a collection of letters from its readers which drew attention to what they perceived to be the differences between the culture of south and north Pembrokeshire. The problems confronting historians in trying to make sense of such information is best summed up by Russell Davies (1998):

> Utilizing a plethora of platitudes which plagued contemporary cultural assessments, the inhabitants of south Pembrokeshire were portrayed as a base people who frequented public houses. In stark contrast, the inhabitants of north Pembrokeshire were deemed to be paragons of virtue whose culture was based on singing festivals, eisteddfodau, and society meetings.

Culture may be defined as the arts, customs and other manifestations of human intellectual achievement which, when regarded collectively, might be said to define a people and a nation also. Yet culture is more than simply a nation's literature, laws, beliefs and religion, it is the sum total of all these and more, but above all, it is a way of life that pervades an entire society and one that takes account of the differences as well as what is shared and held in common. One of the most important elements determining the cultural identity of a nation is its language. The Welsh language has an ancient pedigree and through its use generations of Welsh people have expressed themselves in verse, prose, music, law and religion. The historical and cultural heritage served to preserve in the Welsh a sense of identity which military conquest, political annexation and social assimilation had failed, intentionally and unintentionally, to destroy. Increasingly during the nineteenth century, and paradoxically in view of its decline, the language came to represent the chief difference between the Welsh and their English neighbours and it was this gradual awareness of themselves as a people distinct from either the English, Scots or Irish that came to symbolize and give expression to a growing sense of nationalism. It is this factor in Welsh life that historians refer to as the so-called 'National Revival' or 'National Awakening' and the fact that they tend to date this from 1847 is an acknowledgement of the perceived impact of the controversy stirred up by the so-called Blue Books.

However, to speak in terms of a 'National Revival' in Pembrokeshire is almost to invite criticism since it tends to simplify what is in reality something very much more complex. Although nineteenth-century Pembrokeshire was nowhere near the multicultural society it is today, nor was it a county possessed of a single shared culture; rather it was a shire of broadly three cultures, one or more of which may not have been touched or included in the so-called 'national revival'. By the beginning of the twentieth century it is possible to divide the county between what may be termed, no doubt controversially, the 'Welsh' (native Welsh speakers mainly from the north), 'Anglo-Welsh' (native non-Welsh speakers mainly from the south) and the immigrant foreigners (settled mainly, though not exclusively, in the south) who spoke only English. This threefold division of the population makes more difficult the task of defining the Pembrokeshire Welsh, their culture and sense of identity. To say that this complex social division of the population has contributed to a resistance to, or latterly, a decline in the sense of 'Welshness' and Welsh identity, particularly, it is argued, as more and more people have turned to using the English language, is to deny the Anglicized south a culture. That culture may not have been what we might deem specifically or recognizably Welsh, but it was a culture nonetheless. What the nineteenth century witnessed was the seeding and growth of an alternative culture, an Anglo-Welsh culture if you will, though even this label does not do it justice, which by the early decades of the following century accounted for more than two-thirds of the population of Pembrokeshire. For example, in the 1921 census the population of Anglicized Pembrokeshire was put at 69 per cent as opposed to 31 per cent in the areas traditionally associated with the Welsh-speaking north.

Leaving aside the language issue, arguably, in Pembrokeshire, local patriotism, more so in the south than in the north, has tended to be stronger than any sense of Welsh or native nationalism. The demise of Pembrokeshire and the creation of Dyfed in 1974 prompted an outcry and demonstrated clearly the people's attachment to their county. It was not long ere a popular movement was established to work for the shire's restoration and although this had little to do with the county's re-emergence in the local government reorganization of 1996, it had contributed to raising awareness, a sense of 'Pembrokian' identity if such labels are permissible. Further afield, this sense of identity did not show itself to be especially Welsh in so far as the election results in respect of Welsh devolution in 1979 and 1997 can be trusted. Although it might be argued that in the 1979 devolution campaign Pembrokeshire was no less hostile to the idea of a Welsh Assembly than the rest of Wales, the No vote was especially strong in the county, accounting for much of the 71 per cent recorded for Dyfed. Voter apathy was also a significant factor for, as the results in Dyfed show, of the 245,000 eligible to vote only 160,000 bothered to do so. More telling perhaps are the results of the 1997 devolution campaign for, while the rest of Wales had warmed to the idea, though voter apathy was an even more important factor than before, Pembrokeshire remained distinctly cool, being one of those counties to vote overwhelmingly against the proposal. This may fit what scholars have tended to call the 'three-Wales model' based on a perceived shift in voting patterns noted within Wales since the 1983 election. For example, D. Gareth Evans (2001) has described it thus:

> 'Y Fro Gymraeg' – a Welsh-speaking, Welsh-identifying group based in north and north-west Wales; 'Welsh Wales' – a Welsh-identifying, non-Welsh-speaking group prevalent in the traditional industrial Valleys of the south; and 'British Wales' – a British-identifying, non-Welsh-speaking group dominating eastern Wales, the border lands, south Pembrokeshire and the Anglicized coastal plains.

Even if south Pembrokeshire fits 'a British-identifying, non-Welsh-speaking group' its people are certainly not unaware or necessarily unsympathetic to the reality and notion of Wales and Welshness. Indeed, language and politics aside, the Welsh may be said to be discovering themselves as a people, casting aside the stereotypical images of Wales as a nation of rugby lovers, choral singers and coal miners, to embrace a more confident notion of nationhood as exemplified in the flawed but no less powerful image of 'Cool Cymru' which came to dominate the media perception of Wales in the late 1990s. If the barrier within, between north and south, has finally crumbled so also has the barrier without, if it ever truly existed, between the shire and the rest of Wales. Today, Pembrokeshire takes its place as one of the most beguiling and intriguing places within an united Wales.

References

General Works

Bradley, R. (1984), *The Social Foundations of Prehistoric Britain* (London).

Davies, J. (1993), *A History of Wales* (London).

Davies, R. R. (1987), *Conquest, Coexistence and Change: Wales 1063–1415* (Oxford/Cardiff).

Davies, R. (1998), 'Language and Community in South-West Wales *c.*1800–1914', *Language and Community in the Nineteenth Century*, ed. G. H. Jenkins (Cardiff).

Davies, W. (1982), *Wales in the Early Middle Ages* (Leicester).

Evans, D. G. (2001), *A History of Wales, 1906–2000* (Cardiff).

Evans, H. T. (1915), *Wales and the War of the Roses* (Stroud).

Giraldus Cambrensis (1194), *The Journey Through Wales/The Description of Wales*, ed. and trans. L. Thorpe (London).

Heal, F. and Holmes, C. (1994), *The Gentry in England and Wales, 1500–1700* (London).

Hilton, R. (1985), *Class, Conflict and the Crisis of Feudalism: Essays in Medieval Social History* (London).

Hollister, C. W. (2001), *Henry I* (Yale).

Holt, J. C. (1983), 'Feudal Society and Family in Early Modern England', *Transactions of the Royal Historical Society*, 5th ser., 33 (Cambridge).

Jenkins, G. H. (1987), *The Foundations of Modern Wales: Wales 1642–1780* (Oxford/Cardiff).

Jenkins, P. (1992), *A History of Modern Wales 1536–1900* (London).

Jones, I. G. (1992), *Mid-Victorian Wales: The Observers and the Observed* (Cardiff).

Jones, J. G. (1998), *A Pocket Guide: The History of Wales* (Cardiff).

Kightly, C. (1988), *A Mirror of Medieval Wales* (Cardiff).

—— (1994), *Chieftains and Princes* (Cardiff).

Laws, E. (1888), *The History of Little England Beyond Wales* (London).

Lloyd, H. A. (1968), *The Gentry of South West Wales 1540–1640* (Cardiff).

Lloyd, J. E. (1931), *Owen Glendower* (Oxford).

—— (1935–9), *A History of Carmarthenshire*, Vol. 1 (Cardiff).

Malkin, B. H. (1804), *The Scenery, Antiquities, and Biography of South Wales* (London).

Morgan, K. O. (1995), *Modern Wales: Politics, Places and People* (Cardiff).

—— (1981), *Rebirth of a Nation: Wales 1880–1980* (Oxford/Cardiff).

Rees, V. (1976), *A Shell Guide to South-West Wales* (London).

Roberts, G. T. (1998), *The Language of the Blue Books* (Cardiff).

Rowlands, I. (1981), 'The Making of the March: Aspects of the Norman Settlement of Dyfed', *Proceedings of the Battle Conference*, 3, ed. R. A. Brown (Woodbridge).

Strange, K. (1987), *Merthyr Tydfil in the 1840s* (Bridgend).

Williams, A. H. (1941), *An Introduction to the History of Wales*, vol. 1 (Cardiff).

Williams, D. (1998), *Gower: A Guide to Ancient and Historic Monuments on the Gower Peninsula* (Cardiff).

Williams, G. (1987), *Recovery, Reorientation and Reformation: Wales 1415–1642* (Oxford/Cardiff).

Williams, G. A. (1985), *When Was Wales?* (London).

Winterbottom, M. (ed.) (1978), *Gildas: The Ruin of Britain and Other Works* (London).

Pembrokeshire Specific

Fenton, R. ([1811] 1994), *A Historical Tour Through Pembrokeshire*, facsimile edn ([London] Haverfordwest).

Howell, D. W. (1993a), 'Crime and Protest, 1815–1974', *Pembrokeshire County History, Vol. IV: Modern Pembrokeshire*, ed. D. W. Howell (Haverfordwest).

—— (1993b), 'Leisure and Recreation, 1815–1974', *Pembrokeshire County History, Vol. IV: Modern Pembrokeshire*, ed. D. W. Howell (Haverfordwest).

Howells, B. E. (1987), 'Land and People', *Pembrokeshire County History, Vol. III: Early Modern Pembrokeshire*, ed. B. E. Howells (Haverfordwest).

Laws, E. ([1888] 1988), *The History of Little England Beyond Wales* ([London] Haverfordwest)

Mathias, Roland (1993a), 'The civil war', *Pembrokeshire County History, Vol. III, Early Modern Pembrokeshire*, ed. Brian Howells (Haverfordwest).

—— (1993b), 'The second civil war and interregnum', *Pembrokeshire County History, Vol. III, Early Modern Pembrokeshire*, ed. Brian Howells (Haverfordwest).

Owen, G. (1892–1936), *The Description of Pembrokeshire*, ed. H. Owen, 4 vols (London).

Phillips, L. (1993), 'Pembroke Dockyard', *Pembrokeshire County History, Vol. IV: Modern Pembrokeshire*, ed. D. W. Howell (Haverfordwest).

Philpin, A. (1993a), 'Farming in Pembrokeshire, 1815–1974', *Pembrokeshire County History, Vol. IV: Modern Pembrokeshire*, ed. D. W. Howell (Haverfordwest).

—— (1993b), 'Crime and protest, 1815–1974', *Pembrokeshire County History, Vol. IV: Modern Pembrokeshire*, ed. D. W. Howell (Haverfordwest).

Williams, G. (1967), 'The Protestant Experiment in the Diocese of St. David's, 1534–55', *Welsh Reformation Essays* (Cardiff), 111–39.

Select Bibliography

Charles, B. G. (1973), *George Owen of Henllys* (Aberystwyth).
—— (ed.) (1967), *Calendar of the Records of the Borough of Haverfordwest 1539–1660* (Cardiff).
Davis, P. R. (2000), *A Company of Forts: Medieval Castles of West Wales* (Llandysul).
Houseman, M. (2004), *The Llawhaden Book* (Narberth).
Howell, D. W. (ed.) (1993), *Pembrokeshire County History, Vol. IV: Modern Pembrokeshire* (Haverfordwest).
Howells, B. (ed.) (1987), *Pembrokeshire County History, Vol. III: Early Modern Pembrokeshire* (Haverfordwest).
Howells, B. and Howells, K. (eds) (1972), *Pembrokeshire Life 1572–1843: A Selection of Letters* (Haverfordwest).
Leach, A. L. (1937), *The History of the Civil War, 1642–1649, in Pembrokeshire and on its Borders* (London).
Miles, D. (ed.) (1999), *A History of Haverfordwest* (Llandysul).
Morris, J. (1981), *The Railways of Pembrokeshire* (Tenby).
Owen, G. (1994), *The Description of Pembrokeshire*, ed. D. Miles (Llandysul).
Rees, S. (1992), *A Guide to Ancient and Historic Wales – Dyfed* (London).
Walker, R. F. (ed.) (2002), *Pembrokeshire County History, Vol II: Medieval Pembrokeshire* (Haverfordwest).

Journals and Periodicals General

Archaeologia Cambrensis
Cof Cenedl
National Library of Wales Journal
Studia Celtica
Transactions of the Honourable Society of Cymmrodorion
Welsh History Review

Pembrokeshire Specific

Journal of the Pembrokeshire Historical Society (1985–)
The Pembrokeshire Historian (1959–81)

Newspapers (past and present)

Dewsland and Kemes Guardian
Haverfordwest and Milford Haven Telegraph
Pembroke County Guardian
Pembroke Dock and Pembroke Gazette
Pembroke Dock and Tenby Gazette
The Pembrokeshire Herald
The Pembrokeshire Telegraph
Western Telegraph

Record Offices and Libraries

Pembrokeshire Record Office, The Castle, Haverfordwest
Tenby Museum, Tenby
Pembrokeshire County Library, Haverfordwest

Index

Aaron of Caerleon 29
Abercastle 99
Abereiddi 98
Abergavenny 43
Abergwili 76
Act of Settlement (1662) 71
Acts of Union (1536, 1543) 3, 61,
    62, 63, 64, 65, 67
Adam of Usk 44
Agincourt, battle of 55
Agricola 25
Agriculture Act (1920) 129
Aircol ap Triphun 25–6
Alban of Verulamium 29
Alfred, king of Wessex 28
Ambleston 19
Ambrosius Aurelianus (Emrys
    Wledig) 26
Ammanford 139
Amroth 137
Amwn (of Dyfed) 31
Angle 43
Anglesey 34, 93
Anglicans 101–5, 117, 132, 138
Anglo-Normans 36, 38, 60
Anglo-Saxons 24–5, 29, 30, 33, 37,
    38
Anna (of Gwent) 31
Annales Cambriae 23
Antiquité de la nation et la langue
    des Celtes, L' 15
Aquitani 15
Archaeologia Britannica 15
Armes Prydein 33, 35
Arnulf of Montgomery 38
Asser 28, 35
Audley, Sir Thomas 63–4

Bale, John xi
Ballot Act (1872) 116
Banbury, battle of 58
Bangeston 43
Barlow, John 82, 84
Barlow, Lewis 79
Barlow, William (Slebech) 90
Barlow, William, bishop of
    St David's 75, 76–7, 78, 79
Barlow family 67, 97
Barri, de, family 39
Barri, Gerald de *see* Gerald of Wales
Barrow-Wall, W. 96
Bayvil 30
'Beaker People' 11–12
Beaufort, John, earl of Somerset 46
Beavans, William 3
Belgae 15
Beneger family 56
Bentham, Jeremy 118
Berry, James 89
Bevan, Aneurin 133
Black Death 37, 42–4
Bleiddud, lord of Tenby 35
Blue Books, Treason of the (1847)
    94, 105–7, 142
Boia 32
Boleyn, Anne 59, 75, 76
Bosherton 12
Bosworth, battle of 59
Boulston 55
Bowen, Emmanuel 2
Bowen, George 96, 105
Bowen, Thomas 82
Bowen family 52, 54, 67, 116
Bradley, A. G. 103
Brawdy 137

Brecon 38
Breconshire 74, 104
Breton language 15
Brian, de, family 39
Bristol 99, 108
Britannia 20
Britannia Depicta 2
British Society 107
Britons 17–18, 20, 21
Brittany 15, 31–2
Brittonic languages 15–16, 17
Brut y Tywysogyon 23, 33, 34–5, 39, 40
Buckland, William 8
Bullin, Thomas 111–12
Burgess, Thomas, bishop of St David's 102
Burns, Mary 124
Burns, William Michael 124
Burrium 18
Burton 111
Bush 135
Butler, James, earl of Wiltshire 57

Caesar, Julius 15, 17
Caldy Island 2, 8, 9, 12, 30, 31
Caledonii 17
Calixtus II, Pope 33
Cambrian 122
Cambrian Register 93, 100
Campbell, John 95
Campbell, John, Earl Cawdor 96, 109
Campbell family 116
Canaston Bridge 111
Canon, Sir Thomas 66
Cantref Gwarthaf 4
Cardiff 113, 120, 140
Cardigan 47, 84
Cardiganshire 4, 5, 44, 45, 74, 123
    see also Ceredigion
Carew 4, 35, 39, 41, 48, 55, 70, 83, 84
Carew, Sir John 52
Carew, Richard xi

Carew, Sir Thomas 45, 46, 55
Carmarthen 19, 20, 21, 27, 46, 48, 82, 84, 85, 97, 125
Carmarthen Journal 122
Carmarthen West, constituency 134
Carmarthenshire 2, 4, 5, 19, 44, 45, 46, 56, 59, 62, 74, 82, 87, 97, 105, 123, 125, 135, 139
Carn Ingli 17
Carn Meini 11
Carreg Cennen 46
Carreg Coetan Arthur 10
Castagnier, Commodore Jean 108–9
Castell Dwyran 26
Castell Henllys 16, 17
Castle Flemish 19
Castlemartin 41, 64, 137
Castlemartin, John 48
Castlemartin Yeomanry 110, 112 *see also* Pembrokeshire Yeomanry
Castro family 56
'Catalogue of the Saints of Ireland' 33
Catullus 15
ceffyl pren 113
Celtic Church 29–33
Celts 14–18
Cemais 4, 39, 41, 48, 51, 61, 64
Census of Religious Worship of 1851, The 101, 104
Ceredigion 27, 28, 32
Chadwick, Edwin 118, 121
Champagne, John 43
Champagne family 52
Channel Islands 31
Charles I, king of England 61, 63, 81, 84, 86, 91
Charles II, king of England 87, 89, 91
Charles VI, king of France 47
Chartism 110, 114, 116
Chester 47
cholera 119–20

Churchill, Winston 132, 137
Cilgerran 40, 41, 61, 63, 64, 98
Circulating Schools 105
Civil Wars 61, 63, 81–8, 89, 90, 91
Cleddau, river 2, 39, 97
Clegyr Boia 10
Clement VII, Pope 74
Cobbett, William 116
Cobden, Richard 116
Coedrath 41
Colby, Colonel John 96, 109
Colby Moor, battle of 85
Conservative Party 116, 117, 132, 133
Constans, Emperor 24
Constantine, Emperor 29
Cornish language 15, 77
Cornovii 16
Cornwall 10, 31, 34
Cosheston 43
Council in Wales and the Marches 62, 64, 67
County and Borough Police Act (1856) 125
Court, Sir Francis de 48
Cowbridge 121
Cradock, John 43, 53
Cradock, Richard 53–4
Cradock family 52, 53–4 *see also* Newton family
Cromwell, Oliver 87, 88, 89, 91
Cromwell, Thomas 62, 63, 74–5, 76
Crymych 12
Cuch, river 3
Cunedda Wledig 24
Cymru Fydd 117

Dale 83
Daugleddau 4, 64
David, saint 30, 31, 32–3
Davies, David (Dai'r Cantwr) 113
Davies, Howell 104
Davies, R. Rees 45, 50

Davies, Richard, bishop of St David's 78, 79, 80
Davies, Russell 140
Davies, Simon 140
Davies, Wendy 22–3, 34
Daylight Rock 9
De bello Gallico 15
De Excidio Britanniae 4, 23, 26–7
Deceangli, the 16, 18
Dee, river 25
Deer Park Fort 17
Deheubarth 1, 28, 34, 37, 38, 134
Deísi 23–4, 26
Demetae 3, 16, 17, 18, 19–21, 23, 26
Democratic Party 133
Description of Pembrokeshire, The xi–xii, 60, 93
Description of Wales 37
Deva 18
Devereux, Walter, earl of Essex 69
Dewisland 49, 64
Dialogue of the Present Government of Wales, A 60
Dickens, Charles 124
Dinefwr 46
Dio Cassius 18
Diodorus Siculus 15, 18
Diwygiwr, Y 116
Dodd, A. H. 61, 63, 67
Domesday Book 38
Donnelly, Desmond 131, 133
Dryslwyn 46
Dublin 34, 35
Dungleddy *see* Daugleddau
Dwnn, Griffith 77–8
Dwnn, Owain 56
Dyfed 3–5, 21, 33, 34–5, 36, 38–9, 40
county 1, 134–5, 142
Dyfrig, saint 30, 31

Earwear 66, 82
East Moor 82
Eastwood 95

Edward III, king of England 44
Edward VI, king of England 77, 78
Edwards, Nicholas 133–4
Edwin ab Einion 34
Edylfi 34
Efail-wen 111, 114
Eisenhower, Dwight D. 137
Elen, daughter of Llywarch ap
        Hyfaidd 28
Elizabeth I, queen of England 61,
        62, 78–9, 95
Elliot, John (customs official) 66
Elliot, John (royalist) 82, 87
Ellis, Tom 117
Emlyn 4
European Economic Community
        (EEC) 130
Evans, Benjamin 115
Evans, D. Gareth 128, 142
Evans, John 91
Evans, Rebecca 125
Eynon, John 58

Fairburn, Vice-Admiral 137
Fenton, Richard xii, 53, 93–4, 127,
        128
Ferrar, Robert, bishop of St David's
        77–8, 79
Ffynone 96, 109
First World War 105, 128–9, 136–7
Fishguard 30, 94, 99, 110, 111, 131,
        139
    Fishguard landing 108–10, 135,
        136
fitzGerald family 39
fitzMartin, Robert 39
fitzMartin, William 39
fitzMartin family 39
fitzTancard family 39
fitzWizo family 39 see also Wizo
Fleming, Colonel 86, 87
Flemings 5–6, 39–40, 50, 72
Foel Cwmcerwyn 2

Foel Eryr 12
Foster, Thomas Campbell 112–13
Frenni Fawr Round Cairns 12
Freystop 96–7

Galatae 15
Gauls 15
Gawdon 41
Gee, Thomas 114
Gerald of Wales (Gerald de Barri,
        Giraldus Cambrensis) xii, 36,
        39, 60, 93, 127, 128
Gerald of Windsor 39
Gerard, Sir Charles 84, 85
Gibbon, Levi 113–14
Gildas 4, 21, 23, 26–7
Gilfach quarries 99
Giraldus Cambrensis see Gerald of
        Wales
Glamorgan 34, 87, 97, 105, 125
Glog 98
Glorious Revolution (1688) 90, 91
Gloucester, Humphrey, duke of
        56, 57
Glyn-y-mêl (Lower Fishguard)
        93–4
Glyndŵr Rebellion 37, 42, 44–9,
        51, 55
Glywysing 28
Goat's Hole Cave 8
Godebert 40
Goidelic languages 15
Goodwick 109, 131
Gors Fawr 12
Gower 8
Great Revival (1904–5) 103, 104
Green, Francis xii, 94
Grievance of their Majesties' Sub-
        jects in the Principality of
        Wales, The 67
Griffiths, Grace 2
Gruffudd ap Llywelyn 37–8
Gruffudd ap Rhydderch 37

Gwyn, Hugh 66–7
Gwynedd 28, 37, 38
Gwynne, Ivor 133

Hardie, Keir 117
Harlech 86
Harold, king of England 38
Harold, Sir Richard 52
Harold's Stone 12
Haroldston 3, 52, 53, 54, 78, 111
Harris, Edmund 64
Harris, Howell 103, 104
Hassall, Charles 73, 95–6
Hastings family, earls of Pembroke
        52, 56
Havard, Charlotte 125
Haverford 4, 41, 47, 49
Haverfordwest 1, 41, 50, 64, 66, 70,
        75, 78, 83, 84, 85, 94, 98, 109,
        111, 112, 118, 119, 120, 121, 123,
        124, 125, 126, 139, 140
    constituency 62, 63, 89–90, 117,
        134
Hayscastle Cross 12
Hecataeus of Miletus 15
Hengest 24
Henllan 54, 70, 82
Henry I, king of England 40, 72
Henry IV, king of England 45, 46
Henry V, king of England 47, 55
Henry VII, king of England 53, 58–
        9, 90
Henry VIII, king of England xi, 3,
        59, 61, 74, 75, 77
Herbert, Henry, earl of Pembroke 62
Herbert, William, earl of Pembroke
        (d.1469) 58
Herbert, William, earl of Pembroke
        (d.1630) 62
Herbert family, earls of Pembroke
        62
Hereford 80
Herodotus 15

Hertford, marquis of 82
Hetherington, Henry 116
Hilton, R. 51
Historia Brittonum 23
*Historical Tour through
        Pembrokeshire, An* 93
History of Carmarthenshire, A 8, 81
*History of Little England Beyond
        Wales, The* 13, 93
Hoche, General Lazare 108
Hodgeston 78
Holt, J. C. 71
Horsa 24
Horton, Colonel 87
Howard Association 123
Howell, David 55, 139
Howells, Brian 51
Hoyle's Mouth Cave 8
Hume, Joseph 116
Hundred Years' War 55
Hunt, Henry 'Orator' 116
Hyddgen, battle of 45, 46
Hyfaidd ap Bleddri 28
Hywel ab Edwin 37
Hywel Dda (Hywel ap Cadell) 28, 53
    Laws of 23, 28

'In Praise of Tenby' 35
Independent Labour Party 133
*Introduction to the History of
        Wales, An* 30
*Inventory of the Ancient Monu-
        ments relating to the County
        of Pembroke, The* 127
Ireland 10, 11, 21, 23–4, 25, 29, 32,
        33, 34, 35, 38, 65, 90, 99, 108,
        131
Irish language 15
Isca 18

Jacobites 91
James, duke of Monmouth 91
James I, king of England 61, 63, 81

James II, king of England 90, 91
Jenkins, Geraint H. 88
Johnson, H. R. Vaughan 106–7
Jones, David (historian) 114
Jones, David (Methodist) 104
Jones, Sir Evan Davies 133
Jones, Griffith 105
Jones, Ieuan Gwynedd 71
Jones, J. Graham 8
Jones, Thomas 126
Jones, William Basil, bishop of St
       David's 19
Journey through Wales 37
Julius of Caerleon 29

Katherine of Aragon 74
*Kingdom's Weekly Intelligencer,
       The* 85
Kingswood 41
Knox, Colonel Thomas 108, 109
Knox, William 96

Labour Party 117, 133–4
Lambarde, William xi
Lamphey 61
Land and the Nation, The 129
Landshipping 97, 106
landsker 50, 60
Latin 26
Laugharne 46, 62
Laugharne, Rowland 82, 83, 84–5,
       86, 87, 88, 89
Laugharne, Thomas 87
Laugharne family 54, 67
Laurie, John 132
Lawrenny 97
Laws, Edward xii, 14, 22, 88, 93, 94,
       127, 128
Lee, Rowland 77
Leland, John xi, xii
Letard 'Litelking' 40
Lewis, John 95
Lewis, Robert 115

Leynthale, Sir Roland 47
Lhuyd, Edward 15
Liberal Party 116–17, 129, 131–2,
       133, 135
Liberation Society 116
Life of St David 23
Lingen, R. R. W. 98, 105, 106, 107
Little Hoyle Cave 8
Liverpool 99
Llanhywel 115
Llanllwch 44
Llanrhian 99
Llanstephan 46, 62
Llanteg 43
Llanwnda 30
Llanychlwydog 30, 115
Llawhaden 16, 19, 41, 49, 61, 63, 65
Lloyd, Isaac 89
Lloyd, J. E. 8, 11, 25, 81
Lloyd George, David 117, 129, 132,
       135, 136
Lloyd George, Gwilym 132
Llwyn-gwair 96, 105, 116, 129
Llŷn peninsula 34
Llywarch ap Hyfaidd 27, 28
Llywelyn ap Gruffudd, prince of
       Wales (Llywelyn the Last) 40
Llywelyn ap Iorwerth, prince of
       Gwynedd (Llywelyn the Great)
       40
Lort, John 88, 89
Lort, Roger 82, 83, 87, 88, 89
Lort, Sampson 82, 87, 88, 89
Ludchurch 43
Ludlow 62, 64, 67

Mabinogi 4, 23
Maelgwn Gwynedd 27
Maenclochog 12, 32, 98, 115
Malefant, John 43
Malefant family 52
Malkin, Benjamin Heath 109
Manaw Gododdin 24

Manorbier 4, 36, 41, 48, 83, 84
Manorowen 95
Manx language 15
March, the 36, 41, 50, 54, 56
Maredudd ab Owain, king of
    Deheubarth 33–4
Marloes 9, 17
Marshal, William, earl of Pembroke
    40
Marshal family 40–1
Marston Moor, battle of 84
'Martyrology of Oengus, The' 33
Mary I, queen of England 78
Mary II, queen of England 90
Mathias, Roland 86
Mefenydd 44
Mercurius Aulicus 84
Mercurius Politicus 91
Merthyr Tydfil 117
Messenger, William 1
Methodist Revival 103–4
Meyrick, Lt Col Frederick 135
Milford 140
Milford Docks 100
Milford Haven 2, 47, 66, 83, 99, 100,
    131, 136, 137, 139
Mill Bay 58
Mills, James 125
Milton 55
Monkton 8
Monmouth Rebellion (1685) 91
Morgan, Henry, bishop of
    St David's 78, 79
Morgan, William, bishop of
    St Asaph 80
Morgannwg 38
Moridunum 4, 19, 20
Morris, Edward (Cerrigydrudion)
    135
Morris, Richard 93
Mortimer's Cross, battle of 57
Morton, Henry 66
Moylegrove 115

Municipal Corporations Act (1835)
    124
Mynachlog-ddu 12, 113, 114
Mynydd Carn, battle of 38
Mynyw 32

Nab Head 9
Nanna's Cave 8, 9
Narberth 41, 46, 49, 62, 64, 111, 112,
    115, 122, 139
Naseby, battle of 85
National Assembly for Wales 134
National Society 107
National Union of the Working
    Classes 115
Needham, Sir Robert 90
Nennius 23
Nest, daughter of Rhys ap Tewdwr
    39
Nevern 30, 31, 39
New Moat 90, 116
New Model Army 86
Newcastle Emlyn 46
Newport 10, 16, 63, 70
Newton 53
Newton, Richard *see* Cradock,
    Richard
Newton family 54
Neyland 139
Nichol, William 78
Nicholas, Jemima 108
Non, mother of St David 32
Nonconformists 89, 101–5, 138
Normans 4, 5, 22, 28, 29, 38–9 *see
    also* Anglo-Normans
Northern Star 114

Oakwood Park 130
Offa, king of Mercia 25
Ogam 25, 26
Ordovices 16
Orielton 54, 70, 82, 90, 97, 129
Ormond, James, earl of Wiltshire 1

Owain Glyndŵr 45–6, 47, 48, 49, 51
Owen, Arthur 89
Owen, George (Henllys) xi–xii, 6, 40, 51, 60–1, 64, 66, 67–8, 72–3, 80, 93, 94, 95, 96, 98, 99–100, 127, 128
Owen, Henry xii, 94, 127, 128
Owen, Sir Hugh 97
Owen, Sir Hugh (parliamentarian) 82, 90
Owen, Robert 123
Owen family (New Moat) 90
Owen family (Orielton) 52, 67, 90, 97

Pakington, Hester (née Perrot) 2, 3
Pankhurst, Emmeline 132
Parson, Dr 120
Paviland 8
Pebidiog 4, 61
Peel, Sir Robert 114, 124
Pembroke 4, 8, 38, 39, 40, 41, 47, 48, 50, 55, 56, 70, 82, 83, 84, 85, 86, 87–8, 98, 122, 131
    earls of 5, 41–2, 50, 52, 55, 56, 59, 61, 62, 75
Pembroke, constituencies
    borough constituency 62–3, 89, 117, 132, 134
    county constituency 62–3, 89, 90, 117, 131–2
    single constituency 132–4 *see also* Carmarthen West; South Pembrokeshire and Preseli
Pembroke Dock 111, 130, 131, 136, 137, 139, 140
Pembrokeshire Anti-Tithe League 115
Pembrokeshire Coast National Park 130
Pembrokeshire County Guardian 138–9
Pembrokeshire Herald 119, 122, 138, 139, 140

Pembrokeshire Local History Society 142
Pembrokeshire Yeomanry 135–6
    see also Castlemartin Yeomanry
Penally 32
Penfro 4
Penmaen-mawr (Gwynedd) 11
Pentre Ifan 10, 54, 70
Perambulation of Kent, A xi
Perrot, Alice (née Harold) 52–3
Perrot, David 47
Perrot, Dorothy (née Devereux)
Perrot, Sir James 63
Perrot, Jankyn 58
Perrot, John (d.1349) 43, 52
Perrot, John (Tenby) 55
Perrot, Sir John (d.1592) 62, 69, 70, 78, 96–7
Perrot, Sir Owen 53
Perrot, Peter 52
Perrot, Stephen 48
Perrot, Thomas (Lancastrian) 57, 58
Perrot, Sir Thomas (d.1461) 57
Perrot, Sir Thomas (d.1594) 66, 69
Perrot, Sir William 53
Perrot family 52–3, 54, 56, 67, 70, 96
Pezron, Abbé 15
Phaer, Thomas 66
Philipps, Sir Ivor 136
Philipps, Sir James Erasmus 131
Philipps, Sir John (d.1737) 105
Philipps, John Cosby 132
Philipps, John Wynford, Baron St David's 131–2, 135
Philipps, Sir Richard 82
Philipps, Sir Richard, Baron Milford 96
Philipps family 52, 54, 97, 116
Phillips, James (Cardigan) 88
Phillips, James (historian) xii, 94
Philpin, Audrey 115, 124, 125

Picton 54, 70, 82, 96, 97, 105, 116, 129, 131, 136
Pigwn, Y 18
Pilcornswell 16
Pius V, Pope 79
Plaid Cymru 134
Pliny 18
Pocket Guide: The History of Wales 8
Polybius 15
Pontarddulais 112–13
Poor Law Act (1601) 71, 122
Poor Law Amendment Act (1834) 94, 112, 122, 123
Popton 43, 51
Portfield 119
Porth-gain 98, 99
Potter's Cave 8, 12
Powell, Rice 82, 83, 87, 88
Powys 38
Poyer, John 82, 83, 86–7, 88
Prendergast 82, 111
Preseli hills 2, 10, 11, 12, 17
Prettani 15–16, 17 *see also* Britons
Prichard, Rhys 65
Priory Farm Cave 8
Prison Reform League 123
Prisons Act (1865) 126
Prisons Act (1877) 126
Prix Pill 84
Ptolemy 3, 4
Public Health Act (1848) 120
Public Health Act (1875) 121
Pwll-trap 111
Pwllcrochan 12, 87
Pytheas of Marseilles 15

Quentin, General 108

Radnorshire 74
Raglan 86
Ramsey Island 2, 8, 9, 30, 35
Rebecca Riots 94, 110–15, 122, 135

Rede, Thomas 46
Rees, Revd David 116
Rees, Sir Frederick xi
Rees, Thomas (Twm Carnabwth) 113
Rees, V. 7
Reform Act (1832) 116
Reform Act (1867) 116
Reform Act (1884) 116
Reformation, the 61, 74–81, 90
Report of the Commissioners of Inquiry into the State of Education in Wales, The 105–7
Restoration, the (1660) 89, 91
Return of Owners of Land of 1873, The 129
Reynbot, John 53
Reynish, Mary Anne 125–6
Rhodri Mawr, king of Gwynedd, Powys and Deheubarth 28
Rhos 4, 39, 64
Rhosson Uchaf 93
Rhigyfarch of Llanbadarn Fawr 23, 32–3
Rhys ap Gruffudd 75
Rhys ap Gruffudd (the Lord Rhys) 28, 39, 40
Rhys ap Rhydderch 37
Rhys ap Tewdwr, king of Deheubarth 34, 38
Rhys ap Thomas, Sir 59, 75
Richard, Henry 102
Richard III, king of England 58
Richards, William 73
Robelyn, William 43
Robelyn family 52
Robeston Wathen 111, 124
Roch 4, 51, 61, 83, 84, 91
Roch, Walter 132
Roche, Elizabeth 48
Roche, Thomas 48
Roche, de la, family 39
Romans 3–4, 17, 18–21, 24, 25–6, 29

Roosevelt, Franklin D. 136
Rosebush 98
Rowlands, Ifor 38–9
Royalist Association of West
    Wales 82
Rudd, Anthony, bishop of
    St David's 99
Rupert, Prince 84
Rutzen, Baron de 113

St Bride's 54, 82
St Clear's 46, 111
St David's
    bishops 19, 32, 37, 61, 75, 76–8, 79
    cathedral 23, 31, 32, 34, 38, 76–7,
        99
    city 120, 139
    diocese 5, 32, 65, 74, 76–7, 80
    lordship 41
    religious community 28, 32, 34
St Dogmael's 115
St Elvis 30
St Fagan's, battle of 87
St Florence 41
St Issells 43
Salesbury, William 60, 80
Samson, saint 30, 31–2
Sant, king of Ceredigion 32
Saunders, Erasmus 79
Saxons *see* Anglo-Saxons
'Scleddy' 111
Scotland 11, 24, 34, 91
Scotsborough 58
Scott, Sir George Gilbert 102
Scottish 15
Scourfield family 116
Scurlage, Walter 43
Scurlage family 52, 56
Sealyham 129
Second Walk Through Wales, A 1
Second World War 137
Seisyllwg 28
Seren Gomer 115

Severn, river 25
Seymour, Edward, duke of Somerset
    77
Shirburn, Alice 44
Shirburn, John 44
Shirburn, Nicholas 43
Shirburn family 52
Shrewsbury 47
Silures 16, 17, 18, 19
Simpson 53
Sitriuc, king of Dublin 35
Skokholm Island 2, 9, 35
Skomer Island 2, 8, 9, 17, 35
Slebech 79, 82, 90, 96, 109, 112
Smith, Sir Thomas 72
Society for Promoting Christian
    Knowledge 105
Society of Sea Serjeants 91
Solva 140
Somerset, Henry, duke of Beaufort
    91
South African War 135–6
South Pembrokeshire and Preseli,
    constituency 134
South Wales Daily News 117
Stackpole 4, 12, 41, 48, 54, 57, 82,
    83, 95, 96, 116
Statute of Artificers (1563) 73
Stephen, king of England 72
Stepney, Sir John 82
Stepney family 67
Stevens, William 115
Stonehenge 12
Strabo 15
Strathclyde 34
Sulien, bishop of St David's 32
Sunday schools 106–7
Survey of Cornwall, A xi
Swanley, Admiral 83
Swansea 97, 139, 140
Symons, J. C. 106, 107

Tacitus 17, 18, 20

Talbot, Richard 44
Tancard 40
Tate, Colonel William 108, 109
Teifi, river 3
Teilo, saint 30, 32
Telegraph Almanac 136
Tenby 2, 8, 19, 40, 41, 46–7, 48, 50,
    54, 55, 63, 66, 70, 79, 82, 83, 84,
    85, 86, 87, 98, 100, 118, 130–1,
    139, 140
Terrell, Thomas 132
Thelwall, Simon 84
Thirlwall, Connop, bishop of St
    David's 102
Thorne, Roland 91
Times, The 112, 113
Tithe Rent Charge Recovery and
    Redemption Act (1891) 115
Tre-wern 70
Trecŵn 137
Trefloyne 82, 83
Triphun 25, 27
Tudor, Edmund, earl of Richmond 58
Tudor, Henry *see* Henry VII
Tudor, Jasper, earl of Pembroke 57,
    58, 59
Tudor family 58
Twyne, John xi

Upton 129
Uzmaston 1

Valence family, earls of Pembroke
    56
Valor Ecclesiasticus 75, 76
Vaughan, Sir Henry 84
Vaughan, John (Trawscoed) 84
Vaughan, Richard, earl of Carbery
    82–4
Vaughan family (Tretower) 58
Vernon, Sir William 57
Vernon family 54
Victoria, queen of England 110

Vikings 33–5, 37
Viroconium 18
Vortigern 24
Vortipor, king of Dyfed 4, 25, 26–7

Wales in the Early Middle Ages
    22–3
Wallography 73
Walter, Lucy 91
Walter, Richard 91
Walwyn's Castle 4, 41, 48, 62
Warner, Richard 1
Wars of the Roses 37, 57–9
Welsh Land League 114
Welsh language 5–6, 17, 60, 79–80,
    101, 102, 104, 115, 117, 134,
    140–1
Welsh party 116
Welsh Reconstruction Advisory
    Council 129
Wesley, John 103–4
When Was Wales? 14
White, Griffith 82–3
White family 54, 67
Whitechurch 115
Whitefield, George 103
Whitland Turnpike Trust 111
William I, king of England 38
William III, king of England 67, 90
William of Brabant 40
Williams, A. H. 30
Williams, Diane 8
Williams, Gwyn A. 14–15, 22, 30
Williams, Waldo 134
Wiltshire 11
Wiseman, Andrew 43
Wiseman family 52
Wiseman's Bridge 137
Wiston 4, 41, 48, 54, 63, 70, 81, 82,
    88, 97
Wizo 40 *see also* fitzWizo family
Wogan, Henry (Milton) 55
Wogan, Sir Henry 56, 57

Wogan, John 58
Wogan, Sir John 81, 82, 88
Wogan, Thomas (Lancastrian) 57
Wogan, Thomas (regicide) 82, 88
Wogan, William 55
Wogan Cavern 9
Wogan family 52, 54, 56, 67, 70, 97
Woodstock 55

Wye, river 25
Wylie, J. H. 49
Wyrriot, Thomas 56, 57
Wyrriot family 54, 56, 67

Young, Thomas, bishop of
    St David's 78
Ystrad Tywi 28